Commencement
of the
Central Pacific Railroad
at Sacramento
January 8, 1863

D1156977

COLLIS POTTER HUNTINGTON

Collis Potter Huntington

BY CERINDA W. EVANS

Volume One

✦ ✦ ✦

*"Success in life only means honesty of
purpose and intelligent economy."*

THE MARINERS' MUSEUM · NEWPORT NEWS, VIRGINIA

1 9 5 4

MUSEUM PUBLICATION NO. 24

Copyright, 1954
The Mariners' Museum, Newport News, Virginia

ào

ACKNOWLEDGMENTS

The author acknowledges with profound gratitude her indebtedness to all those whose aid in research, kindly interest, and generous encouragement contributed so greatly to the writing of this book.

DEEDS

TO COLLIS POTTER HUNTINGTON

The splendor of the deed enfolds our dreams;
Its glory with the grace of starlight gleams.
The flames of genius still make fair the night
And clear the pattern of our lives with light.
Here, though life's road winds grim through silt and sand,
The shining temples of achievement stand;
Faith paints the grandeur of the splendid deed
With hues that bear a balm for hearts that bleed.
So men forgetting war may bend above
Inscriptions written for the fanes of love,
Hark exaltation of life's fair refrains
That urge new bravery from lives in chains,
And whisper from the cells where faiths are furled
The miracle of deeds that light the world.

A.M.H.

CONTENTS

ILLUSTRATIONS

COLLIS POTTER HUNTINGTON

Chapter I

INTRODUCTORY

THE LIFE OF Collis Potter Huntington, great railroad builder and financier extraordinary, is inseparably interwoven to a remarkable degree with the history of his country from the middle of the nineteenth century.

It was said of him at the time of his death in 1900 that he had done greater things and more of them in the strenuous work of developing the resources of America than any other man; "no ten men, in truth, have done so much" to bring the United States to a position among nations intellectually, financially and commercially second to none.

He was both brain and backbone of the greatest transportation system the world has ever seen, its railroads extending from the Atlantic to the Pacific, from Yuma north to Portland, Oregon, and from San Francisco east to Ogden, Utah. This railroad with its branches and ramifications aggregated over ten thousand miles of track. The steamship lines in connection therewith to Mexico, Central and South America, the Far East and through coastal waters extended over twenty thousand miles of water route, bringing the United States into closer relations with our Latin neighbors and other foreign countries.

Especially is Mr. Huntington considered among the chief creating and controlling forces to whom the rapid development and civilization of the Pacific Coast is due through the establishment of rail communication with the Eastern States. As early as 1875, it was said that the railroad had added $300,000,000 to the value of taxable property in California, and in 1893, the assessed value of taxable property had increased to $1,071,000,000. Today the West rivals the East in population, material progress, and in intellectual growth; in schools, colleges, great universities; in art and scientific institutions.

The railroad had reduced the time of travel from New York to San Francisco from several months to a few days, and had opened to settlement by emigrants a vast tract of the best agricultural land in the country. It carried large quantities of much needed machinery to the mining fields, causing new mines to open up that yielded large amounts of gold and silver which materially influenced our foreign exchanges. As the railroads were built, mile after mile, there were located depots, warehouses, repair shops, etc., forming the nuclei of settlements that grew into villages, towns, and even large cities. Here were established the homes of the employees of the railroad and of those engaged in mercantile and other industries; here they built their homes, schools, churches and other institutions.

At least two of these cities were planned and founded by Mr. Huntington himself: Huntington, West Virginia, where the repair shops and warehouses of the Chesapeake and Ohio Railroad were located; and Newport News, Virginia, the eastern terminus of that railroad, and where Mr. Huntington established the largest and best equipped shipyard in America.

It has been estimated that at least one hundred thousand men have been employed in these various industries of Mr.

Huntington, which with their families amount to several hundred thousand persons maintained by the Huntington interests alone.

Of the seven transcontinental railroad lines in operation at the time of Mr. Huntington's death, his were the only roads that had never defaulted in their financial obligations nor passed through an enforced reorganization. When the great financial depression and panic of 1873 struck this country, only the financial genius of Collis Potter Huntington saved his roads from disaster, while other important roads were falling all around him. His letters from New York to Mark Hopkins in Sacramento during that time reveal his strenuous efforts to meet the needs as they arose and the terrific strain under which he labored. An intimate associate said of him, "He did more to stabilize Wall Street during that panic than any other man. Take it all in all, he was the most remarkable man we have ever had in Wall Street."

The great achievements of Mr. Huntington were not easily secured. In addition to the usual problems, endless perplexities, and grilling application that of necessity accompany such undertakings, before the first rails of the Central Pacific were laid, he with his associates in the venture were attacked by a fierce antagonism aroused by jealousy, envy, malice, and personal grievances that opposed every step, grew in hostility and bitterness through the years, and culminated in the venomous outburst against him at the time when the Refunding Bill for the Central Pacific was before Congress in 1896. But the clear vision of his objective, his marvelous ability, great courage and indomitable spirit, and his incredible patience carried him through to a magnificent success.

Chapter II

ANCESTRY

THE HUNTINGTON FAMILY is of ancient English lineage and was founded in America by Simon Huntington who had married Margaret Baret of Norwich, England.

He sailed for America with his wife and three small sons in 1633, but was stricken with the smallpox, died en route and was buried at sea. The mother and sons landed at the Massachusetts Bay Colony, and from the three sons, Christopher, Simon and Samuel, came the three branches of the Huntington family that have spread throughout America, members of which are noted for their work as legislators, jurists, inventors, educators, and artists.[1]

Collis Potter Huntington was a descendant of the second son, Simon, the line being as follows: Collis Potter Huntington, son of William and Elizabeth (Vincent) Huntington; grandson of Joseph and Rachael (Preston) Huntington; great grandson of John and Mehitabel (Metcalf) Huntington; great[2] grandson of Lieutenant Samuel and Mary (Clark) Huntington; great[3] grandson of Deacon Simon and Sarah (Clark) Huntington; and great[4] grandson of Simon and Margaret (Baret) Huntington, the emigrants.[2]

Collis Potter Huntington was born October 22, 1821, at Harwinton, Connecticut, a small town in Litchfield County that was settled in 1731 and incorporated as a township in 1837 with a population of about 1,100. The name was de-

Elizabeth Vincent Huntington, Mother of Collis P. Huntington

rived from the names of the three Connecticut towns, Hartford, Windsor and Farmington.

His father, William Huntington, born in 1774, at Harwinton, was a man of large frame, standing six feet two inches
in height, and of a striking appearance. He possessed unusual
intelligence and was the inventor of a carding machine that
sold for $100. He was of stern character, original and inde-
pendent in his views. His methods of training his children
were strict and practicable, requiring of each child some part
in the performance of household and other duties. He claimed
that if a boy had a working knowledge of the three R's, he
could make his own way in the world and he put this idea
into practice with his own sons. His advice in business dealings was: "Do not be afraid to do business with a rascal, only
watch him; but avoid a fool, for you can never make anything
out of him." He died November 8, 1860.[3]

Elizabeth Vincent Huntington, wife of William Huntington and mother of Collis Potter Huntington, was born in
August 1791, at Martha's Vineyard, the great[2] granddaughter
of William and Susanna (Browning) Vincent, early settlers
on Martha's Vineyard. She was a woman of exalted character, ambitious for her children that they develop into intelligent and useful men and women.[4]

Some years after her death when presenting a beautiful
chapel to Harwinton in her memory, Mr. Huntington spoke
feelingly of his mother as one of the best women who ever
lived. He regarded her influence as the greatest single factor
in forming his character and controlling his acts. When he
left home to make his own way in the world his mother said
to him: "Son, always remember that your future will be
largely as you make it. Do anything you have a mind to do,
but never ask anybody's opinion of what is right or wrong,

for if you do it will be because you want an excuse to do something that your own conscience does not approve."

One of her grandsons, Willard Vincent Huntington, said of her: "She was a woman of beautiful disposition. I can truly say I never saw a frown on her face." She died March 1, 1871, at Warsaw, New York, at the home of her eldest daughter, Mary, Mrs. Daniel Sammis.

Collis Potter Huntington was the sixth child of a family of nine children. The other members of the family were: Mary, born February 17, 1810, married November 4, 1838, Daniel Sammis, a farmer living at Warsaw, New York; Solon, born January 13, 1812, married June 2, 1840, Harriet Saunders, and resided at Oneonta, New York; Rhoda, born October 13, 1814, married May 10, 1834, Riley Dunbar, a rake maker, living in Wolcottville, Connecticut; Phoebe, born September 17, 1817, married October 4, 1840, Henry Pardee, a dealer in shoes in Oneonta, New York; Elizabeth, born December 19, 1819, married April 5, 1842, Hiram Yager, a farmer in Kortwright, New York; Joseph, born March 23, 1823, died single, February 23, 1849; Susan L. born August, 1826, married November 16, 1849, William Porter, a physician living in New Haven, Connecticut; and Ellen Maria, born at Torrington, Connecticut, August 12, 1835, married August 6, 1862, at Oneonta, the Rev. Isaac E. Gates of Preston, Connecticut, who later became one of Mr. Huntington's most trusted lieutenants.[5]

Ellen Huntington, the youngest child, was educated in private seminaries in Galway and Hamilton, New York. She was a writer of some prominence, and published several volumes of verse, some of which were translated into other languages. Some of her poems were set to music and became popular hymns.[6]

Chapter III

BOYHOOD IN HARWINTON

AMONG THE HILLS of Harwinton, Connecticut, lies a small but pretty valley known as Poverty Hollow, a region of small farms and several saw mills. Here was located the 80-acre farm of William Huntington and the house in which Collis Potter Huntington was born. The farm was mostly woodland, meadow land and pasture. The house was a plain white, story-and-a-half frame structure with a large cellar and having a huge stone chimney at one end. The gable end faced the road, and at the front of the house was the well with its picturesque bucket and sweep.

Across the field about twenty yards from the house stood the barn. The beautiful Lead Mine Brook flowed westward down the valley across the Huntington property. A small stream flowed into this brook upon which stood the wool-carding mill owned by William Huntington. About five hundred yards down the valley stood the one-room school house where Collis went to school. All these buildings have long since disappeared.[1]

From early childhood Collis led a busy life. He has said that he could not remember the time when he was not doing something useful. One of his early tasks was to assist his father in building a stone wall which fifty years later was in a state of good repair. He hauled wood from a nearby hill with a team of oxen when he was so small he had to stand on a box to place the yoke upon their sturdy necks. His interest in books at that early age is shown by his purchase of a copy of Patrick's Narrative of a Shipwreck on the Coast of North Africa with the first sixty cents he ever earned.[2]

When only nine years of age, he was employed by a neighbor to pile a quantity of wood in a wood-shed which he did very carefully, picking up the chips and putting them into barrels. His employer was pleased with the job and gave him a dollar and said, "You have done this so well, I shall be glad to have you pile up my wood next fall." While pleased with the dollar and the word of praise, the small boy told a friend, "He doesn't suppose I am going to pile up wood for a living the rest of my life, does he?"[3] Which remark shows that even at that early age, he had visions of greater usefulness.

The school term in Harwinton was only four months in length and all the schooling the young lad ever had was the few years he attended this school. His favorite studies were arithmetic, geography and history. He loved to pore over maps and thus acquired a rather extraordinary knowledge of the topography of the country which he found most useful later in life. Thus was laid the slender foundation of knowledge upon which he himself was to build a broader education, a wider knowledge of men and world affairs than most university men possess.

He had inherited his father's physique and was tall and unusually strong for his age. His favorite sport was wrestling with the other boys.

In the latter part of 1895, a man named T. E. Nunan, who claimed to be a kinsman of Mr. Huntington and a former resident of Harwinton, visited Poverty Hollow and afterward wrote an article for the San Francisco *Call* published in the issue of February 2, 1896, and entitled: "Birthplace and Early Life of C. P. Huntington."

Nunan was accompanied on his rounds by Lyman Mather, the only schoolmate of Collis remaining in Poverty Hollow. He was only a year younger than Collis but feeble and penniless, a pauper kept at the expense of the town.

"I remember Collis well," said old Mr. Mather. "He and I are about the only ones living of all that used to go to school down here. At school he was a regular harum-scarum. He was a wild sort of fellow allus a-stubbin around barefoot in summer. And he was a regular dare-devil; if there was any danger anywhere, he would jump right plumb into it fust thing. He was allus having trouble with his teachers. William K. Peck was one of the teachers. Collis was a big fellow, he looked like a perfect mountain to me. Oh, he was bright enough, but he had rather cut-up than study."

Another boyhood friend of Collis that Nunan tells about in his narrative was Erastus Baldwin who had gone to California about twenty-five years before and for a while worked as a section hand on the Central Pacific Railroad. At the time of Nunan's visit, he was seventy-four years of age, hale and hearty, and operated a mill in Poverty Hollow where he was regarded as the village philosopher. He claimed supremacy in wrestling in his school days even over Collis Potter Huntington.

"Col and I were boys together, and we've been men together," said Mr. Baldwin. "We used to have some good wrestling bouts in those days. The Poverty Hollow boys were a big strong lot of fellows, and Col was the biggest and toughest of the lot. I was going to school in Campville then, and over there we had a teacher who was pretty spry, and who knew a good deal about wrestling in a sort of scientific way. This teacher used to give us lessons, and I got so there was nobody in our school who could handle me, even if I was the smallest of the lot."

"We got a challenge from the Poverty Hollow boys and we came one Saturday to wrestle it out. Several matches were tried and Col got the best of everybody he tackled. Finally he tackled me and I gave him the prettiest throw you ever saw in your life!" (The historian laughed so loud, the Hollow laughed with him in echo.) "By jingo!" said Col, "you be a good 'un if you be small!" "I threw him every time he stood up until he said he had enough." He added, "You speak to Col about that when you go back to California."

After reading Nunan's article in *The Call,* Mr. Huntington wrote a letter to a friend in San Francisco which was published in *The Call* and reproduced in the Sacramento *Record-Union* in the issue of March 3, 1896:

I suppose you have seen published in one of the San Francisco papers lately an article signed by a Mr. Nunan which purports to be an authentic account of my early life. It amused me a good deal, because a good deal of it was true, but some of it was not . . . I do want to put Mr. Nunan right in one or two statements of his narrative. Where, for instance, he remarked that one of the boys at school threw me in wrestling. That's a mistake, for no one in the Hollow ever threw me or ever could, and in a rough and tumble scrimmage, I could 'wipe up the floor' with half the boys in school taken together.

The writer of the article also says, on the authority of someone in the poorhouse who says he was a playmate of mine, that I was not a good boy in school. I think I was a pretty good boy, although I did have a tussle a couple of times with the teachers, and I laugh over it to this day when I think of it. I believe the writer's poorhouse friend is right in saying that this teacher's name was Peck. The penalty in our school for bad spelling, as fixed by Peck, was one blow of a heavy ferule on the palm of the hand for every word misspelled. I was never in those days, and am not today, much of a speller,

Lead Mine Brook on the Old Huntington Property
at Harwinton, Connecticut

Small Brook which Flows Into Lead Mine Brook
on Which Was Located the Huntington Carding Mill

Stone Wall which Collis Helped to Build at the Age of Six

although I believe I worked harder in that direction than those who were fortunate enough to find it an easy task; and I objected to the punishment, for it did not seem to me a fair thing to do.

So one day I agreed with four other boys that when the spelling lesson came up we would all miss every time. We did so, and as the good spellers 'went up,' as it was called, the bad spellers of course 'went down' to the foot of the class. We five boys had arranged between us that the first boy called out for punishment should refuse to put out his hand and open the fight right there. It happened that the first boy called in this connection was not the right boy for the business; but the next was, and that was myself. I commenced business without any delay, and only one of the four came in to help me; but we two went for that teacher and whipped him.

There was another teacher whose name, if I recollect right, was Ely. The first day this teacher came to school he brought with him a bundle of whips which he stood behind his desk. When he returned from dinner—we had dinner at noon in those days—the uncanny looking things were not there, or rather I should say they were cut up into small pieces. He asked one and another of the boys who had done it, and they all answered that they did not know, although of course they knew very well. When he asked me if I knew, I said yes; but when he asked who it was I refused to tell him. He said he would put me out of school if I did not tell, but I didn't and we sailed in, and there was fun for the boys for a few minutes. I was able to gather him up and take him out without harming him much.

Now there may have been something wrong about those two schoolboy squabbles, but somehow I do not remember them as being so, and few recollections of my life have given me so much innocent satisfaction, or so often caused a smile, as the remembrance of my tussle with Mr. Ely.

Chapter IV

A TRAVELING SALESMAN

AT THE ANNUAL BANQUET given to the executives of the
Southern Pacific Company and other friends on April 23,
1892, at the Palace Hotel, Mr. Huntington referred to the
work of his early years as follows:

My story is old. It commenced in the early part of this century
amongst the hills of New England. There I started in life and business with advantages over many of the others who started with me,
for I had not a liberal education and I had no money, whilst many
of my boy neighbors had both, which prevented them from doing the
hard and homely work which was nearest to them. I had no such
obstacle between me and the useful work that needed to be done; so
I took the work that lay nearest to me with an effort to do it better
than it had ever been done before; and from the standpoint of each
day's labor, looking upward and onward, ever anxious to spy out
something better than what had preceded it. I can say that I have
been fairly successful as all will be, I am confident, who work with
the honesty of purpose that actuated me.

At the age of fourteen, his school life ended. His father
consented that he should support himself, and he went to
work for Orsen Barber, a neighbor farmer, for seven dollars
a month, his board and clothes. At the end of the year he had
saved his whole year's salary, $84.00.[1]

The next year he went to work for another neighbor,
Phineas W. Noble, a grocer in whose store he acquired the

rudiments of trade, buying and selling, which in later life developed into a skill in handling merchandise which few men could equal.[2]

After he had accumulated $175.00, and with the assistance of Mr. Noble who was a good customer of several New York firms, he received credit for a stock of watch findings, jewelry and silverware, amounting to $3,000.00, to him a large sum. To these were added, according to Nunan, a supply of pins, needles, knives, tape, thread and little combs. He carried his wares in two tin boxes that were about two feet long and sixteen inches deep. He held one by each hand with a strap over his shoulders for additional support. By working with vigor, ingenuity, and persistence, he disposed of the goods with satisfactory results.

In 1872, a lady living in Tulare, California, displayed some cutlery which she said she had purchased from C. P. Huntington, twenty odd years before. The article goes on to state that when he had made enough money, he purchased a horse which he packed and drove before him.[3]

Later the young salesman purchased a large number of "clock notes" at a heavy discount from a merchant in New York who had employed a hundred salesman to dispose of his clocks in the Southern States. Although regarded as a risky venture, he was very successful in his collections. He thus gained experience in negotiation, and developed a keen insight into human nature, coming in contact, as he did, with a great variety of persons. He saw much of the bad features of slavery to which he developed a strong opposition. His tact, courtesy, keen mentality and attractive personality made a favorable impression and won for him many friends.

Several times he came to the home of Mr. Robert Lee Randolph in Winchester, Virginia, where he was always cordially received. Mr. Randolph's son, the late Rt. Rev. A. M. Randolph, Bishop of Virginia, told a friend about the impression the young merchant had made on his father. "He has great ability and strong character," said Mr. Randolph, "and will likely make his mark in the world." The Bishop had lived to see father's prophecy fulfilled greatly beyond expectations.[4]

Between the ages of sixteen and twenty-one, young Huntington had traveled extensively through the states east of the Mississippi River, and was familiar with almost every county in these states. This knowledge was of great value to him in later years when he was building railroads through this section and acquiring valuable coal fields.

During his travels he came in 1837 to Newport News and the banks of the James River and Hampton Roads. He thought then that there could be no better place for a city, and many years later he was able to develop this dream.

Chapter V

A MERCHANT IN ONEONTA

By THE TIME the young traveling salesman had reached his majority in 1842, he had accumulated sufficient funds to enter into a partnership with his brother Solon in Oneonta, New York. Solon had come to Oneonta with his bride in 1840, and opened a store of general merchandise in a stone building that had been occupied for many years by the Mendel Brothers. The firm of Huntington Brothers was enterprising and prospered rapidly. In addition to the store the two men were engaged in various manufacturing enterprises, while Solon became also an extensive land owner.

Oneonta was a post office and township located on the Susquehanna River in Otsego County, New York, about seventy-five miles W.S.W. of Albany. The Act creating the township was passed by the state legislature at Albany, April 17, 1830. The township was formed by taking a portion of each of the townships of Milford, Otego, Huntsville and Davenport. In 1840, the population numbered 1,936 inhabitants and the village contained schools, three or four churches, numerous stores, and several factories, foundries, and mills. It was incorporated as a village after an election on the fourteenth of October 1848, ordered by the county judge, James Hyde, upon application by some of the leading citizens among whose names was that of Collis P. Huntington.[1]

In September 1844, Mr. Huntington married Elizabeth Stoddard of Litchfield County, Connecticut, a member of the well-known Stoddard family of New England, with whom he lived very happily. In paying a tribute to her devotion and helpfulness, Mr. Huntington told how she got ready to leave Oneonta and make the overland journey to California—a trip requiring several months—on two hours notice, and he added that she bore the discomforts of the journey with greater cheerfulness than himself.

They occupied a house in Oneonta at the corner of Chestnut and Church Streets, a square one-story-and-half building with a piazza extending along its whole front and partly down the sides. The piazza was flanked by fluted wooden pillars that reached from foundation to roof. The second story was reached by a rather steep stairway to four sleeping rooms each opening from the square central room at the head of the stairs. The upper floor was lighted from the windows on the sides of the observatory surmounting the center of the roof which, while providing plenty of light to the middle room, left the side chambers in semi-obscurity. Each of these sleeping rooms, however, had a swing window opening directly over a trap door in the ceiling of the piazza by means of which when open, the darkness of the rooms was modified. A profusion of lilacs bloomed in the yard every spring.[2]

After Collis and his wife had left Oneonta to reside in Sacramento, California, his mother and sister Ellen came to reside in this house. There Ellen was married in 1862 to the Rev. Isaac E. Gates, a young Baptist minister, who had but recently been graduated at Hamilton University. In the

Elizabeth Stoddard Huntington, First Wife of Collis P. Huntington

The C. P. Huntingtons and Friends at Niagara Falls, ca. 1866

spring of 1866 the mother went to reside with her daughter, Mary, living at Warsaw in the western part of the State of New York.[3]

On December 2, 1848, the first village election was held in Oneonta in which Collis P. Huntington was elected to the office of Street Commissioner, and Solon was elected Pound Master. On the sixteenth of September 1849, the trustees leased to Solon a piece of ground for the purpose of being used as a pound lot for the full term of twenty years in consideration of one dollar.[4]

A volunteer fire company had been organized in Oneonta and young Huntington appointed as its Chief. The company had a small engine and made frequent practice trips down the streets. Mr. Harvey Baker who lived in Oneonta at the time relates the following incident which occurred about 1845.

The fire company under command of Chief Huntington came down to the mill race between the saw mill and the grist mill for practice, as was often the custom. After practicing for some time throwing water in various directions, someone proposed to try the stream on the grist mill window in its westerly gable. I was then half owner of the mill property with Messrs. Collier and Goodyear, and had it under my charge. Mr. Huntington himself had the hose pipe in hand and asked me:

"Shall I try it?"

"Yes, fire away; I will risk the window," was my prompt reply.

No sooner said than done, the glass and sash were shattered in an instant.

"Don't throw water in the mill, as I have grain there," was my immediate appeal, but the position was so oblique that scarcely any water entered it. A bin of from one hundred to one hundred-fifty bushels of wheat was nearly under the window, but it received no damage. Mr. Huntington offered to pay me for the window but I assured him it was my risk and not his. The quickness of its destruction was a source of much satisfaction as well as surprise to the fire company. Mr. Huntington made a splendid head officer for the fire company.[5]

Collis Potter Huntington was a tall, splendidly formed young man with great muscular power. One day not long after he had arrived at Oneonta while driving a carriage and pair, he passed a hotel and was hailed by the proprietor:

"Huntington, are you busy? If not, I wish you would come in here and give me a hand."

The proprietor went on to tell him that there was to be a dance in the hall of the hotel that evening and some boys of another town had said they were coming over to dance with the girls though uninvited and unwanted, and he wished to stop them.

Huntington put his horses in the stable and went into the hotel. That evening sleighs containing eighteen young men drove up to the door with much noise and jingle of sleigh bells. They came into the hotel and went over to the bar for several rounds of drinks. Huntington, reading a newspaper, was seated at the entrance to the stairway leading to the hall upstairs from which sounds of dancing could be heard.

The young men left the bar and the leader of the gang came across to where Huntington was sitting and said: "Stranger, we would like to pass to go upstairs." There was no reply, and the request was repeated. At the third repetition, the young man took hold of Huntington's chair as though to move it. As he told the story to his son, Mr. Huntington said,

I got to my feet very rapidly and was able to strike with both hands. The room was very crowded, but at the end of the fracas,

Oneonta, Main Street, 1870

S.S. Cresent City of the New York, Havana & New Orleans Line, 1849

I grasped the last one, folded his head and feet together and tossed him through the window. The rest struggled to their feet and got out.

This story was verified by old friends in Oneonta.[6]

Mr. Huntington's memories of Oneonta and its associations must have been very pleasant judging by his use of the name in after years. An early locomotive of the Central Pacific Railroad was named Oneonta; his two private railroad cars were named Oneonta I and Oneonta II; his yacht, a small motor boat on Raquette Lake in New York, was called Oneonta. Between Los Angeles and San Marino in California is a town, Oneonta Park, said to have been so named, however, by Henry E. Huntington, Collis Potter's nephew and Solon's son, who was born in Oneonta.

On the Columbia River in Oregon there is a stream flowing through high walls of rock known as the Oneonta Gorge, and a nearby waterfall called the Oneonta Cataract. While not confirmed, the opinion is strongly held by some persons that these names and that of the S. S. *Oneonta* of the Oregon Steam Navigation Company that operated on the Columbia River were given by Mr. Huntington whose railroad extended to the Columbia River. The name Oneonta is defined by Gannet as meaning "Place of Peace."

The years at Oneonta had developed Collis's trading ability and strengthened his habits of thrift. When, therefore, gold was discovered in California, he decided to go, not as a miner seeking gold, but as a merchant selling the supplies and the machinery needed by the miners. In October 1848, he shipped around the Horn a quantity of goods for trade, and in the spring of 1849, he took passage for California by way of Panama.

Chapter VI

THE SAGA OF PANAMA

THE GOLD SEEKERS from the East usually organized themselves into groups or companies both to travel together and to
work together in the mines. This gave them, so they claimed,
the advantages of agreeable companionship, assistance in
cases of illness or emergency of any kind, and enabled them to
take a large supply of provisions. There were 124 such mining
companies from Massachusetts alone that left for the gold
fields of California in 1849. This scheme, however, did not
work successfully. It usually resulted in the few strong aggressive members having all the responsibilities while the weak
and indolent idled away the time gambling and in much
dissension. Almost invariably the company would break up
upon arrival at San Francisco.[1] When it became known in
Oneonta that Huntington was really going to California, he
was asked to organize and become the leader of a company
or companies for the expedition. He declined, however, to
assume responsibility for the welfare of others on such a long
and difficult journey in a venture where success was so
uncertain.

Three general routes of travel were open to California
in those days: (1) the all-water route around Cape Horn or
through the Magellan Strait; (2) the land and water route
through the Isthmus of Panama or through Mexico; and,

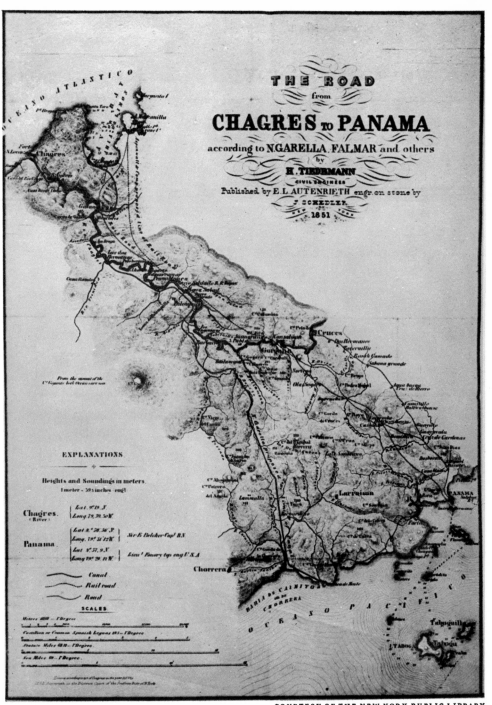

Map of the Isthmus of Panama, 1851

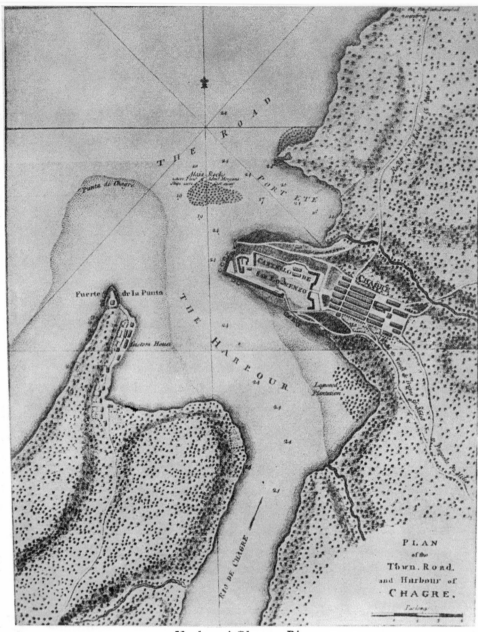

Harbor of Chagres River

(3) the overland route by Santa Fe and the Gila River, known as the Old Spanish Trail, or the South Pass over the Rocky Mountains at 7,000 feet above sea level.[2] Mr. Huntington chose the land and water route and sailed March 15, 1849, from New York on the S.S. *Crescent City* for the Isthmus of Panama. It was the beginning of a long and tiresome journey of five months to reach the Golden Gate.

The first landing place on the isthmus was at Chagres, a village or collection of huts on the right bank of the Chagres River. The entrance to the harbor at the mouth of the river was made difficult by a number of shifting sand bars and rock ridges known as the Laja reef so that steamers usually anchored off the Chagres and landed their pasengers in boats or lighters. The harbor once entered, however, the vessel was perfectly secure.[3] Guarding the entrance to the harbor was a high rocky bluff facing the sea on which were the ruins of the historic castle, San Lorenzo, erected in the latter part of the sixteenth century by the engineer, Juan Antonelli, by order of Philip II of Spain.[4]

The climate of Chagres was said to be among the worst in the world, having tropical temperatures, torrential rainfall, with bilious, remittent and congestive fevers rampant. Occasionally yellow fever and cholera took heavy toll. The sole trade was in the forwarding of goods across the isthmus. Accommodations were scanty and most inferior, and passengers usually hurried up the river without stopping an hour among the verminous huts unless forced to do so.[5]

The ascent of the Chagres River amid most beautiful scenery to Gargono or Cruces a few miles farther, was made in native boats, long slender cayucas, fashioned usually from the trunks of the espeve tree, a compact wood with but little grain that did not crack or splinter when dragged over the rocks of the rapids. They were hollowed out by means of fire and the machete.[6] A palm leaf thatch or *toldo* afforded the passengers shade while the baggage piled amidships was covered with oiled cloths, *encerrados* as they were termed. In the lower reaches the river was a muddy, sluggish stream which higher up became swirling rapids flowing through an almost impenetrable green jungle. Few signs of civilization could be seen; now and then a group of huts or the hacienda of a ranch where passengers sometimes camped en route. The journey was not a long one, the time required depending upon the heaviness of the cayuca and the number of active boatmen and varying from ten to thirty-six hours.[7]

When the passengers from the S. S. *Crescent City* arrived at Chagres, they found there passengers from previous steamers, who had been having trouble in procuring boats to ascend the river, as high as $30 being charged for a single passage to Gorgona, forty miles away. A committee of three from the *Crescent City* was appointed to go ashore and contract for boats to take about a thousand passengers up the river. Huntington, Hastings of Detroit, and a man named Parbert were selected for the committee. Before accepting his appointment, Huntington said:

Gentlemen, it is well enough to go ashore, but I know that as soon as we land, everybody will try to hire his own boat. I do not want to go on a fool's errand. I propose to contract for boats for as many as are willing to pay ten dollars apiece, and for no others.

The force of his proposition was seen and nearly everybody paid his ten dollars into the fund.

The committee went ashore and made a contract with the native boatmen to take each passenger and his baggage to Gorgona for seven dollars. United States currency was worth at that time about twenty-seven per cent more than Spanish money. Parbert and Hastings went up the river in the first boat in order to engage horses and mules for transportation from Gorgona to Panama, taking the money to be paid to the boatmen at the end of the route. Huntington remained behind and followed in the last boat three days later.

About half-way up the river to Gorgona, Huntington was met by some returning boatmen, who on recognizing him, became furious, exclaiming, "Mucho malos Americanos! Mucho malos Americanos!" and demanded back the money out of which they claimed to have been defrauded. Parbert, it appeared, had bought Spanish money on his arrival at Gorgona, left it in the hands of another person to pay for the boats, and had himself gone to Panama, pocketing the difference of exchange. Huntington pacified the swindled boatmen as well as he could and hurried on to Panama. With intense indignation, he confronted Parbert and compelled him to give back to every passenger his proportion of the money withheld.[8]

The road from Gorgona to Panama, about twenty miles in length, was a mere bridle path with numerous holes and swampy places. The usual method of travel was on horse or mule with another mule to carry the baggage and a muleteer to act as guide. A few persons occasionally chose to make the trip on foot. After a toilsome journey of some eight or ten hours, Panama was reached. From thence passengers embarked for San Francisco and the gold fields.

The city of Panama is situated on the shores of the beautiful Bay of Panama. Before the influx of visitors it contained from 5,000 to 7,000 inhabitants. Accommodations for travelers were very scarce. While healthier than Chagres, Panama was by no means a safe place for strangers. Passengers frequently had to wait weeks for a passage to San Francisco, and, unless provided with ample means, their resources were often exhausted before the opportunity to sail arrived, and then they were unable to go.[9]

When the passengers from the *Crescent City* reached Panama, no vessel was there to take them North, and before Mr. Huntington had secured passage from Panama three months had elapsed, and thousands of Americans had fallen ill. Cholera, dysentery, and yellow fever had claimed many victims.

In a letter to his brother Solon in Oneonta, dated May 9, 1849, Collis wrote:

We are here on the Isthmus of Darien waiting for the *Humboldt* to sail and hoping she will sail soon for if she does not she will have to get another set of passengers as death is carrying off the Americans most fearfully. A gentleman told me yesterday, and he has a chance to know, that there are from eight to ten deaths a day . . . This climate tells most fearfully on Northerners at this season of the year.

Numerous organized companies arrived with their captains and lieutenants, but the members generally quarreled among themselves when they reached the isthmus. Many came to Huntington to sell out so they could return home and he bought their outfits whenever he could see a chance to make a profitable trade.[10] Others who had means took passage to a South American port and sailed thence to San Francisco, making a more rapid and a more comfortable journey.[11]

Huntington offered to transfer freight and baggage across the isthmus and quickly secured enough orders to pack the donkey which he purchased. Back and forth across the isthmus he went, walking the twenty miles from Panama to Gorgona twenty-four times in making his twelve trips.[12] He would start early in the morning, making half the distance before the heat became intense, then the remainder during the late afternoon and night. He never felt one touch of any of the illnesses that attacked other men.

Hearing of a little schooner that was offered for sale at Estebula he went on foot to see her. With a young man named Carmichael from Montgomery County, New York, he went up the Bogota River and walked some thirty-nine miles under a hot sun. Arrived there, he purchased the vessel, the *Emma*, and loaded her with supplies—rice, potatoes, flour, sugar, dried beef, etc. Carmichael in the meantime had been attacked with brain fever and was delirious during the five days passage back to Panama. Huntington nursed him all the way, but the sick man died soon after they reached Panama and was buried there. Many others, a large proportion, in fact, fell victims to the tropical fever. Huntington gained ten pounds in weight because as he said, "I always keep too busy to be sick." The supplies and the little *Emma* were sold at a profit.[13]

After about three months at Panama, Huntington paid one hundred dollars for his ticket. Three hundred dollars would have bought a first-class passage. The voyage from Panama was a long two months. The first part was rainy and dreary enough, and were spent by many between seasickness and homesickness. Mr. J. E. Gordon, one of the few survivors living in the year 1900, recalled Huntington as "a sunshiny companion when skies were cloudy and seas rough. He was a genial young man, and travelers liked him," he said.

The dreadful diet to which the steerage passengers were subjected brought everyone next door to starvation before the ship reached San Francisco. Indeed, some of Huntington's fellow passengers did not survive that diet which was the worst of its kind. The bill of fare was reduced to this:

Sunday—Coffee, dough, tea
Monday—Coffee, beef, tea
Tuesday—Coffee, beef soup, tea
Wednesday—Coffee, rice, tea
Thursday—Coffee, dough, tea
Friday—Coffee, pork, tea
Saturday—Coffee, salt pork, tea

With hardtack every day and bean soup for dessert.

If trouble and danger bind men together this voyage was enough to build up friendships. The people who came in the steerage of the good ship *Humboldt* held together all those years with a clannish persistence in a society organized by Mr. Huntington, the Society of the Humboldters. He had been the prime mover in all their reunions and arranged that they should meet at a banquet each year on the thirtieth day of August, anniversary of the day of their arrival at San Francisco. Year by year the number dwindled and on August 30, 1899, only four men sat down together. Huntington could not be present often, but he would send them a word of good cheer, sometimes a substantial check.[14]

Portraits of the following Humboldters appeared in the San Francisco *Call*, September 2, 1900, page 11, from the collection of James L. King: R. E. Raimond, James Irvine, James Anthony, W. R. S. Taylor, John Wright, Benjamin P.

Cayucas on the Chagres River

*The Humbolters: Passengers Who Arrived at San Francisco
on the Ship Humboldt, August 30, 1849*

Flint, R. B. Turner, A. B. Perkins, W. W. Light, Madison Spaulding, S. W. Shaw, A. M. Kennady, C. P. Huntington, J. E. Gordon, R. E. Cole, J. H. Alvord, H. Iskelheimer, Simon Mattingly, Levi P. Rashford, A. A. Bennett, Isaac E. Davis, J. B. Lewis, Richard Kirby, Addison M. Starr, D. W. Hunt, John Clar, Dr. John W. Morse, Jonathan Kittredge, Captain McArthur and R. E. Hendricks.

Biographical sketches of the following Humboldters by Thomas B. Merry appeared in the same issue of *The Call*: Jonathan Kittredge, R. E. Raimond, James Anthony, W. R. S. Taylor, A. B. Perkins, Alexander M. Kennady, S. W. Shaw, Addison M. Starr, Levi P. Rashford, A. A. Bennett, Dr. John F. Morse and Richard Kirby.

The *Humboldt* passengers debarked at San Francisco August 30, 1849, going their several ways. Collis Potter Huntington had left New York on the fifteenth of March, had traveled twenty-five hundred miles to Chagres River, sixty miles across the Isthmus of Panama from Chagres to Panama, and thirty-five hundred miles from Panama to San Francisco. He had left New York with $1,200 in cash, and earned enough on the way to pay all his expenses and have $5,000 in cash upon his arrival at San Francisco.

Chapter VII

A MERCHANT IN SACRAMENTO

ON THE THIRTIETH DAY of August 1849, the *Humboldt* sailed
through the Golden Gate after a long and tiresome journey
from Panama. Some of the Humboldters borrowed money
from Huntington in order to celebrate their arrival in fitting
manner by a "good square meal." Huntington himself
"dined" upon crackers and cheese. When he was asked how
much he would take for his chances of success in California
he replied, "I would sell out in a minute for $10,000."

The streets of San Francisco were full of people, hurrying
to and fro, and of as diverse and bizarre character as one
could imagine. Yankees of every possible variety, native Californians in serapes and sombreros, Chileans, Sonorans, Kana-
kas from Hawaii, Chinese with long queues, Malays with
their creeses, and others of unrecognizable nationality. On
every side stood buildings of all kinds, just begun or half
finished, the greater part of them mere canvas sheds, open
in front, and covered with all kinds of signs in all kinds of
languages. In the Plaza, the American flag was flying from
a high pole in front of a long one-story adobe building used
as the Customs House.[1]

More than two hundred vessels of different kinds were anchored in the harbor, most of them deserted by their crews,
the gold fever having carried them off to the mines.[2]

Prices were staggering. Parker House, the main hotel, rented for $110,000 yearly; the second floor being sublet to a gambling fraternity for $60,000. A small cellar office twelve feet square and only six feet deep brought $250 a month. A single cot amid dozens of others jammed together in a shed rented for $5 per day. Food, too, was exorbitant, $20 to $25 per week for meals at inferior boarding houses. A "filling" meal in the best restaurants cost from $8 to $10. Money was loaned at fourteen per cent monthly.[3]

Huntington did not remain long in San Francisco, but sailed for Sacramento on a schooner, paying his passage by helping to load the vessel. Arriving in Sacramento, he immediately went to the mine fields where one day's work was enough to convince him that he preferred another method of seeking his fortune. After spending some time in studying the locations of the various mines, he returned to Sacramento, determined to establish a store dealing principally with miners' supplies consisting largely of hardware, powder and provisions.

Sacramento was located at the head of ship navigation on the Sacramento River at the junction of its tributary, the American River. A few miles above the city, a sand bar extended across the river and from that point up the river was so shallow as to be navigable only by vessels of light draft. The city had an excellent levee to protect it from the dangerous floods that frequently sweep down the rivers, alongside of which ships could lie in safety and upon which they could discharge their cargoes without the expense of lighterage.[4]

This levee, built by the city, was at that time three feet high, six feet wide at the crest and four yards across at the base. It began on high ground near Sutterville, ran west to

the east bank of the Sacramento River, then north to the
mouth of the American River; from there it extended nearly
a mile along the south bank of the American River, then east
to high ground. This levee and several others were swept
away by heavy floods before the river was tamed.[5]

The river in front of the city was a quarter of a mile wide,
giving ample room for the working of vessels. At the time of
Huntington's arrival, the levee for a mile along Front Street
was lined with vessels, in some places they were two deep.
There were large numbers of steamers, ships, barks, brigs,
schooners and other small craft. Vessels could come from
the Bay, a distance of one hundred four miles, in twenty-four
hours, and the longest passage seldom exceeded four days.
Steam tugs were expected soon to ply the river.[6]

The town of Sacramento at that time was in the form of a
square, one and a half miles to a side. The streets were laid
at right angles; those running east and west were "named
for the alphabet"; those running north and south "named
for arithmetic." There were but few houses in Sacramento
in the spring of 1849; in the fall of 1850, however, the population was ten thousand, most of them living in tents.[7]

The fortunate location of Sacramento made it the most
important town for the mine fields of the Yuba, Feather and
Bear Rivers, Deer Creek, Cosumme, Dry Creek and the
upper Sacramento, together with the contiguous dry dig-
gings. From this extensive mining country, good roads (in
the dry season) converged to Sacramento City. Along the
roads hundreds of teams toiled daily to supply this vast region
with provisions, clothing, miners' tools and other necessary
articles. To supply the Sacramento market thus continually
depleted, steamers and other vessels arrived daily from San

Francisco bringing merchandise that had been discharged from that port and reshipped to Sacramento. However, two hundred vessels had at that time been cleared from the States for Sacramento direct. This proved most advantageous as the cost of shipping from San Francisco to Sacramento exceeded the cost of shipping from New York to San Francisco.[8]

In contemplating this flow of merchandise, Mr. Huntington realized that in this was his opportunity. Where camps were located, towns must spring up and more and more provisions, lumber and innumerable articles of hardware would be required. "More distinctly than all else he realized that where Gold is King, as in a mining country, Extravagance and High Prices make up his Court." Mr. Huntington left home a merchant and a merchant he remained.[9]

As lumber in California in 1849 cost a dollar a foot, Mr. Huntington's first store of general merchandise opened in October 1849, was in a big tent, the roof and sides of which were made out of old sails. As his business expanded, as it speedily did, other tents were added and soon it took five of them to hold his stock. Rivals in the trade were soon outdistanced by the establishment of team service to the various mining camps. Young as he was, he soon gained the sobriquet of "Old Huntington" in compliment to his sagacity. When men had goods to sell and it seemed impossible to find a buyer, it was common saying: "Go to Old Huntington, he will always make an offer." He wore at the time a wide-brimmed Panama hat which came down almost to his shoulders which helped to identify him.

His maxim of trade was this: Anything that can be bought for less than production, that is not perishable, and that is an article in general use, is worth buying and holding. The story of one of his purchases will illustrate this. He once bought a lot of bar steel at a time when there was no manufacturing in California. Nobody wanted steel and the owner was glad to get rid of it at a cent a pound. For four years he stored it in his back yard under old sails; but when quartz mining was reached, everybody wanted steel, and he sold the major part of it at one dollar a pound, and his patience had its reward.[10]

There were many stories current among old Sacramento men of Mr. Huntington's early business career all showing the remarkable sagacity, quickness to see and grasp opportunities, his sterling honesty and love of fair play which have been his most conspicuous traits. He was once asked to buy a large tent, the property of a company intended to go to the mining fields, but they had disagreed and wanted to divide their property and separate. He offered them $150 for it, which they accepted provided they should have a day in which to remove their other possessions. Huntington agreed, picked up a piece of charcoal and marked on the tent in large letters "For Sale." In two hours he had sold it for $250 to the amazement of the previous owners still sitting under its shade, who had not thought of this simple device.

When the San Francisco harbor was filled with ships deserted by their crews, Huntington was offered large quantities of ships' bread at a very low price, and he bought all he could get, foreseeing that the ships would sail away some time and would need supplies. When this happened, he sold the bread at great advance, while others wondered why they had not foreseen this event.

Old Californians said that in those early days when anyone in Sacramento or San Francisco was stuck with a consignment of something which had no sale, he went to Huntington

San Francisco in November, 1848

San Francisco in November, 1849

who was pretty sure to buy if the article was cheap enough and very certain to sell it for a handsome profit. Those who knew him in those days say he was always content with a fair profit, especially when selling at wholesale, and he became known as the man who never misrepresented the article he wished to sell. His customers increased rapidly because he left them also an opportunity to make a fair profit. There is a story told of him that he once bought several hundred grain cradles which had lain a long time in the owner's loft. Mr. Huntington unpacked them, showed them on the street and presently, as he had foreseen, there was a brisk demand for them at $18.00 each. "You might get $30.00 for them," said a friend, "are you not making a mistake?" "Not at all," replied Huntington, "I paid $5.00 and I want to sell them all. They are too bulky to keep. It is better to let the others have a chance to make some money."[11]

In order to keep well supplied with merchandise Huntington made frequent trips by boat to San Francisco. He would climb Telegraph Hill and scan the harbor with a pair of strong binoculars for ships that had come into the harbor during the night. He would be among the first to come alongside a ship in his small boat carrying a bag of gold dust with which he paid for his purchases. He divided his time in the earlier days between his principal business house in Sacramento and three trading posts at Weaver Creek, Marthelness Creek, and Mud Springs. He frequently traveled by night as well as by day, back and forth over a country beset with dangers peculiar to a new and comparatively lawless mining community. At times he carried large sums of gold and in one case of emergency he walked fifty-four miles in one night carrying with him forty-five pounds of gold dust.[12]

While handling so successfully the larger transactions of his business, he did not overlook the small details. "Watch the small economies," was the motto of his life. Said he:

> I have always looked after the little things of my business; weightier matters will take care of themselves. I told one of my clerks in Sacramento to pick up a four-penny nail that had been lying on the floor for some time, remarking to him: "The time taken by you to pick it up is worth more than the nail, perhaps, but if you don't save the four-penny nail, pretty soon you will attach no value to a six-penny; next, an eight-penny will follow it, and finally you will not care for spikes."[13]

Among the 10,000 inhabitants of Sacramento in 1850 there were only two families, those of William H. Watson and Dr. Birdsall, most of the population being made up of young men adventurers and a few good business men. The place had all the vices of the usual pioneer settlement: gambling dens, saloons on every corner, houses of ill fame, and all the evil which they developed. Home life was unknown; few men withstood the lure of the temptations that surrounded them. Mr. Huntington retained his early New England habits: he did not drink, or smoke, or gamble. He slept in his store and was up and at work before the earliest of his clerks.

To protect these young men from the dangers on every side, they were required by contract to remain in the store from supper time until breakfast. The upper story of the frame building had been furnished with comfortable lodgings, well lighted, and supplied with a collection of books and newspapers with which to pass the time. The books had been purchased at an auction for $29.00, and later they formed the nucleus of the first free circulating library in Sacramento.

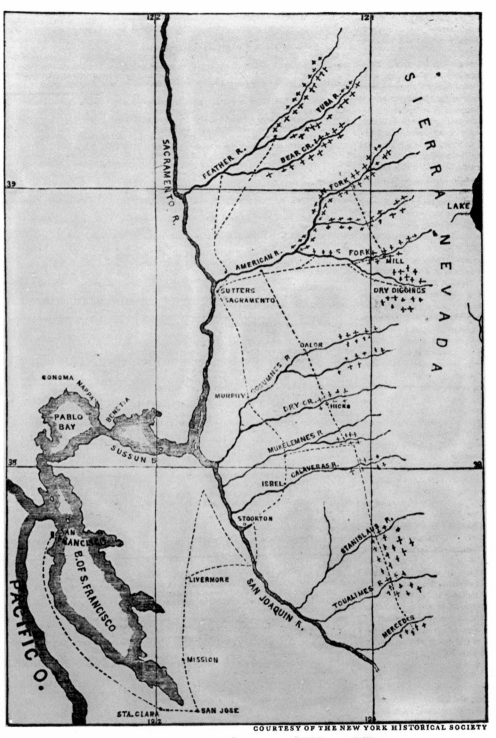

Map of the Gold Region of California, ca. 1855

The meals served to Mr. Huntington and his clerks at the same table were superior to any that the restaurants of Sacramento could furnish.

For years his store was probably the only one in Sacramento that remained closed on Sundays, both in regard for the sacred observance of the day and for the health and recreation of his employees. A number of these young men, schooled to usefulness and integrity under this roof, afterwards became good business men and worthy citizens of California. They acknowledged a profound obligation to their employer.[14]

Huntington was scrupulously honest, and to use a homely phrase, "did not allow anyone to run over him." The miscellaneous business that had been started in a tent, a jobbing as well as retail business in foodstuffs, powder, hardware—in short, all the necessities of a pioneer community grew after a while into a permanent hardware store at 54 K Street.

In 1851, Mr. Huntington made a trip back to the East. Upon his return, he was accompanied by Mrs. Huntington, making the long trip overland. For a time they lived at 45 K Street, then moved to the upper floor of the 54 K Street building.[15] Later they had a dwelling erected on M Street, between 3rd and 4th which they occupied until they left Sacramento in 1863 to reside permanently in New York. Many years later the M Street house was torn down and replaced by a hotel for Japanese, many of whom had settled in that district.

Chapter VIII

HUNTINGTON AND HOPKINS

HUNTINGTON'S MERCANTILE ESTABLISHMENT in Sacramento was opened in October 1849, in a tent on K Street under his own name only, C. P. Huntington. On May 1, 1850, he was joined by Daniel Hammond, and the firm became known as Huntington and Hammond. Mr. E. Schultz joined the firm in June of the same year and the firm's name became Huntington, Hammond & Company. In March 1852, both Hammond and Schultz retired to open a store of their own at Mr. Huntington's suggestion, and the name of the establishment again became C. P. Huntington.[1]

On the night of November 2, 1852, a terrible fire swept through Sacramento destroying most of the inflammable buildings with their contents. C. P. Hutington is listed as one whose loss in building and merchandise amounted to $50,000. The loss of Hopkins & Miller's store next to that of C. P. Huntington was estimated at $55,000.[2]

On May 1, 1853, F. A. Massol and Henry Merwin joined Mr. Huntington and the firm's name became Huntington, Massol & Company. By limitation the partnership expired in two years, and Massol and Merwin went into business on J Street between 3rd and 4th Streets.[3]

Mr. Huntington had become acquainted with Mr. Mark Hopkins of the firm of Hopkins & Miller next door, and the two men had formed a warm and lasting attachment for each other. Mr. Hopkins had formerly been in business at Lockport, New York. He and E. H. Miller, Jr., had formed a partnership at an early date in Sacramento. The firm was dissolved in 1853, and Hopkins returned to the East, but drifted back again to California. He had said that the only thing that would ever induce him to go into active business again would be a partnership with Huntington. As this was agreeable to them both, the firm of Huntington & Hopkins was formed in 1855, and the two friends remained associated in business twenty-three years until the death of Mr. Hopkins in 1878. About this partnership Mr. Huntington said:

> During that period, we did a business amounting to hundreds of millions of dollars in hardware, railroad building, and various other enterprises, but not an unkind word, so far as I can remember, ever passed between us. Mark Hopkins was one of the truest and best men who ever lived. He had a keen analytical mind and was thoroughly accurate. He was strictly an office man, had general supervision of the books, contracts, etc. When our articles of partnership were drawn up and signed, each took a copy and placed it in his private safe, and there these contracts remained unexamined and unread by either of us during our entire association. I have never seen mine since. I believe it is in the old safe in Sacramento yet.[4]

Mark Hopkins told an acquaintance that they had never owned a dollar's worth of stock in a mine, never sent out a drummer to get business (this was before the reorganization in 1868), and had never sued a man for debt. A large percentage of the business of the house was on credit, and sooner or later these accounts were nearly all collected.

The House of Huntington & Hopkins was conducted on the "most approved business principles." It came into prominence rapidly and was recognized as sound both economically and morally. Perhaps no other house in the State had a higher mark of commercial credit in the reports of commercial agencies. This credit proved of incalculable benefit in the early years to the Central Pacific Railroad Company. Its name became early the best guarantee of promises to pay. The House of Huntington & Hopkins was never for a moment impaired, and its name spread to every town and mining camp on the coast and it did an immense business. The fluctuations in trade and the competition in California were extreme in those days and business houses lasted on the average about two years, occasionally as long as five years. Neither the House of Huntington & Hopkins nor its successor, Huntington, Hopkins & Company ever saw a piece of their paper dishonored, a remarkable tribute to their ability and integrity.[5]

The population of California had been drawn from both free and slave states, and the first issue which confronted them in forming the new state was whether it should be slave or free. The Compromise of 1850, known also as the Omnibus Bill, decided that, however, and California was admitted to the Union as a free state in 1850.

To the leading men of the free state party, Huntington was "bound by the strongest ties that bind men in a common cause," and he espoused the free state side of the controversy with characteristic energy and enthusiasm. He was mainly instrumental in establishing, maintaining, and shaping the policy of the first out-and-out Free Soil newspaper in the State, *The Times,* with James McClatchy as proprietor and editor. It was published from the quarters furnished free in the upper story of Huntington & Hopkins at 54 K Street.

Portrait of Collis Potter Huntington, ca. 1855

The enterprise had been carried through in spite of great opposition, aided by a group of men whose custom it was to meet there for discussion of political and other problems of public interest.[6]

When the election of Lincoln to the Presidency by the Republican Party had made the paper safe and self-sustaining, they presented the plant and good will to its publishers. The store became a sort of rendezvous for the rising Republican Party on the West Coast. They had sustained E. P. Tracy and Colonel Edward D. Baker in their Republican canvas for office. Said one of them: "The last thing we were accustomed to do before starting on a tour was to call at Huntington & Hopkins to get the necessary funds to meet our traveling expenses."[7] Among this group were two men who later came to be associated with Huntington & Hopkins in the construction of the Central Pacific and other railroads, Charles Crocker and Leland Stanford, the latter the unsuccessful candidate for Governor of California in 1859, and the successful candidate for the same office in 1861.

Both members of the firm of Huntington & Hopkins were very active in forming the Central Pacific Railroad Company in 1861 to build the western end of the first transcontinental railroad. After the promise of a loan from the Government was procured in 1862, and the work had begun in 1863, Huntington removed to New York as purchasing agent and financier of the new company. He continued also as purchasing agent for Huntington & Hopkins.

As time passed and he became more and more involved in supplying the needs of the railroad company, the employees of Huntington & Hopkins assumed greater responsibilities. Finally W. R. S. Foye, one of their most trusted men, wrote to Mr. Huntington who in turn wrote to Mr. Hopkins on January 11, 1867, as follows:

Mr. Foye writes that he is not altogether satisfied with his position. I have written to him to have a talk with you and state just what he wants. Mr. Foye has been with us a long time and has always been faithful to our interests. While I leave the whole matter with you, I think we should be liberal with him.

Later, on February 2, 1867, he writes:

I shall be very glad to hear that you have made arrangements for Foye to stay with us.

On March 12, 1867, he writes:

It costs a fearful amount of money to pay all the bills of this railroad and the store, and it keeps me very busy. I sometimes think I would change my place for any other in the world.

In a letter dated March 29, 1867, he refers to the sale of the store as follows:

As to selling out our store or a portion of it, I quite agree with you, and think we have too much to do to do it well—at least I will speak for myself. I do not know of any other parties that I had rather sell it to than Foye, Miller, and Gallatan. I think with you that it would be well (at least for a time) to keep one-fourth interest ourselves. And if you wish to sell one-half or three-fourths interest, do so. As to the plan for the stock and the manner of payment, I shall leave entirely with you, feeling that my interest is as safe in your hands as in my own. While I would like very much to go to Sacramento and take you by the hand and talk over matters as in years gone by, but if I should sell all my interest at 54 K, I think that I had rather you would do it while I am here, than do it myself there. I do not think I could sell all my interest there and walk out of the old store without dropping a tear on the threshold, for the old place is somehow dear to me with all my losses there by fire and flood.

After the sale had taken place, Mr. Huntington wrote to Mr. Hopkins in a letter dated December 8, 1867:

I am satisfied with the sale that you have made of the four-fifths of our stock and hardware, and if the Boys do the best that they know (as I doubt not that they will) they ought to make their fortunes by giving the business their undivided attention. Now I hardly think it is for the interest of Huntington, Hopkins & Company that I should do the buying now. I will not turn my back to anyone as a buyer when I have the time, but the first is the business of the different railroads that I represent which is enough for any one man to do . . .

I would like very much to see you and talk over matters, but it has seemed so necessary for the last three years that you should be there and I here, that I could not devise any means by which we could get together without business and railroad suffering.[8]

These letters reveal Mr. Huntington's warm affection for Mr. Hopkins and an abiding faith; they reveal a deep sentiment (at which his critics would scoff) expressed when planning to sell the hardware store he had founded; and they show his genuine interest in the welfare of the young men in his employ.

Chapter IX

HUNTINGTON, HOPKINS & COMPANY

THE FIRM OF Huntington & Hopkins was reorganized on January 1, 1868, admitting to partnership Albert Gallatin, William R. S. Foye, Charles Miller, and Horace H. Seaton, who had all been in the employ of the firm and largely identified with its business. The new firm's name was thereafter known as Huntington, Hopkins & Company.

Albert Gallatin (no relation to Albert Gallatin, Jefferson's Secretary of the Treasury) was born at Sparta, Livingston County, New York. He came to California in 1860 and tried mining on the Salmon River without success. He arrived in Sacramento in 1861 without a dollar, and applied to Huntington & Hopkins for work. He accepted the job of porter, the only one available at the time, from which humble position he rose to that of salesman. He testified later to the interest Mr. Huntington took in his welfare and the pains he took to advance him in the business. In 1864, he engaged in the hardware business with George P. Howe at Dayton, Nevada, but sold out to his partner in 1867 and resumed the duties of salesman for Huntington & Hopkins. The next year he became a member of the firm.

W. R. S. Foye was a native of Wiscasset, Maine, and received a good business education in Boston. He came to California in 1856 and engaged as salesman with the firm

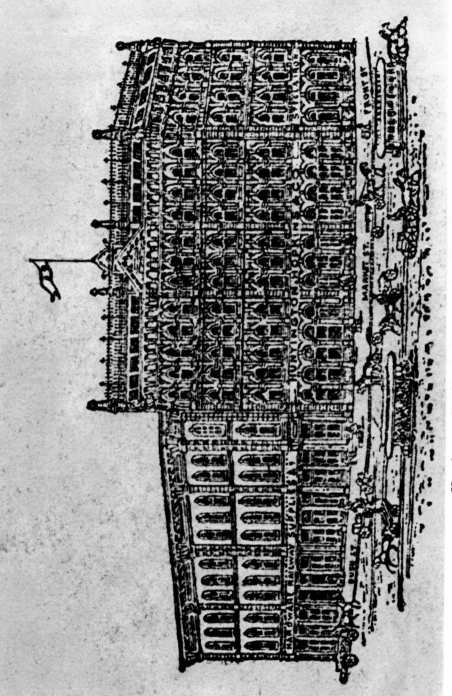

Huntington, Hopkins & Company, San Francisco

Iron Safe of Huntington, Hopkins & Company

of Huntington & Hopkins. He was a modest retiring man but had the reputation of being a shrewd, careful business man.

Charles Miller was born in Green County, New York, and came to California in 1856. He was at once employed as bookkeeper for E. H. Miller & Co., and remained with them until 1860, when he was installed as bookkeeper for Huntington & Hopkins. In 1862, he resigned and entered the employ of Hooker & Company, of which firm he subsequently became a member, and with it was absorbed into that of Huntington, Hopkins & Company.[1]

Horace H. Seaton of Newark, New Jersey, a nephew of Mrs. C. P. Huntington, was a bookkeeper with the firm at the time of its reorganization and became one of the new partners. He withdrew from the firm in 1876 and his interest was absorbed by the firm. The death of Mark Hopkins in 1878 further reduced the number of members in the firm.

About the time of reorganization the company bought the stock and good will of Hooker & Company, a firm that had been doing hardware and metal business in Sacramento for many years. The junior partners assumed full charge. Their stock of heavy and shelf hardware, builders' hardware, mechanics' tools, mining supplies, powder, fuse, cutlery, bar and sheet iron, gas and water pipe, etc., etc., was full and complete. The trade was principally with jobbers who found that they could purchase from Huntnigton, Hopkins & Company to better advantage than upon their own account.

By 1878, the old frame building at 54 K Street had given place to a large building with a frontage of 80 feet on K Street extending back 160 feet to an alley; across this was the iron warehouse having a frontage of 30 feet and running back 160 feet to L Street. To this was added an extensive shed which sheltered a large quantity of goods. The buildings were of brick with two floors and basement, all built in the most substantial manner and furnished with iron covers for the sky lights.[2]

In 1885 the store had grown into an immense three-story building. In the east half were the offices, counting rooms, sample and sportsman's departments, etc. The basement was utilized as a vast storeroom for various classes of goods. The west half of the building was devoted to a general salesroom with entry, receiving, and stock clerk's offices. A large building 140 feet by 180 feet, running from L Street to the alley and connected with the main store on K Street by archways, was used for storerooms.[3]

Upon the completion of the Western Pacific Railroad in 1870, it was decided to establish a branch house of Huntington, Hopkins & Company at San Francisco. At that time, Russell & Erwin Manufacturing Company, an Eastern firm of large means, desired to sell their branch house in San Francisco which they had operated a number of years without profit. Huntington, Hopkins & Company purchased their stock and good will and established a branch house at the junction of Bush and Market Streets. In 1881, they purchased the lot at the corner of Front and Market Streets and erected thereon a four-story, Iron front building, connecting it with their other store, making an entire frontage on Bush, Market, and Front Streets of 250 feet. Finding this location insufficient to accommodate their fast-growing business, they erected a four-story and basement brick building, 187½ feet square, on their lots on the east side of First Street near Market Street. Having an opportunity in 1888 to purchase the two lots on Fremont Street connecting with the First Street property, they started the construction of a five-story and basement building, the first story composed of granite and iron columns, the four stories above of sandstone and patent stone brick. This group of buildings made Huntington, Hopkins & Company one of the largest and most complete stores of its kind in the United States.

All goods were received and shipped from the center of the building under cover, there being a driveway through the entire building with space to turn heavily loaded trucks in the center. There were three sidewalk elevators, one of them capable of lifting a truck with bars of iron twenty-two feet long; four elevators for use in the four-story building and two for the five-story building. In addition, there were two hand-package elevators for the rapid handling of packages requiring quick delivery.[4]

Huntington, Hopkins & Company were among the first in their line to sense the change from the old method of dealing in merchandise, and were among the first to send out traveling salesmen through California, Oregon, Washington Territory, British Columbia, Nevada, and Arizona. In this way they not only retained but increased their trade, notwithstanding the opening of the Atchison, Topeka & Santa Fé Railroad into Southern California and the Northern Pacific Railroad into Oregon and Washington Territory, making direct connection with eastern cities. Their goods were sold and shipped all the way from Alaska and British Columbia to ports along the Mexican and Central American Coasts; also from Nevada, Arizona, Utah, and Idaho. The ramifications of their trade included even manufacturing countries beyond the seas.

Their methods of business from the first differed from those afterwards in vogue. Instead of letting newspapers into their confidence and encouraging astounding and boastful stories of their accomplishments, they preferred to keep quietly and patiently at work without regard to the ways of others in the trade or for popular applause. Scores of their competitors, who were advertising the great things they were going to accomplish, fell by the wayside.

In February 1888, the firm was incorporated under the name of Huntington-Hopkins Company with Mr. Gallatin as President to reside in San Francisco; Mr. Miller, Vice-President and Purchasing Agent to reside in New York; Mr. Huntington, Treasurer; and Mr. Foye, Secretary, in charge of the Sacramento house. Mr. Seaton, having withdrawn in 1876, and Mr. Hopkins' death in 1878, left these the only surviving members of the firm and also the only stockholders of the new company.

It has been said that the true merchant is not content merely with buying goods at one price and selling them at another, but that he creates commerce by promoting manufactures, stimulating consumption, and directing trade into economic channels. Mr. Huntington was just such a merchant, the Sacramento *Union* declares in the issue of December 5, 1886, and gives the following instances as proof:

For many years England manufactured the files used in America. There was a belief among American iron-makers that no one could make files but the English. During the War Between the States when the Confederate warship *Alabama* was driving American commerce from the seas, the English manufacturer was reaping a rich harvest by manufacturing hardware for America and shipping it in

English bottoms. The house of Huntington & Hopkins, being the largest importers of hardware on the Pacific Coast, Mr. Huntington determined if possible to find a manufacturer whose wares equalled those of the English. He sent an agent to the great foundries and machine shops at Pittsburgh to learn what American files were used and stood the test of the English files. His inquiry developed the fact that one brand of files manufactured in this country was equal to the best English brands, but that the manufactory was small, making it difficult for machinists to obtain this brand of American files.

Mr. Huntington sent for the manager to ascertain if the capacity of his manufactory could not be increased by the extension of credit in the way of capital based upon large orders. The answer was in the affirmative, whereupon Mr. Huntington supplied the manufacturer with sufficient capital to enlarge his works and gave him orders which justified the enlargement. As a result, American files could successfully compete with the established brands of the old world.

Another instance relates to drill steel. When the Central Pacific Railroad was being constructed and the vast work of tunneling the mountains was in progress, Mr. Huntington was determined to find a steel which would answer as a substitute for British drill steel. The foreman of the work followed the traditional method of ordering English steel only; but the use of American steel supplied by Mr. Huntington broke down the old barriers of prejudice and the house has steadily adhered to the purchase of the American article where brands equal in quality to the English brand could be found.

Mr. Huntington's knowledge of American manufacturers was equal, if not superior, to that of any other man on the continent. He had traced the history of American manufactures until he was familiar with the details of every step by which American brands of axes, forks, and edged tools have come into use. His accounts of the struggles that American manufacturers have had in reaching a high state of perfection occasionally furnished subjects of his conversation, among which was the interesting incident of the John Collins axe.

Mr. Collins began in a small way to manufacture his axes. At that time the English axes were those almost solely in use in America. Collins took his axes to the leading hardware house in New York, soliciting contracts to supply their trade. The merchants declined to give him the price he asked; whereupon Collins informed them that his axes would be offered to their trade and would go into universal use. He continued manufacturing axes, sending them throughout the country, selling them to woodsmen and others at retail. The axe was superior to the English manufacture, and soon orders poured in on the wholesale houses for the Collins axe. The leading hardware house in New York to which Collins had originally applied had none of the Collins axes to supply the trade, so instead of ordering axes direct from Collins, the company bought a few of his brand and sent them to England for reproduction. The imitation was a failure and the very large order given the English manufacturers remained on their hands. Throughout South America, Australia, and South Africa the Collins axe came into common use as well as in the United States of America.

These incidents could be extended and relate to the manufacture of screws, butts, house hardware, locks, saws and planes. In fact, as relates to saws, Spear & Jackson of London once held control of the American market with their English brand, not only in America, but in nearly all the colonies of Great Britain. The house of Huntington, Hopkins & Company has thrown the influence of the Pacific Coast in favor of American manufactures everywhere and thereby assisted them to get upon a firm footing, and in this sense, it is preeminently a house of merchants.

The history of the house of Huntington, Hopkins & Company is in part the history of the earlier days of the first great transcontinental railroad. From the time they began their great work in the construction of the Central Pacific, and later in the construction of other railroads, the firm was most active in furnishing many of the necessary supplies. As the work progressed and its scope widened, however, it became more and more apparent that additional assistance in the management of Huntington & Hopkins was urgently needed. Hence the enlargement of the firm as above described into the great mercantile house of Huntington, Hopkins & Company of Sacramento and San Francisco.[5]

Chapter X

PACIFIC RAILROAD PROJECTS

ON JANUARY 25, 1885, Mr. Huntington wrote a letter to the Honorable James W. Throckmorton, Chairman of the Committee on Pacific Railroads, which began as follows:

From the time when President Jefferson dispatched an expedition overland under Captains Lewis and Clark, to examine and report upon the Northwest Territory, newly acquired by treaty in the early part of the century, down to the acquisition of California as a result of the war with Mexico, the only communication with the Pacific was by voyage around Cape Horn. The commercial intercourse with the two sides of the continent was confined to the exchange of a few furs and peltries by an occasional trading or whaling ship. The intervening territory between the advanced outposts of European settlement on the East, and the fur trading and cattle herding Missions of the West was known to consist for the most part of desert plains and still more sterile mountain ranges, the whole fertile portions of which were occupied by warlike Indians, jealous of the intrusion of the white man upon their domain over which then roamed vast herds of bison which served them for subsistence. The transit across this formidable country was limited to an occasional armed exploring or emigrant party to the Oregon Territory. Not until the discovery of gold in California was the overland journey deemed practicable for purposes of migration, and was then accompanied with grave perils from the elements as well as the wild and treacherous Indians. The shorter route by sea voyage and portage across the isthmus was the reliance for the carriage of passengers, mails and property.

The moving of heavy burdens which theretofore had been practicable only by the power of gravity, the wind, or the muscular force of tamed animals, had in the meantime been undergoing a revolution by the successful application of the steam engine in hauling loads upon an improved roadway and vehicles adapted thereto. As might be expected, there were imaginative minds who speculatively began to predict the wonders this new agent might perform.

On July 4, 1828, was laid the cornerstone—yes, cornerstone—of the Baltimore and Ohio Railroad, America's first railroad for passengers and freight, and soon thereafter proposals began from various parts of the country for a railroad to the Pacific, several of which are here briefly outlined:

On February 6, 1832, an article appeared in *The Emigrant,* a weekly newspaper published in Ann Arbor, Michigan, suggesting a railroad from New York to Oregon along the shores of Lake Erie and Lake Michigan, to be a national project. It was said to have been written by the editor, Judge S. W. Dexter.

Dr. Samuel Bancroft Barlow of Granville, Massachusetts, wrote a letter to *The Intelligencer,* a newspaper published in Westfield, calling attention of the public to this proposal and suggesting that three years be spent in surveys.

In 1835, Samuel Parker made a transcontinental trip from Buffalo to Oregon and stated in his journal that there would not be any greater difficulty in the way of constructing a railroad from the Atlantic to the Pacific . . . than in passing the Green Mountains between Boston and Albany.

In 1836, John Plumbe of Dubuque, Iowa, proposed the building of a railroad from Lake Michigan to Oregon. A public meeting was held in Dubuque in March, 1838, to promote Plumbe's project.

In 1836, an article on the subject written by Lewis Gaylord Clarke appeared in the *Knickerbocker Magazine.*

In 1837, Hartwell Carver of Rochester, New York, grandson of Jonathan Carver, the explorer, in an article published in the New York *Courier and Inquirer* proposed a transcontinental railroad having its western terminus on the Colorado River.

In 1843, Lilburn W. Boggs, Governor in 1836 of Missouri Territory, wrote an article for the St. Louis *Republican* on the Pacific Railroad, estimating the cost, which was never published. In 1846, Mr. Boggs moved with his family to Napa Valley, California.

On January 28, 1845, Asa Whitney laid before the Senate the first of several memorials on behalf of a plan for a Pacific Railroad. He asked Congress for a strip of land sixty miles wide from Lake Michigan to the Pacific. After ten miles of railroad had been built, a section of land five miles long would be sold to settlers, the proceeds to reimburse the builder of the road. This plan to continue until the entire track had been laid. By 1850, fourteen states had endorsed the scheme. The Government was not called upon to defray any part of the cost, and the capital for the work was to be created as the work progressed. The weakness of the plan was in the uncertainty of the sale of the land which, spread over a long period of time would produce funds insufficient for building a railroad.[1]

It will be noticed that each of these plans had Oregon as the western terminus. At that time the southern boundary of Oregon was the southern extent of territory on the West Coast claimed by the United States, and the chief communication with the Atlantic was by voyage around Cape Horn. The Oregon boundary had been in dispute between the United States and Great Britain for many years, but emigration had proceeded so rapidly that there were thousands of settlers in that territory; and as early as July 3, 1843, a provisional government had been organized. Considerable anxiety had been felt throughout the East lest Oregon set up the separate government of a new nation with its cities, ports and harbors as a commercial rival to the United States. Hence the greater need felt to link that territory to the eastern states with bands of iron. The Northwest boundary question was not settled until June 18, 1846.

The annexation of Texas had taken place December 29, 1845. On July 4, 1846, Captain Fremont and the settlers at Sonoma, California, declared their independence from Mexico. On July 7, Commodore Sloat, USN, raised the United States flag at Monterey, and two days later both Fremont and Sloat with their followers entered the Bay of San Francisco. These events changed the aspect of the railroad question and the terminus of the Pacific Railroad from Oregon to San Francisco and its matchless harbor; although formal treaty with Mexico was not concluded until February 2, 1848, by which Arizona, Upper California, Nevada, New Mexico, Utah, and parts of Colorado and Wyoming were ceded to the United States. From then the proposals for a Pacific Railroad multiplied.

The San Francisco *Californian,* in the issue of October 27, 1847, suggests the following Southern route for the Railroad to the Pacific: Leaving the Mississippi River about 100 miles above New Orleans to San Diego, about 1,500 miles distant. The route is exempt from difficulties throughout.

On May 13, 1848, John Marsh in the *California Star* proposes a route from California toward the East. From the Bay of San Francisco, up the valley of the San Joaquin, through the range of low hills at the end of the valley, along the road between Los Angeles and New Mexico, up the valley of the San Juan, to the junction of the Silver River, to the town of Abaca in New Mexico across the ridge separating the waters of the Gulf of California from the Gulf of Mexico, onto Santa Fé, and from thence to the Missouri River.

"New Route Across the Continent," a heading in the Placer *Times* for November 24, 1849, given to the report of an exploring expedition under direction of Lieutenant Whitney published in *The National Intelligencer,* a route from the Gulf of Mexico to the great West was open for Southern States.

Four conventions to consider a Pacific Railroad were held during 1849, in Chicago, Boston, St. Louis and Memphis, and another during 1850 in Philadelphia. The St. Louis Convention opened October 15, 1849, and was attended by several hundred delegates from fifteen states. It resulted in resolutions advocating a "Central National Railroad from the Valley of the Missouri to the Pacific Ocean," the construction of which was to be provided by the General Government. A committee was appointed to communicate the resolutions to the Memphis Convention and to request their concurrence.[2]

The convention that met in Memphis, November 10, 1849 was presided over by Lieutenant Matthew Fontaine Maury, USN, who said in his address that as fortifications were built by the National Treasury, so should railroads be constructed "to promote the welfare of the Union, in subserving the interests of commerce, and in advancing the prosperity of the people." Resolutions for Government action were adopted by the convention.[3]

On February 15, 1853, William McK. Gwinn, United States Senator from California, introduced a bill in the Senate calling for three railroads to the Pacific Coast. One commencing on the western border of Texas, another on the border of Missouri, and a third to start from Wisconsin, to be called respectively the Southern, the Central, and the Northern Pacific. This bill passed the Senate but was ignored by the House.

The Shasta *Courier* for May 6, 1854, states that at a Pacific Railroad meeting at Chico, Butte County, resolutions were drawn calling the attention of the General Government to Noble's Pass across the Sierra Nevada Mountains.

The Sacramento *Union,* April 13, 1858, relates that Mr. Phelps of Missouri, Chairman of the Committee on the Pacific Railroad, introduced a bill in the House to aid in the construction of a railroad from St. Louis to San Francisco; the road to pass through Albuquerque and over Tejon Pass; one-half of the road to be built by California and one-half by Missouri, to be assisted by Government bonds after ninety miles of the road had been built.

An item dated September 19, 1857, from the Washington correspondent of the Sacramento *Union* for October 24, 1857, refers to the Southern Atlantic and Pacific Railroad organized last winter by a group of gentlemen of the Southern States. The President of the company, the Honorable Vernon K. Stevenson of Kentucky, seems confident of procuring a grant of land from Congress to aid in this great enterprise.

In 1861, a bill was offered in Congress authorizing the construction of a Pacific Railroad by a corporation proposed to be formed in Vermont. It failed to secure the consideration of either the House or Senate.

Chapter XI

UNITED STATES RAILROAD SURVEYS, 1853-1855

By the Act of Congress of March 3, 1853, the Secretary of War, Jefferson Davis, under the direction of the President, was authorized by Congress to employ a portion of the Corps of Topographical Engineers, and such others as he may deem necessary, to make explorations and surveys to ascertain the most practicable and economical route for a railroad from the Mississippi River to the Pacific Ocean.

Five routes were mapped out practically along the overland roads of that period as shown on the Ravenstein map in Marcy's *Prairie Traveler*, 1863. The surveys were placed in charge of experienced engineers whose names and brief estimates are given below:

1. Northern route from St. Paul to Vancouver, in charge of Isaac I. Stevens, Governor of Washington Territory, with Captain George B. McClellan, USA. Estimates: 1,684 miles of track, cost $130,781,000.

2. Route near the 41st and 42d parallels, Council Bluffs to Benecia, California, in charge of Captain J. E. Fremont with Captain Howard Stansbury and Lieutenant E. B. Beckwith. Estimates: 2,032 miles of track, cost $116,095,000.

3. Route near the 35th parallel, Fort Smith to San Pedro in charge of Lieutenant A. W. Whipple. Estimates: 1,892 miles of track, cost $169,216,265; branch road, Mohave to San Francisco, 400 miles of track, cost $19,935,000.

4. Route near the 32d parallel, Fulton to San Pedro, in charge of Captain John Pope with Lieutenant John G. Parke and Major William H. Emory. Estimates: 1,618 miles of track, $68,970,000; extension to San Francisco, 440 miles of track, cost $25,100,000. Extension of No. 4 from mouth of Gila River to San Francisco, in charge of Lieutenant R. S. Williamson. Estimates?

5. Route near 38th and 39th parallels, Westport, Kansas, to Tehachapi Pass, California. Estimates: 2,100 miles of track, "cost so great, road impracticable." Same route by Cochetopa Pass, Colorado, and Madeline Pass. Estimates: 2,100 miles of track, cost prohibitive.[1]

An appropriation of $150,000 was made for these surveys, which was increased by $40,000 through the Act of May 31, 1854, and further by $150,000 through the Act of August 5, 1854.

The reports of these various surveys were published in twelve quarto volumes in thirteen parts, and beautifully illustrated with maps and colored lithographed plates of scenes along the routes, and the natural history of the regions. The noted botanist, Asa Gray, made a catalog of plants; and a collection of insects, mammals, birds, fishes, mollusca and crustacea was made on the survey.

On February 14, 1855, the House ordered 10,000 copies of the reports to be published; and later, March 25, 1860,

10,000 extra copies of Governor Stevens' final report made in 1859 was ordered. The cost of the publication of the reports was in addition to the $340,000 appropriated for the surveys.[2]

While these surveys threw a flood of light on the interior of the continent, the results did little or nothing to promote a transcontinental railroad.

Chapter XII

CALIFORNIA RAILROADS, 1850-1860

DURING THE FIRST DECADE after California had been admitted to the Union in 1850, a number of railroad companies were organized in the State of California: one was completed, with several extensions started, and others in the process of construction. Two of the most pretentious roads never got beyond the surveys.

The first railroad company organized in California was the San Francisco and San José Railroad Company, to connect the two cities, and intended to become a link with the great Atlantic and Pacific Railroad. The first meeting was held at San José on Saturday, September 6, 1851; directors were elected, and commissioners appointed to receive subscriptions to stock. Capital stock was fixed at $1,250,000 of which $150,000 had been subscribed and $50,000 paid in.[1] By December 6, of the same year, a survey had been completed and articles of association written. The distance was estimated at fifty miles and the cost at $1,600,000.[2]

Years went by and no further action had been taken towards carrying out the conditions of the charter. By 1859, four stages were running daily between San Francisco and San José, charging a fare of $3.00 and unable to accommodate all the passengers. Traffic would increase four or five hundred-fold once a railroad were constructed.[3] But it was not until April 29, 1861, that the ground was first broken for this railroad, nearly ten years after its organization.[4] It was finally opened on January 16, 1864.

The Sacramento Valley Railroad was the first railroad to be constructed on the Pacific Coast. The line extended from Sacramento twenty-two and one-half miles to Folsom, a mining town and the starting point of a number of stage lines. The company was organized on November 9, 1854, and opened for business, January 1, 1856. Theodore D. Judah was the engineer for the road and was recognized as their active agent until October 6, 1860.[5] The cost of the road was about $60,000 per mile. The firm of Pioche, Bayerque & Company of San Francisco, owned considerable stock in this road.[6]

An extension to this road known as the California Central from Folsom to Marysville, a distance of forty miles, was constructed during the years of 1858 to 1861, at a cost of $2,000,000; and a short line from Lincoln, a new town on California Central, to Gold Hill, seven miles from Auburn, was built during the same years. A third extension, the Auburn Railroad from Folsom to Auburn, thirteen miles in length, was begun in 1861;[7] and a fourth extension, the Sacramento, Placer & Nevada Railroad, was organized June 1, 1861.[8] This road also was to be an effort towards building an Overland Road, and articles of incorporation were filed in the Office of the Secretary of State, August 17, 1852. The line was surveyed from Folsom via Auburn to Nevada City, sixty-eight miles long; and the survey was extended to Henness Pass over the Sierra Mountains. However, the enterprise was found to be too gigantic a task for the means of the incorporators and the project was abandoned. The report of the survey through Henness Pass was not preserved.[9]

The Market Street Railroad of San Francisco was organized November 28, 1857, under an Act of the California Legislature passed April 6, of the same year. The road to be extended to Hayes Valley via Mission Dolores, capital stock $250,000, to be completed by April 1, 1859. The firm of Pioche & Bayerque were the chief promoters of this road.[10]

The San Francisco, Stockton & Sacramento Railroad, the project of a San Francisco & Stockton Company, was scheduled to run from Sacramento to Stockton, forty-five miles, over a level plain; from Stockton to a point opposite Goat Island along the Bay, passing by Martinez along the south shore of Carquinez Straits to Contra Costa, seventy miles distant, for a deep water terminal, where connection by ferry could be made with San Francisco. The whole distance from Sacramento to Contra Costa was one hundred fifteen miles, or fifteen miles nearer than by steam navigation.

The plan was to level Goat Island and form a plateau from its surface extending toward the Contra Costa shore, a mile and a quarter distant. As there was little or no current inside the island, except that caused by the tides and the water was quite shoal at low tide, except for a distance of about one hundred feet which could be filled up or bridged across, communication could be established between the island and the shore.[11]

The intention of the promoters of this road was to secure foreign capital to construct the road within the next thirty years, as California capitalists would not invest in railways so long as money could be loaned on good security at two per cent per month. The builders would have to organize under the laws of California, and once invested, the road would become taxable property and controlled by the laws of the State. To secure foreign capital to build this road an agent, F. P. O'Byrne, was sent to Europe for that purpose. A company was organized in London and announced that they were about ready to begin operations, but before doing so certain changes would have to be made in the Railroad Law of California: (1) the clause requiring the directors of a railroad to reside in the State; and (2) the section requiring a certain number of the directors to be American citizens. No such law existed in England; there the shareholders have the right to choose their own directors without specification of citizenship.

In order to overcome these difficulties, O'Byrne was obliged to guarantee that the people of San Francisco and Stockton whom he represented would have a bill passed in the Legislature granting the right of the San Francisco, Stockton & Sacramento Railway Company formed in London, and having its principal office there, to build the road with such rights and privileges as may be granted the Atlantic & Pacific Railroad Company, it being the intention to make this enterprise a part of the railroad across the continent to connect California with the Eastern States.[12]

An editorial in the Sacramento *Union* for April 21, 1858, says that an immense amount of English capital had been sunk in California through the inefficiency, unfaithfulness and dishonesty of the local Boards of Directors to whom it was intrusted. The shareholders of the new company intend to have a voice in the disbursement of their own money by means of a home Board of Directors. The San Francisco,

Stockton & Sacramento Railroad must form a link with the great Atlantic & Pacific chain; it will be beyond rival competition for at least a quarter of a century and pay a handsome dividend on the money invested.

This was the third California Railroad projected with the intention of becoming the Western section of the first transcontinental road, only one of which—the San Francisco & San José—was ever built.

The plan for the San Francisco, Stockton & Sacramento Railroad is of particular interest in view of the later antagonistic attitude toward the Central Pacific Railroad Company and their plan to use Goat Island.

The Shasta *Courier* for Saturday, October 26, 1861, remarked dejectedly: "There are always ten roads completed on paper to one finished in fact."

Chapter XIII

SAN FRANCISCO RAILROAD CONVENTION, SEPTEMBER 20, 1859

ON APRIL 5, 1859, the California Legislature adopted a concurrent resolution calling for a railroad convention to promote the interest and secure the protection and security of the people of California, Oregon and Washington.

This convention opened September 20, 1859, in the Assembly Hall, at Kearny and Post Streets, San Francisco, and was attended by delegates from different sections of California, from Oregon, and from Washington Territory. The sessions were presided over by John Bidwell, and lasted several days. The discovery in July of the great Comstock lode east of the Sierras furnished another urgent reason for a railroad over the mountains.

After long and careful consideration, the convention recommended the following: (1) That the western terminus of the road should be at San Francisco, from that point to San José, thence to Stockton, and thence by the most practicable route across the Sierras; (2) that the states of California and Oregon should create a fund of $15,000,000 and $5,000,000 respectively to aid in the enterprise; (3) in favor of an amendment to the state constitution of California permitting the state to loan her credit to the work; and (4) the abolition of the individual responsibility clause with regard to stockholders in a corporation.[1]

Theodore D. Judah, engineer, was the delegate from Sacramento. He had made several preliminary surveys over the Sierra Nevadas, and due to his information on the subject, he was appointed as the accredited agent of the convention to present its proceedings to the President of the United States, the heads of the Departments, and the Congress at Washington. He was instructed also to bring to bear all legitimate influence to procure favorable action for a Pacific Railroad bill.[2] Judah left San Francisco October 20, 1859, on the S. S. *Senora* with the memorial which he was to lay before Congress.[3]

He reached Washington in time for the opening of the 36th Congress. As a result of his work, a bill was drawn up by the Honorable John C. Burch, representative from California, which was printed at private expense and copies sent to each senator and member of the House. This bill embodied the following principal features: (1) the construction of a railroad between the Mississippi River and the eastern boundary of California; (2) a guaranty by the Government for the payment of five per cent interest per annum for thirty years on the bonds of the company; (3) an issue of bonds by the company not to exceed $50,000,000, to constitute a first lien upon the property, assets, etc., the said company to become entitled to the Government's guaranty only as the work progressed; (4) the road to be completed in ten years; (5) a right of way granted, together with a strip of land four hundred feet wide on the line of the road, and 5,000 acres of land for depots, watering stations, etc.; (6) every alternate section of public lands for twenty miles upon each side of the road to be set apart and sold at proper times to obtain funds for payment of the interest guaranteed by the United States and for the partial liquidation of the principal; (7) the remaining alternate sections on each side of the road to be granted to the company constructing the road; and (8) the company to carry the mails of the United States at a price not exceeding $600 per mile per annum.[4]

It should be observed that the western end of this road as planned, from San Francisco to the eastern boundary of the state of California, was to be constructed by the fund of $20,000,000 provided by California and Oregon without aid from Congress except for land grants. The Government was asked to aid in the construction of that part of the road from the Mississippi River to the eastern boundary of California.

Although the delegates to Congress from both California and Oregon worked earnestly to forward the measure, the bill was not even considered; nothing was accomplished. Judah returned to San Francisco and made a report to the Committee of the Railroad Convention, charging nothing for his work or expenses, save a bill for $40.00 for printing the Burch railroad bill.

Theodore Dehone Judah, Engineer

Chapter XIV

CENTRAL PACIFIC RAILROAD COMPANY, ORGANIZATION

SENTIMENT for a Pacific Railroad increased steadily as the years passed. By 1861, sectional differences had the country in such turmoil that a transcontinental road was felt by many to be an urgent necessity in order to save the Pacific Coast for the Union. With the outbreak of war in April the demand became imperative.

We have seen how California had planned three railroads, each of which was intended to be the western end of the great Atlantic and Pacific Railroad, only one of which was in the process of construction; and to further the enterprise, San Francisco had held a convention, had offered to build a railroad across the Sierra Nevada Mountains herself and had sent the engineer Judah to Washington to enlist the aid of Congress, but all to no avail.

The various projects for a Pacific Railroad had included lines along the Northern, Central and Southern routes, but because of the intense sectional differences, no route could be decided upon. The Central route had the greatest number of advocates in California, but the great obstacle was in finding a way across the Sierra Nevada Mountains. The Henness Pass over these mountains had been explored but no report of the survey had been preserved.

The surveys of the War Department had thrown a flood of light on the interior of the continent, and were of considerable topographical value, but they did not show a route for a railroad over the Sierra Nevadas that was practicable or even possible.

When Judah returned to California from Washington in 1860, he set about making a more thorough search for a pass and a suitable approach to the Sierras. He was accompanied on this survey by Dr. Daniel W. Strong, a druggist at Dutch Flat, who suggested the route and contributed largely in paying the expenses of the trip. After completing this survey, a circular letter was issued under date of November 1, 1860, directing the attention of the public to some newly discovered facts with reference to the route of the Pacific Railroad through California. A practicable line had been discovered from Sacramento upon the divide between the Bear River and the North Fork of the American River via Illinoistown and Dutch Flat through Donner Lake Pass on the Truckee River which gives nearly a direct line to Washoe. The projected railroad might connect with the Sacramento Valley Railroad at Folsom or with the California Central at Lincoln. Said Judah, "I will undertake to build a railroad over this route in two years for $70,000 per mile from Sacramento to Washoe."[1]

Judah then went to San Francisco to lay his plans before the capitalists there and to induce them to form a company to take hold of the work and push it forward, but he made no impression upon his hearers. He had been given one opportunity without success, and no financial support of any kind was offered him.

"If Congress does not pass a bill," they said, "no railroad could be built; if a bill were passed, the road could not be completed for ten or twenty years."

Another reason for this attitude was the provision in the constitution of the state making stockholders liable for their proportion of all debts and liabilities of any company in which they had stock.[2]

Judah said to a friend, "The capitalists of San Francisco have refused to make an investment for which in less than three years they shall have cause to blame their lack of foresight."

For several years, the Pacific Railroad and its wonderful possibilities had been a subject of frequent discussion by Messrs. Huntington & Hopkins and others who frequented their store; so that when a meeting on the subject was called by Judah to be held in the St. Charles Hotel, Mr. Huntington was present. Judah told his listeners of his several reconnaissances over the mountains and his desire to make a more thorough survey with instruments, and he solicited subscriptions to that work. Small sums of money were offered, barrels of flour, sacks of potatoes, etc. Huntington listened attentively but subscribed nothing. He had been over those mountains and knew the difficulties. As a member of the Board of Wagon Road Directors, appointed at a Convention in Sacramento, he had gone with its president, J. H. Nevett, on a tour of inspection in June, 1857, to locate a new wagon road over the Sierras from Placerville to Carson Valley.[3] He had contributed liberally toward building that road and to an overland telegraph line. He had but little faith in Judah's methods; he felt that more forceful and vigorous measures were needed.

As he was leaving the meeting, Mr. Huntington drew Judah aside and said to him: "If you want to come to my office some evening, I will talk to you about this road."

The meeting took place the following evening at the home of Edwin D. Prentice, Mrs. Huntington's brother-in-law, on K Street, between 9th and 10th. At this meeting—the first inception of the road—there were present Huntington, Hopkins, Judah, W. H. Stoddard and Mr. Prentice who took part in the early history of the road, but died in 1862.[4]

As a result of this meeting, Huntington undertook to secure six other men who would join him in a pledge to pay the expenses of a thorough instrumental survey across the mountains which Judah had estimated would cost $35,000. Mr. Hopkins was in much doubt about the gigantic difficulties of the mountains being overcome, but he was willing to follow his partner's lead. Mr. Huntington talked with Leland Stanford who agreed to join the enterprise and pay one-seventh of the cost of the survey.[5]

Charles Crocker had frequent conversations with Judah on the subject of the survey after the meeting at St. Charles Hotel in Sacramento. One day, meeting Huntington, who was soliciting subscriptions, he said, "You appear to be taking great interest in this matter." "Yes," said Huntington, "and I want to talk to you about it. We are trying to form a syndicate, and your name has been favorably mentioned."

"Well," replied Crocker, "I think anything you and Uncle Mark undertake is worthy of attention."[6]

Lucius A. Booth, Charles Marsh, and James Bailey came into the agreement. These seven men bound themselves to pay the initial cost of the survey.

On Tuesday, April 30, 1861, after frequent and earnest discussions among the group, the Central Pacific Railroad Company of California was organized under a general law of the state, with a nominal capital of $8,500,000, to construct a railroad from Sacramento to the eastern boundary of the state, a distance of 115 miles. For that distance $1,000 per mile had been subscribed and ten per cent paid in as the law required. Articles of Association were adopted, officers and a board of directors elected, and a board of commissioners appointed.

The officers elected were Leland Stanford, president; C. P. Huntington, vice-president; Mark Hopkins, treasurer; James Bailey, secretary, soon to be succeeded by Edward J. Miller, Jr., a former partner of Mark Hopkins; and T. D. Judah, chief engineer.

The Articles of Association were as follows:

1. The name of the association shall be the Central Pacific Railroad Company of California.

2. The number of years the same shall continue is fifty years.

3. The amount of capital stock of this company shall be eight million, five hundred thousand dollars.

4. The names of the nine directors of the company are C. P. Huntington, Leland Stanford, Charles Crocker, Mark Hopkins, Theodore Judah, L. A. Booth, James Bailey, all of Sacramento; D. W. Strong, Dutch Flat; and Charles Marsh, Nevada.

5. The places from and to which the proposed road is to be constructed are the City of Sacramento and the eastern boundary of the State of California.

6. The counties into and through which the road is intended to pass are Sacramento, Placer and Nevada.

7. The length of the road, as near as may be estimated, is one hundred and fifteen miles.

8. The names of the five commissioners to open books of subscription to the stock are B. F. Moore, Dutch Flat; Edward J. Bricknell, Illinoistown; E. G. Waite, Nevada; E. G. McLaughlin, Grass Valley; Samuel Cross, Sacramento.

9. We the undersigned, do hereby subscribe to the above Articles of Association our names and the amounts of stock taken by us respectively, in the Central Pacific Railroad Company of California: James Bailey, Mark Hopkins, C. P. Huntington, T. D. Judah, Leland Stanford, Charles Crocker, all of Sacramento, one hundred fifty shares each; Charles Marsh, Nevada, D. W. Strong, Dutch Flat, fifty shares each; E. J. Bricknell, Illinoistown, forty shares; E. L. Bradley and R. M. Trim, Dutch Flat, twenty-five shares jointly; B. Bricknell, Illinoistown, twenty shares; C. Cole, Wm. G. English, Chas. G. Hooker, Milikin Brothers, Lord, Holbrook & Co., L. A. Booth, Samuel Cross, all of Sacramento, N. W. Blanchard, B. F. Moore, both of Dutch Flat, E. G. Waite, John Williams, T. Ellard Beans, J. N. Lumay, all of Nevada, E. McLaughlin, Grass Valley, ten shares each; John F. Morse, P. H. Russell, N. L. Drew of Sacramento, P. T. Mathewson, Dutch Flat, William Loutzenheim, Grass Valley, five shares each. Total, 1,250 shares.

At the next meeting of the company, Judah proudly displayed a design for a railroad office that he had drawn. It was elaborate and complete and could be built, he said for about $12,000.

"It is an admirable plan when we can afford it," said Mr. Huntington, "but now, when we are not doing much business, a building like this shall have to suffice."

And he drew a plan of a plain, box-like building, one story in height. The four sides were nailed together one afternoon and roofed over the next day, at a total cost of $150. When the building became too small for its original purpose, it was removed and used as a paint shop.[7]

City offices were opened on the second floor of the 56 and 58 K Street Stanford buildings adjoining the Huntington & Hopkins hardware store at 54 K Street. Later a door was cut through to the second floor of the 54 K Street building and the offices enlarged.[8]

On Friday June 28, 1861, the Central Pacific Railroad Company filed their certificate of incorporation in the office of the Secretary of State at Sacramento. Samuel Brannan (to be heard from later) had joined the company, purchasing two hundred shares; also, Edwin B. Crocker, a brother of Charles Crocker, who became the chief counsel for the company. Leland Stanford had been nominated for Governor of California on June 19, 1861.[9]

Many years later in an interview, Mr. Huntington said:

> We did not know definitely where we would build to, but expected the road would be a part of the transcontinental system. To those who had considered such an enterprise, the Rocky Mountains had seemed no serious obstacle, but the Sierra Nevadas had always been a formidable barrier in the way. I felt that, once crossed, our road would then become the nucleus of a Pacific System. I used to say to my immediate associates, "Don't let us talk about a Pacific Road. Let us always keep in control of what we build and pursue such a conservative policy as will not bring us into financial difficulties or harm our credit." Had I then known as well as I do now the character of the country east of the Sierra Nevada, I would have arranged from the start to build to the Missouri River. The desire for a transcontinental railway was general. Everybody on the West Coast wanted better and cheaper facilities for returning to visit their homes in the East . . . Senator Benton and other prominent men were strong advocates of a railroad to the Pacific Coast, in order to bring California closer to the eastern states. The depredations and loss of life by the Indians among the emigrants, who traversed the 2,000 miles of plains in wagons, was a serious consideration. Between

the Missouri and Sacramento Rivers, a distance of 1,800 miles, there was not a single navigable stream and a vast portion of this territory was unknown and uninhabited except by savages.[10]

During November, 1861, the Central Pacific group organized and incorporated the Nevada Railroad Company, which was authorized to construct a railway and telegraph line through the Nevada Territory, a distance of 275 miles, under an Act of the Nevada Legislature entitled: "An Act granting certain persons the right to construct a railroad from the Western to the Eastern boundary of Nevada." This was approved and signed by the Governor on November 25, 1861. A subsequent act, passed by the Nevada Legislature later in the year, extended the time for making the survey and filing the maps thereon as required by the first named Act.

On the 28th day of September, 1863, a few days before sailing for New York, T. D. Judah sold to Charles Crocker for $10,000, his "rights of property and estate . . ." together with all the "rights thereunto belonging to or in any way appertaining" in this company. James Bailey, who withdrew from the company at the same time, sold his rights, etc., in the Nevada Railroad Company to Asa Philip Stanford, younger brother of Leland Stanford on the same date.[11]

Chapter XV

CENTRAL PACIFIC RAILROAD COMPANY, SURVEYS

SOON AFTER its organization, the company ordered the surveys and examination of routes over the Sierra Nevada Mountains, under the superintendence of Theodore D. Judah, engineer. Using instruments for the first time, five routes were surveyed: (1) a route from Folsom via Greenwood and Georgetown to the headwaters of the Middle Fork of the American River; this route had the advantage of the Sacramento Valley line, twenty-two and one-half miles already in operation, but was rejected on account of the heavy grades to the Truckee River; (2) a route via Dutch Flat and Donner Lake Pass to the Truckee River; (3) a route via Nevada City and Henness Pass; (4) a route via Downieville and Yuba Gap; (5) a route via Oroville, Bidwell's Bar, Middle Fork of the Feather River and Beckworth's Pass.

According to the Sacramento *Union* for November 11, 1862, Mr. Huntington accompanied the surveying parties on the survey of the Feather River:

The only thorough reconnaissance of that route that has ever been made, so far as we are advised, was made last August [1861] by T. D. Judah, engineer of the Central Pacific Railroad Company, accompanied by C. P. Huntington, one of the directors, A. A. Sargent, California delegate to Congress, and Charles Marsh, as far as Long Valley, down the Middle Fork of the Feather River to the neighborhood of Nelson's Creek. At that point the canyon of the river commences. Huntington and Judah determined to explore that canyon, a feat, they were informed by those living along the river, that had never been performed by mortal man. They employed a Chinaman to aid in conveying blankets and provisions. They were seven days working their way through the canyon from Nelson's Creek to Bidwell's Bar, a distance of seventy miles.

The entire distance was through rock-granite, slate and marble, the walls rising from two to three thousand feet, cut through on an extremely crooked line with angles of every variety. Between thirty and forty tunnels in solid rock would be required to turn points, and the bed for a railroad blasted in the wall of rock for nearly the whole distance. No trail practicable for mules had ever been found across the canyon of the Middle Feather between Nelson's Creek and Bidwell's Bar; so Huntington and Judah were told by miners who live up on the benches and descend into the canyon by steps, in some cases by ropes. The miners also assured them that the water in the river rose the past winter fully seventy-five feet. This examination of the canyon demonstrated at once its utter impracticability for railroad purposes.

In addition to the expensive and difficult construction, the route was sixty-five or more miles longer than the Dutch Flat and Donner Lake route.

The field work of the surveys was completed in August, 1861, and by October maps and profiles of the routes had been drawn, estimates made, and other information such as the amount of snowfall, etc., gathered. The Dutch Flat and Donner Lake Pass route was selected as being the most practicable with as many as thirty advantages over the other routes. Huntington, Stanford and Crocker went over the proposed route with Judah, making explorations to the summit and beyond, discussing the difficulties and the paying prospects of the enterprise. Huntington found that in Judah's estimate he had put too much earthwork in the first place and not enough rock. Huntington went over the figures and made such changes in the classification as his judgment dictated. The final cost of the work showed the accuracy of his corrections. These surveys to the eastern boundary of California cost the company $66,740.[1]

Judah made a report of the Donner Pass route on October 1, 1861, giving his estimate of the cost as follows:

Sacramento to the State line	140 miles	$12,380,000
State line to Salt Lake	593 miles	29,035,000
Total cost, Sacramento to Salt Lake	733 miles	$41,415,000
Union Pacific:		
Council Bluffs to Salt Lake	1,125 miles	58,455,000
Total, Central Pacific and Union Pacific	1,858 miles	$99,870,000

On October 9, 1861, the Board of Directors of the Central Pacific Railroad Company passed a resolution, sending Judah, the engineer, to Washington with the report of the survey of the Dutch Flat and Donner Pass route and with maps, profiles, estimates of materials, costs, etc.:

Resolved, that Mr. T. D. Judah, the Chief Engineer of this company, proceed to Washington on the steamer of the 11th instant, as the accredited agent of the Central Pacific Company, for the purpose of procuring appropriations of land and United States bonds from the Government to aid in the construction of the road.

The California delegation to Washington at the time of the 37th Congress, 2nd Session, 1861-1862, were James A. McDougall and Milton S. Latham of the Senate and Aaron A. Sargent, Timothy G. Phelps and a Mr. Law in the House. Judah traveled to Washington with Mr. Sargent which gave them frequent opportunities for discussion of the subject. Upon his arrival at Washington, through the maneuvering of the California delegates, Judah was appointed (1) secretary of the Senate Committee on Pacific Railroads; (2) clerk of the House Committee on Pacific Railroads; and later (3) clerk of the main House Committee on Railroads. The materials concerning the surveys were on display in a room in the Capitol building for inspection by the senators and representatives. Not all the congressmen saw these materials, however. As late in the session as May 1, 1862, Samuel Shellabarger, representative from Ohio, offered an amendment to the bill concerning surveys because he did not know that a survey over the Sierras had been made.[2]

Chapter XVI

PACIFIC RAILROAD BILL

AT THE SECOND SESSION of the Thirty-seventh Congress, Collis Potter Huntington made the first of his innumerable appearances in Washington on behalf of his railroads. He had been deputized by his associates with full power of attorney to do anything he might think best for the interests of the company. They felt that his diplomatic skill, his engaging personality, and his mastery of detail made him the logical man for such a mission. The subject of the Pacific Railroad had been before Congress for ten or more years in various forms of legislation without success, and it was considered most important to have on hand their most persuasive and convincing member.[1]

The long-smoldering hostility between the North and South had burst into flame on April 12, 1861, and the country was engaged in a bitter civil war. On November 28, H.M.S. *Trent* had been stopped on the high seas by a United States warship, and two Confederate agents, Mason and Slidell, on the way to England, forcibly removed to the great resentment and protests of Great Britain. Soon thereafter, the Asiatic fleet of Great Britain consisting of sixteen ships of 291 guns occupied the harbor at Victoria, Vancouver; and a Russian fleet of seven vessels of 192 guns sailed into San Francisco

Bay. The nation at last awoke to the fact that its Government was powerless to protect its Pacific Coast possessions in case of war with a foreign power. There was no way on earth to get troops, munitions and other supplies there on short notice. A railroad across the continent was an absolute necessity, and many Congressmen desired immediate legislation to that end, while others opposed it as an impossibility.

The debates on this Pacific Railroad Bill as recorded in the *Congressional Globe* furnish interesting and sometimes amusing reading. Let no one think that Congressmen do not need to be instructed on bills under discussion. Some of the amendments proposed for this bill show how important such information can be, and that is where Huntington's work was directed. Some of the proposed amendments that failed were as follows: (1) That the Government should be represented on the Board of Corporators and on the Board of Directors. (2) One half the capital stock shall be in good faith subscribed for, and a sum of not less than $10,000,000 shall be actually paid thereon and deposited in the Treasury of the United States as a guaranty for the work, to be refunded to the Pacific Railroad Company. (3) An amendment to require fifty miles of road constructed instead of forty before receiving subsidy bonds from the Government. (4) An amendment that the railroad forever remain a highway for the use of the Government free from any charge whatever for the transportation of troops or property of the Government. (5) An amendment to build forty miles of road in the mountains first before building in the plains. (6) An amendment to consolidate the two companies, etc., etc.

Mr. Huntington's method of dealing with Congressmen, as he himself has said, was to meet them individually and in short talks call attention to some vital part of the enterprise with his most impressive arguments and then leave the member to think it over.[2] Some of the points for emphasis were: (1) that the men of the Central Pacific Railroad Company were reliable and capable men; (2) the country would be more readily prepared in case of war between the United States and a foreign power; (3) the railroad would furnish much needed transportation in the present War Between the States; (4) a great saving of time and money would result in the transportation of troops, supplies and mails; (5) the great importance of uniting the West with the East as one people; (6) the Eastern States would profit by speedy transfer of gold and grain from the West; (7) the value of trade with the countries of the Far East.

Many Congressmen, even after an examination of the maps and profiles of the Dutch Gap and Donner Lake route, did not believe that a road could be built there. Lovejoy of Illinois said in the House:

I do not believe the road will ever be built over the more difficult portions of the route.[3]

Campbell of Pennsylvania, a member of the House Select Committee testified:

It may be we cannot construct this road through the passes of the Sierra Nevada and Rocky Mountains for the next fifteen years.[4]

Even General William Tecumseh Sherman expressed his doubt in no uncertain terms:

A railroad to the Pacific? I would hate to buy tickets on it for my grandchildren.[5]

Some Congressmen were doubtful about the ability of the members of the Central Pacific Railroad Company to construct a railroad. Senator Collomer said:

It will take a Samson to build this road, but this bill would give the office to a Samson without his beard (*sic*).[6]

Said Morrill of Vermont who fought the bill bitterly:

There is no man in this house who doesn't know that if this road is ever to be built, completed and run, it is to be done by the Government of the United States. There is not a capitalist who will invest a dollar in it, if he is to be responsible for its construction.[7]

Senator Clark of New Hampshire was most emphatic:

I believe that if the Good God were to make that road for you right through, you could not form a company in the country that could run it without failure.[8]

A most important part of Huntington's work in Washington was to convince those men that, although not professional railroad builders, the leaders of the Central Pacific Railroad Company were substantial business men with a reputation for carrying through any project undertaken by them.

The importance of the railroad to the Government was recognized and variously discussed. Said Campbell of Pennsylvania:

This grand undertaking will do more to unite us as one people; will accomplish more by extending civilization over the continent— for commerce and civilization go hand in hand—than any other enterprise of modern times; civilization of that high type which shall spread the cultivated valley, the peaceful village, the school house, and thronging cities through the mighty solitudes of the West; while the gold and grain of California and an intermediate continent flow in commingled tide to the marts of the Atlantic.[9]

Phelps of California said in a speech:

If we would avoid the hazard of losing our Pacific possessions in case of war we must provide the means of defending them in one of only two ways. Either we must have a railroad across the continent by which troops and munitions of war can be readily transported to the coast, or we must maintain a sufficient force there in time of peace to meet the exigencies of war. To keep such a standing army on that coast for a few years only would equal the entire cost of constructing a first class road from the Mississippi to San Francisco. . . . Two good reasons for passing the bill for this road: it is a military necessity, and is essential to our internal development. Another reason, beyond the western terminus lie Japan, China and the East Indies with their more than 400,000,000 inhabitants whose commerce, the most tempting prize ever within the reach of any country, may be secured thereby.[10]

William D. Kelley of Pennsylvania said:

Not until we have completed a Pacific Railroad will this nation assume its proper position among nations.[11]

Said Sargent of California:

Cost of land transportation for an army in peace, $20,000,000; in war, six times as much, $120,000,000. Journey across the plains, six months or more; across the deserts, impossible.[12]

Said Campbell of Pennsylvania:

The Government is now paying between seven and eight million dollars yearly for Pacific transportation.[13]

The views expressed by the Congressmen in regard to the repayment of the bonds subscribed by the Government are of especial interest in connection with the attitude of later members of Congress, Government railroad investigators, the Thurmond Act of 1878, and the Refunding Bill of 1896. Said Phelps of California in his speech before the House, April 9, 1862:

If the aid to be given toward the building of this road were a donation instead of a loan of the credit of the Government on unquestionable security, it would be a mere bagatelle considering the great results to be achieved by its construction.[14]

William D. Kelley of Pennsylvania asked:

Can there be any question that our country can bear such an augmentation of its annual expenditure? Or will it harm us if posterity, blessed by this work, should perchance have to pay the principal of the credit involved?[15]

Albert S. White of Indiana on repayment:

I contend that although this bill provides for the repayment of the money advanced by the Government, it is not expected that a cent of the money will ever be repaid. If the Committee intended that it should be repaid, they would have required it to be paid out of the gross earnings of the road, and not the net earnings. I undertake to say that not a cent of these advances will ever be repaid, nor do I think it desirable that they should be repaid.[16]

Said Latham of California:

I would sink $100,000,000 to build the road and do it cheerfully and think I had done a great thing for my country, if I could bring it about. What are seventy-five or one hundred millions of dollars in opening a railroad across the central regions of this continent that shall connect the people of the Pacific and Atlantic and bind us together? Nothing.[17]

Senator Howe of Wisconsin said:

I have studied the railroad system of this country and make the prediction here today and let it go upon the record that the man is not born in this country, nor is there born the grandfather of the man in this country who will ever see this nation get back this money. It is an impossibility. The road will never be worth it. I do not expect any of our money back. It will come back in no other way than is provided for in this bill and that is provision for carrying the mails and doing certain other work for the Government.[18]

Senator Howard of Michigan gives statistics:

When the road shall have been completed, assuming the bonds issued to be $62,880,000, the maximum estimate, the entire interest will be but $3,773,800 per annum. The exact cost to the Government of the transportation services provided for in this bill amounts to $7,357,000. . . . I call the attention of the senators to this pregnant fact not to be ignored or avoided, that the difference between the interest, $3,773,000 and the present cost $7,357,000 with the five per cent reserved to the Government by the bill, would necessarily pay the Government bonds and interest before the Government bonds would mature.

Senator Wilson of Massachusetts expected no return:

As to the security the United States takes in this road, I would not give the paper it is written on for the whole of it. I do not suppose it is ever to come back except as the road does the business we need—carrying our mails, troops and munitions of war. I vote for the bill with that expectation and understanding. . . . In my judgment, we ought not to vote for the bill with the expectation or understanding that the money which we advance for this road is ever to come back in the Treasury of the United States.[19]

James Buchanan, President of the United States, in his Third Annual Message, December 19, 1859:

I venture to assert that the additional cost of transporting troops, munitions of war, and necessary supplies for the army across the vast intervening plains to our possessions on the Pacific Coast would be greater in such a war than the whole amount required to construct the road. And yet this resort would be inadequate for their defense and protection.

The bill was finally passed by Congress, the House, seventy-nine to forty-nine, on May 6; the Senate, thirty-five to five, on June 20. The House concurred in a Senate amendment on June 24, and the bill was sent to President Lincoln for his approval, and became a law on July 1, 1862. Immediately after, Huntington sent the following telegram to his associates: "We have drawn the elephant, now let us see if we can harness him."

Chapter XVII

ACT OF CONGRESS, JULY 1, 1862

THE ROLLINS BILL for a Pacific Railroad before the Thirty-seventh Congress, Second Session, was entitled: "An Act to aid in the construction of a railroad and telegraph line from the Missouri River to the Pacific Ocean." Its purpose was stated: "to secure to the Government the use of the same for postal, military and other purposes." This became a law July 1, 1862.

Two companies were authorized to build the road: the Union Pacific Railroad Company to build the section from the Missouri River to the eastern boundary of California; the Central Pacific Railroad Company of California to build from the Pacific Coast, at or near San Francisco, or the navigable waters of the Sacramento River, to the eastern boundary of California. Should the Union Pacific reach the eastern boundary of California before the Central Pacific, the Union Pacific was authorized to continue construction in California with the consent of that state. Likewise, if the Central Pacific reached the eastern boundary of California before the Union Pacific arrived, it was authorized to continue construction through the territories toward the Missouri River until it connected with the Union Pacific.

The Act granted to the Central Pacific a right of way through public lands of two hundred feet on each side of the road, and the right to take from adjacent public lands earth, stone, timber and other materials for use in the construction of the road. The Indian titles of all lands along the road were to be extinguished.

The Company was granted every alternate section of public land designated by odd numbers to the amount of five alternate sections per mile on each side of the road within the limits of ten miles, not already sold, reserved or otherwise disposed of by the United States, and to which a pre-emption or homestead claim may not be attached. All mineral lands were to be exempted, but lumber thereon was granted to the company.

After the completion of every forty consecutive miles of railroad, three commissioners appointed by the President of the United States shall examine the road, and upon their certificate of the completion of forty miles, patents shall be issued covering the right and title to lands on each side of the road.

Also, upon the certificate of the commissioners, the Secretary of the Treasury shall issue to the Company United States bonds of $1,000 each, payable thirty years after date, bearing six per cent per annum interest (payable semi-annually), to the amount of sixteen bonds per mile for such section of forty miles, the bonds to constitute a first mortgage on the line to secure payment thereof.

Grants are made upon condition that the bonds are paid at maturity, the road and telegraph line kept in repair and use, and the Government to have preference in use at a reasonable price for such service, not more than private individuals. All compensation for Government services to apply to the bond and interest debt. After the completion of the road, five per cent of the net earnings to be annually applied to the debt *until both bonds and interest are paid.*

Assent of the Company required within six months of the passage of this Act. Road to be completed by July 1, 1876.

Route of road designated and a map filed in the Department of the Interior within two years of the passage of this Act. The Secretary of the Interior shall cause the lands within fifteen miles of the route to be withdrawn from pre-emption, private entry and sale; and the Secretary shall cause the lands to be surveyed and set off as fast as may be necessary.

Fifty miles of said road shall be completed within two years after filing assent to the provisions of this Act, and fifty miles every year thereafter.

For one hundred fifty miles eastward from the western base of the Sierras, one hundred fifty miles westward from the eastern base of the Rocky Mountains, points to be fixed by the President of the United States, the number of bonds shall be *treble* the number per mile [$48,000] and between the sections named, the number of bonds shall be *double* per mile [$32,000] to be issued upon the completion of every twenty miles.

No more than 50,000 of said bonds shall be issued under said act to aid in constructing the main line of railroad and telegraph.

Tracks to be of uniform width on both sections, gauge to be determined by the President of the United States, and to be used as one connected continuous line.

Twenty-five per cent of the $16,000 bonds to a mile, and fifteen per cent of the $32,000 bonds to the mile to be reserved and remain in the United States Treasury undelivered until the road is completed.

Rates of fares on the road may be reduced when the net earnings exceed ten per cent (exclusive of the five per cent to be paid the Government).

Annual report to be made by the company.[1]

The bill contained elaborate and detailed instructions in regard to the organization of the Union Pacific Company. The Central Pacific had already been organized and incorporated under the laws of California more than a year before this bill became a law.

Chapter XVIII

PERSONNEL OF THE COMPANY

SOON AFTER the organization of the Central Pacific Railroad Company on April 30, 1861, it became evident that the strength of the company and the hopes for its ultimate success lay in four outstanding members of the group, of whom a writer has said: "They were all remarkable men individually and remarkable in their combination." These four men were merchants of Sacramento, none of them wealthy nor had any of them ever before been engaged in the railroad business. Two of the men of the firm of Huntington & Hopkins were known in the financial world to a limited extent and had established a substantial credit in the East which proved to be of great benefit to the company.

The unchallenged leader of the company was Collis Potter Huntington who had been largely responsible for its organization and who had been elected Vice-President of the company. He had already developed into a skilled trader and financier, and with the full power of attorney from his associates "to buy, sell, bargain, convey, borrow or lend," he left for the East in December, 1862, to assume his three-fold job of financier, purchasing agent, and legislative adviser, any one of which would have been a full-time job for the average man. At times he confronted difficulties of almost unbelievable magnitude. Nor did he neglect the railroad itself, making frequent trips back to the scene of operations during the difficult and precarious year of 1863; each time correcting some error, settling a dispute, or solving some monetary problem. Said Mr. Huntington before the Senate Committee of the Pacific Railroads, March 1896, p. 151:

I labored almost day and night for seven years, back and forth. I would go to California and stay there ten days, and then I would come back to New York and be gone only thirty days, during which time I would have made 1,400 miles by stages and stayed ten days in California.

Mark Hopkins, the oldest of the four, born September 1, 1813, at Henderson, New York, was the Treasurer of the company. He was meticulous and scrupulous as to detail and accuracy; his associates had great respect for his opinion and judgment. Huntington who held him in deep affection, once said of him: "He was one of the truest and best men that ever lived. I do not know what we should have done without him; he always seemed to know just what was the best thing to do in all cases."

Leland Stanford, born near Albany, New York, on March 9, 1824, was a wholesale grocer in Sacramento, a leader in the Republican party and a candidate for the office of Governor of the State of California. He was elected President of the Company, his associates doubtless being aware of the possible advantages of having the corporation headed by the Governor of the State. During his term of office in 1862 and 1863, he approved a number of bills that favored railroad legislation.

Charles Crocker, born at Troy, New York, September 16, 1822, was a successful dry goods merchant in Sacramento when made a director of the Central Pacific Railroad Company. In the fall of 1862, he resigned from the directorate, and under the firm name of C. Crocker & Company, handled most of the construction work to the state line. He was a man of strong physique, great energy and determination and possessed remarkable ability in handling gangs of workmen.

Theodore Dehone Judah was born March 4, 1826, at Bridgeport, Connecticut, and was educated at Rensselaer Institute at Troy, New York. In 1854 he came to the Pacific Coast as the engineer of the Sacramento Valley Railroad which position he held until October 6, 1860. His announcement that he had discovered a practicable route for a railroad over the Sierras aroused the interest of Huntington and led to the organization of the Central Pacific Railroad Company to which he became the chief engineer.

Two other members of the company that held secondary but important positions with the company and served many years were E. B. Crocker and E. H. Miller, Jr. Edwin Bryant Crocker, an older brother of Charles Crocker, was born at Jamesville, Onondago County, New York, April 26, 1818. He was a member of a law firm in Sacramento and was appointed by Governor Stanford to a position on the Supreme Court of California. When his term of office expired, he accepted the position as chief counsel of the Central Pacific Company. In June, 1869, he suffered a paralytic stroke and retired from the legal department of the railroad, but in 1870, he became a member of its board of directors.

Edward J. Miller, Jr., a former partner of Mark Hopkins before the latter's connection with the firm of Huntington & Hopkins, succeeded James Bailey as secretary of the company. Bailey had resigned in the fall of 1863, when efforts were being made to raise money among the company to keep construction moving.

Four other members of the original board of directors of the organization, who withdrew in the fall of 1863, are referred to by Mr. Huntington when he was before the Senate Committee on Pacific Railroads in March, 1896. A member of the committee had charged that they were completely under the control of the four associates, and Huntington said:

Lucius A. Booth was one of the best men in California, as independent as we were. Charles Marsh was a good man and a wealthy man. He was a good miner and engineer. Dr. Strong was a good man. I do not think he had any great deal of money. James Bailey was a man of means. Mr. Judah had less money; he was the engineer. They were all men of prominence in California, and men who were not controlled by anyone, I guess, but themselves. They were all good men.

Chapter XIX

THE WESTERN PACIFIC
RAILROAD

By THE 9TH SECTION of the Act of 1862, the Central Pacific Railroad Company was authorized to construct its railroad from the Pacific Coast, at or near San Francisco, or the navigable waters of the Sacramento River, to the eastern boundary of California, upon the terms and conditions and with all the advantages contained in the Act.

On December 4, 1862, the Central Pacific Railroad Company assigned to Timothy Dane and others the right to construct all that portion of the railroad and telegraph lying between the city of Sacramento and the city of San Francisco, which the said Central Pacific Railroad Company was authorized to construct by the Act of 1862, together with all the Central Pacific Company's rights, grants, donations, etc.[1]

This action of the Central Pacific Railroad Company is further explained by Collis P. Huntington in his testimony before the U. S. Pacific Railway Commission, volume 1, page 12:

When we [he and Judah] were in Washington, trying to get through the bill to give us aid, a certain party said that we must cut off our part at Sacramento and they must have the part between Sacramento and San Francisco, or else we must begin at San Francisco. . . . We consented. We commenced at Sacramento, and assigned that part of the road, as agreed to, to Charles McLaughlin, and a man by the name of Houston, as I remember, and Judge Dane, and a number of others, and then located the road. We had nothing to do with them at the time . . . They finally . . . got embarrassed and did not see their way clear to complete the road to San Francisco; and said if we would take it and finish it to San Francisco, we could have it, and they would keep the land grant. They had built from San José toward Sacramento to a distance of about twenty miles.

The Western Pacific Railroad Company was incorporated December 13, 1862, for the purpose of constructing a railroad from San José through the counties of Alameda, Santa Clara and San Joaquin to the city of Sacramento; the length to be 137.5 miles and with a capital stock of $5,400,000. The right to extend the road from Sacramento to San Francisco was given to the company with all rights, grants, donations, etc., given the Central Pacific Railroad Company west of the western base of the Sierras and subject to the same conditions. The officers of this company were Timothy Dane, president; E. S. Holden, vice president; E. T. Pease, secretary; R. Chenery, treasurer; and W. J. Lewis, chief engineer. The first twenty miles were to be constructed one year from July 1, 1865, and the whole road within four years thereafter. The time was extended two years by Congress. The aid in Government bonds amounted to $1,975,560. San Francisco gave $200,000 outright, San Joaquin county subscribed $250,-000 in stock, and Santa Clara county, $150,000.[2]

The Sacramento *Union* for December 22, 1862, had this optimistic view of the situation:

From recent numbers of the San Francisco newspapers, it appears that the railroad jealousies which have been exhibited in that city have been removed by an action of the Board of Directors of the Central Pacific Railroad Company in assigning the right to build

under the Pacific Railroad bill, and with the Government subsidy
of $16,000 a mile, to a company organized to build a railroad from
San Francisco by way of San José and Stockton to Sacramento
there to connect with the Central Pacific Railroad. This new organization is called the Western Pacific Railroad Company, and
both it and the Central Pacific will open their books for subscriptions
at an early day. The route . . . from Sacramento to Stockton, to
Livermore Pass, to near San José, to San Francisco. San Francisco
is so happily situated that she can afford to be somewhat indifferent
to the question of routes. . . . It is difficult to estimate the advantages
which San Francisco will gain by the road to Washoe alone. [Rail-
road jealousies removed? Alas!]

Chapter XX

DUTCH FLAT AND
DONNER LAKE WAGON ROAD

ARTICLES OF ASSOCIATION for this road were dated November 27, 1861, between L. Stanford, C. Crocker, Huntington & Hopkins, E. L. Bradley, and D. W. Strong. The road was to run from Illinoistown [Colfax] in Placer County, California, to Virginia City and Washoe Valley in Nevada Territory. The agreement was to continue for the period of ten years from date, unless sooner dissolved by the unanimous vote of the shareholders, and for such further time as might be agreed upon.[1]

The Articles of Association show that four hundred shares of stock of $1,000 each were issued and apportioned as follows: Sanford and Crocker, eighty shares each; Huntington and Hopkins, together one hundred shares; E. L. Bradley, twenty shares; and D. W. Strong, forty shares. An amendment extended the time to twenty years unless sooner dissolved. No shareholder was to sell, assign, or transfer his stock, or any interest he may have, to any other person other than some shareholder in the company. Officers of the company for the first year were Charles Crocker, president; Mark Hopkins, secretary and treasurer. Date of amendment, August 18, 1863.

The wagon road was designed for the following purposes: (1) to aid the heavy work over the mountains and avoid delay on the construction of the Central Pacific Railroad; (2) for the transportation of freight from Washoe and Virginia City to the end of the railroad at Dutch Flat and points farther along as the line lengthened over the Sierras; (3) to take supplies to the construction forces on the east of the Sierras by ox and mule teams; (4) as a toll road to control freight shipments over portions of the road as completed. Three toll gates were established on the road from Dutch Flat to the top of Dog Mountain, a distance of sixty-seven and one half miles: Dutch Flat, Polley's Station, and Donner Lake. Authorized rates of toll were established on May 12, 1865.

The Wagon Road was started in the spring of 1863 under the direction of Dr. D. W. Strong; but on October 30, 1863, he made an assignment of thirty-six of his forty shares, as witnessed by Horace H. Seaton, and withdrew from the Central Pacific Railroad Company.[2]

After Dr. Strong's resignation, the wagon road was put in charge of R. H. Pratt[3] and made into an excellent highway.

The wagon road was completed and open for through travel on June 14, 1864, at a cost of $350,000, which was borne by the associates as individuals and was not charged to the railroad company.[4] Mr. Pratt was then made one of the managing officers of the railroad, and served for twenty-five years as Assistant General Superintendent.

Charles Crocker advertised the opening of the wagon road in the Sacramento *Union,* and the most sinister motives were attributed to the railroad company by the San Francisco newspapers. They charged the company with getting money

THE GREAT

DUTCH FLAT

SWINDLE!!

The City of San Francisco

DEMANDS JUSTICE!!

THE MATTER IN CONTROVERSY, AND THE PRESENT STATE OF THE QUESTION.

AN ADDRESS

To the Board of Supervisors, Officers and People of San Francisco.

Facsimile of the Titlepage of a Pamphlet

American River Canyon in the Sierras

under false pretenses; that they had no intention of building a part of the transcontinental line; their purpose was to build the railroad only to Dutch Flat as an adjunct to their wagon road.

A pamphlet was issued August 18, entitled: "The Great Dutch Flat Swindle! The City of San Francisco Demands Justice!" which the Sacramento *Union* credited to one Horace Dawes. The pamphlet was answered by a San Francisco supervisor, H. de la Montanya, who said:

The author very prudently conceals his name as few citizens in the state would voluntarily imperil their reputation as a truthful, honorable man by signing a publication containing so many gross misrepresentations, demagogue insinuations, wilful fabrications, and unmitigated slanders. . . .[5]

Sacramento was at that time having a disagreement with the Sacramento Valley Railroad and had forcibly removed its tracks from Front Street. The Alta *Californian* of San Francisco said:

The Sacramentons are determined to have no railroad but Dutch Flat. . . . The Capital City has aided in the raid upon this county for $600,000, upon Placer County for $250,000, and upon the state for millions, all for the benefit of that scheme. . . . It will yet prove its ruin. There will never be a railroad via Dutch Flat to Nevada Territory. There are obstacles which cannot be overcome. The Pacific Railroad will follow another route, not through the City of Sacramento or anywhere in the vicinity.

After the railroad was constructed over the mountains the wagon road was abandoned and presented to the counties through which it passed. The wagon road business was a losing one. The tolls did not amount to enough to pay for the road.[6]

Chapter XXI

RAISING FUNDS FOR CONSTRUCTION

NOT ALL THE PROVISIONS of the railroad bill were acceptable to Mr. Huntington and his associates, but they decided to accept them with the hope of procuring amendments to the most objectionable features later on. Acceptance of the bill was required within six months from the date of the Act, and the Central Pacific Company filed its acceptance in the office of the Secretary of the Interior on December 1, 1862.

The Act required that forty miles of the road be completed and approved by the three railroad commissioners before any aid could be had from the Government. Some means had to be taken to raise the necessary funds to construct those forty miles.

No stock was issued by the company prior to the Act of 1862, but there had been about one hundred subscribers to stock when issued, representing less than a million dollars. In his interview before the Senate Committee on Pacific Railroads in March , 1896, Mr. Huntington told of some of the difficulties faced at that time in the effort to secure the necessary funds:

When the Central Pacific Railroad was built, it was thought that the people who embarked their money and their time in it were taking great risks. Many of the men in New York and Boston of large means, I endeavored to get to join us in the building of the road, but no one was willing to join us in the undertaking. Such men as Moses Taylor, William E. Dodge, Commodore Garrison, and many others, I spent hours with in the endeavor to induce them to take an interest, and the reply made by Commodore Garrison was in about the words in which they all answered: "Huntington, the risk is too great, and the profits, if any, are too small, we cannot take the risk."

I called upon many of the rich men of California like D. O. Mills, Eugene Kelly, John Parrott, and others, but none of them would join us, some saying the risks were too great, and the others that we were crazy. All the people of California, however, wanted the road; the Government wanted it and all those in the East who had friends in California wanted it, so that each could go to the other without the inconvenience and hardships of the long and tedious sea voyage. Finally, I went among my old friends in New York and Boston and asked them to invest money in this enterprise, and they said, "Huntington, we do not want to go into it, but if you will guarantee the interest on these bonds for ten years, we will take them." I said, "I will guarantee them, because if the Central Pacific ever stops short of completion, C. P. Huntington will be so badly broken that you will never spend any time picking him up."

In the manuscript of Charles Crocker in the Bancroft Library, p. 29, we find:

There was not a bank that would loan the company a cent. They had no faith in it. We procured from D. O. Mills, a banker, who was personally known to all of us, a paper testifying to our responsibility and our honor as men and merchants, and that whatever we agreed to do, he believed that we would faithfully carry it out.

Eighteen miles of the Central Pacific Railroad were built under the Act of 1862. We actually spent our own money building that road up to Newcastle, and it left everyone of us in debt.

In the testimony of Leland Stanford before the U. S. Pacific Railway Commission, pp. 2630 and 2635:

It [the stock] had no value at the time it was issued, and it had no value when the road was completed. Of course it afterwards became valuable. Of the very few people who subscribed for stock at the beginning, most got out, and this included most of those who had taken stock just to help us along. Afterwards, it went down, and I myself bought as an accommodation to a stockholder, 2300 shares at ten cents on the dollar, full paid stock. Finally, it was not sold at all because nobody would have it . . .

At that time we had given up all hopes of realizing anything from the stock of the company. The profit to us as investors in the railroad passed away. We had given up all hopes of that. It was then the simple question of whether we could overcome the difficulties which beset us and succeed in building the road.

At the time of the organization of the company, 1,250 shares of stock were subscribed by the members. Later two hundred shares were taken by Samuel Brannan. On October 22, 1862, committees were appointed to solicit subscriptions in Sacramento. The stock was disposed of very slowly.

Charles Crocker went to Virginia City and tried to sell stock. The capitalists there asked him if the enterprise would produce two per cent a month profit, and when Crocker said that it would not, they refused to go into a speculation that would not promise that much interest.[1]

To James Bailey, then secretary of the company, was assigned the task of collecting subscriptions to stock in San Francisco. He was joined by Mr. Marcus D. Boruck, editor of the *California Spirit of the Times*, a San Francisco weekly. In a lecture on the subject, "The Press," delivered in the Assembly Chamber of the State Capitol at Sacramento on Thursday evening, February 28, 1895, Mr. Boruck tells of the results of his work there:

An effort was made to secure subscriptions to the stock of the road almost at its inception from the merchants, business men, and capitalists of San Francisco, but the purchased press of San Fran-

Officers of the Central Pacific Railroad Company

cisco opposed it in every way. There was no "octopus" then. There were no rates to denounce because there was no necessity to fix rates. There was no road, but still the battle was waged against the road. Stanford, president of the road, requested me through the secretary, Mr. Bailey, to assist him in procuring subscriptions to the stock from among the merchants, business men, shippers, capitalists and others in San Francisco. I did so. This was in October, 1862. We opened an office in Platt's Hall on the corner of Montgomery and Bush Streets. Mr. Bailey returned to Sacramento and left me in charge. We received one subscription from San Francisco and only one. That was from a Frenchman for ten shares. We never saw him before and he has never been seen since. At the end of twenty-two days, without a single subscription from San Francisco, the books were closed and removed to Sacramento.

During the year 1863, the State of California approved the following legislation in favor of the Pacific Railroad Companies, subject to the will of the people: (1) authorized the San Francisco board of supervisors to subscribe $1,000,000 to the capital stock of the Central Pacific and Western Pacific companies; (2) authorized the board of supervisors of Placer County to subscribe $250,000 in stock to the Central Pacific Company; (3) authorized the board of supervisors of Sacramento County to subscribe $300,000 in stock to the Central Pacific, and the city of Sacramento to grant thirty acres of land for depots, warehouses, etc., which included 1,300 feet fronting on the Sacramento River; and (4) authorized a state donation of $10,000 per mile for fifty miles.

This last was repealed in 1864, and the state agreed to pay the interest at seven per cent on $1,500,000 of the company's bonds. The company issued the bonds and the state paid the interest for twenty years, when, the bonds becoming due, the company paid them off. In return for this, the railroad was required to transport without charge public passengers, convicts going to state prison, lunatics in charge of state officials, materials for the construction of the new state Capitol, articles for exhibition at state fairs, and, in case of war, invasion, or insurrection, state troops and munitions. The state received, also, the deed to a large granite quarry on the line of the railroad.

The $1,000,000 was readily voted at the polls during May, 1863, by the citizens of San Francisco, in spite of the opposition of the newspapers of that city; $600,000 was apportioned to the Central Pacific, and $400,000 to the Western Pacific. The board of supervisors refused to take action, however, and legal proceedings were resorted to by the Central Pacific Railroad Company. A compromise was affected by which outright gifts of $400,000 was made to the Central Pacific, and $200,000 to the Western Pacific.

After litigation which cost the railroad company $100,000, the court ordered delivery of the bonds which were finally handed over to the companies in April, 1865, two years after the voters had decided to do so. The delay affected seriously the progress of the road. The chief reason for the outright gift instead of the purchase of stock was that the city treasury might not be held responsible in case the company failed. Had they purchased the stock and held it, they would have been repaid in full measure.

Of the four hundred bonds received from San Francisco, three hundred fifteen were sold at 751.60, bringing in $236,-745. The remaining eighty-five bonds were disposed of at par in payment for rolling stock which gave the company $321,745.

The Placer bonds were sold for about seventy and realized about $160,772. The Sacramento bonds were sold for sixty-five and the three hundred brought about $195,000.[2] Proceeds from these bonds were received in 1864.

During the investigation of the Central Pacific Railroad Company in 1887, by the U. S. Pacific Railway Commission, the following persons gave testimony concerning the efforts of members of the company to obtain funds. Lloyd Tevis, vol. 6, p. 3132, of the report:

The capital of those gentlemen was very limited—I refer to their individual means—because they were borrowing money in the market all the time and of anybody who would lend it to them. They applied to me, I might say hundreds of times. I occasionally loaned them money, and assisted them in procuring money from others. I loaned them at the rate of three per cent a month. [This was after the road had made some progress.]

Marcus D. Boruck, vol. 6, p. 3421:

I know at one time—for seventeen days, I think—they did not have a dollar in the treasury with which to prosecute their work.

Darius O. Mills, banker, vol. 6, p. 3493:

Mr. Huntington went to New York—and he was considered a very shrewd man—to get those bonds started among moneyed men of New York. He did succeed in a small way after a while and it grew. With the exercise of great energy, and I may say, by using a great deal of tact and ability, he got them started so he could make use of them.

Under the laws of California, stockholders are individually liable to the extent of the debts and liabilities contracted or incurred while they are stockholders, regardless of the amount paid. This was a great difficulty in obtaining capital in aid of the road. It also frightened off foreign capital from investments in California.[3]

Chapter XXII

HUNTINGTON, FINANCIER
AND PURCHASING AGENT

COLLIS POTTER HUNTINGTON left Sacramento in December, 1862, for the East to purchase the necessary materials and equipment for the Central Pacific Railroad. All materials for construction, except timber, must come from the Atlantic States via the Isthmus of Panama or Cape Horn to San Francisco Bay, there transferred to river boats or barges for ascending the Sacramento River; thence hauled over the Central Pacific Line as far as completed, and later when needed, carried in wagons beyond the end of the track. All iron must be of American manufacture.

The greater portion of the timber used was found in the Sierras where saw mills were located for the purpose; other timber came from the coast counties of California and from Oregon.

Upon his arival in New York, Mr. Huntington called upon several iron manufacturers and locomotive works, but received no encouragement. They considered the scheme too large and too doubtful and not worthy of business consideration. The bonds could not be sold, as no part of the line had been completed, and the Government had first lien on it whenever it was built. However, money must be raised some way.

Mr. Huntington then thought of visiting Boston and calling upon Oliver Ames & Sons, a firm dealing in hardware or the shovel business there, and of whom the firm of Huntington & Hopkins were customers. Mr. Huntington, however, had no personal acquaintance with either of the Ames brothers. He called there and told Oliver Ames he had a proposition to lay before him. Ames appointed a time for an interview the next day. When the time came, Mr. Huntington laid his proposal before Ames which was to borrow $100,000 or $200,000 and give a large amount of bonds of the proposed railroad as security. Oliver Ames asked: "You mean to give bonds of something not yet in existence? I will have to look into this matter and think it over." He then made another appointment for the next day.

When Mr. Huntington again presented himself, Mr. Ames told him that after he had heard the proposition the first thing he had done was to examine the books of his firm to see how Huntington & Hopkins stood, and he said, "I must say that no firm or customer that we have on our books has been more prompt in meeting their obligations in every way, shape, or manner than the firm of Huntington & Hopkins during the time they have been dealing with us. Now do you intend to carry on the construction of this work in the same manner as you have carried on your business operations?" Huntington answered that he certainly intended to do so.

"Well then," said Ames, "I do not hesitate to loan you the $100,000 or $200,000 that you require in cash. I will do so and take your bonds provided that Huntington & Hopkins take the same interest in the affairs of the road, and look after my interests as they have done when I have sold them goods." And he added, "I think I can be of more benefit to you in other ways than even loaning you this money. I can give you letters to the different iron and locomotive men and others. I am acquainted with nearly all of them. I think these letters will be of advantage to you in making contacts with them."

The purport of the letters was that he, Oliver Ames, had confidence in the enterprise and in the men who were undertaking it to such an extent that he had taken a good many of their bonds as an investment, and he considered them perfectly good on account of the men at the head of the enterprise.

When Huntington presented these letters to the different iron and other manufacturers, he had no trouble getting all the material he wanted and all the credit he wanted. That was the starting point of his success in the East. Ames told him that he had a brother [Oakes Ames] in Congress who might be of great assistance in furthering the interests of the road.[1] Said Mr. Huntington in this connection:

We had endorsed paper to one party (Oakes Ames) of $1,250,000, personal security. They said, "Here, we know you, and while we don't know what you are worth, we are satisfied you would not have endorsed the paper if you were not worth the money." On this credit I procured the aid desired.[2]

Huntington's first attempt at negotiation of bonds of the Central Pacific Railroad Company was with the Boston firm, Flint, Peabody & Company, an old shipping firm. Flint had approached Huntington while in California and proposed to aid him in selling a million and a half of bonds. Huntington hesitated because he understood that Flint was connected with the sale of the bonds of Wilson's railroad at Marysville, which were worthless. Flint, however, assured him that he was not connected with that matter, and Huntington told him that he would receive $20,000 for selling a million and a half of Central Pacific bonds.

After Huntington had taken up his work in the East, he visited Flint in Boston occasionally to learn how matters stood. Flint would say that things were working out nicely, but it took time. Huntington began to investigate and found that Flint was the agent for the bonds of the railroad from Folsom to Marysville and consequently was not in good standing, and could accomplish nothing. With some difficulty he succeeded in getting the bonds away from Flint and afterward sold them himself.[3]

On March 20, 1863, Huntington sent a dispatch to his associates saying that he had purchased 5,000 tons of rails, enough for the first fifty miles of road.[4]

Eventually, he enlisted the young brokers, Fisk & Hatch, in the sale of the Government bonds. They specialized in such securities and acted as the Central Pacific's financial agent in the East, taking bonds and returning cash. The company failed in the panic of 1873, but recovered later.

One of Huntington's notable purchases of material, showing his shrewdness in avoiding a rise in prices, and evading competition, occurred in his negotiation with a middleman named Davis. The iron manufacturers had become convinced that the Central Pacific, the Union Pacific, and other railroads would soon require large quantities of iron, and at a meeting in New York discussed the situation with a view of an advance in price.

Mr. Davis, who controlled the largest quantity of rails, asked Mr. Huntington how many tons he would require during the year. Mr. Huntington, suspecting their plan and pretending irritation replied: "I have rails on the way to lay one hundred fifty miles of track, but my people find they cannot lay more than one hundred miles this year." When Davis told him that Durant of the Union Pacific expected to lay 60,000 tons, Huntington laughed and said: "You know he will do nothing of the kind, the Kansas branch is in litigation," and he went on to give reasons why none of the roads would lay rails. All of which was proved to be true.

Davis went back to the iron makers with this opinion, and they decided not to advance prices. Whereupon, Huntington called upon the different men for prices and when he had heard from them all, telegraphed to each, and in one day, purchased 60,000 tons of rails.

These rails would require a large number of ships for transportation and the problem was to secure a sufficient number at satisfactory prices. He called in his ship broker and said to him:

"I want a good ship; go out and see what you can find."

The broker went out and returned with the names of three or four and named the rates for each. Huntington shook his head:

"It is too high; ships are coming in all along. Try again."

The broker went out again, and again the third time, coming back with the names of twenty-three ships. Huntington noted down the vessels, and suddenly said,

"I'll take them."

"Take them! Take which?" asked the bewildered agent.

"I will take all those ships," was the reply.

"But I cannot let you have them all; I must have two or three of them myself."

"Not any of these, I have engaged them for myself," was the obdurate answer.

The vessels took out to California some 45,000 tons of rails which the shipowners said would have cost him at least ten dollars a ton more had they known what he intended, a clear gain of $450,000 for the railroad company.[5]

Several accounts are given of Huntington's efforts to raise money among his associates. The following purports to come from the Huntington manuscript in the Bancroft Library, pp. 9-12:

At the start a construction company was formed consisting of Stanford, Hopkins, Booth, Marsh, Peel, Judah, and Huntington. Each man was to furnish one-seventh of the means to build the road to Newcastle, which they were to own equally. But Peel receded from his agreement after the work had commenced, being afraid to risk his share, $34,000 in gold, worth thirty per cent premium. Huntington then said that Peel must buy him out, or sell out to him; but Peel refused to do either. Huntington had another alternative, which was to stop work, which he did, going along the line and ordering nine sub-contractors to cease and pay off their men. These sub-contractors thinking there must be some real cause for this arbitrary action, offered to buy out the company, and build the road for themselves. "All right," said Huntington, "I give you two weeks to do it in." But the only man they found who was likely to become their capitalist, Charles McLaughlin, when he learned that Huntington was to sell out, declined to furnish the money, as Huntington knew very well he would do. The nine sub-contractors returned, Peel having sold out and the road was finished to Newcastle.[6]

Mr. Huntington returned from the East upon another occasion and found the treasury almost depleted and the necessity of raising more money or stopping work. A meeting of the company was called and Mr. Huntington said: "Huntington and Hopkins can out of their own means pay five hundred men during a year; how many can each of you keep on the line?" Before the meeting had adjourned these men had resolved that they would maintain eight hundred men on the road out of their own private fortunes. Dr. Strong was unable to furnish his share of the expense, and withdrew, as did Bailey, Marsh, and Booth.[7]

Chapter XXIII

CONSTRUCTION OF THE CENTRAL PACIFIC RAILROAD, 1863

GROUND WAS FORMALLY broken for the commencement of the Central Pacific Railroad on January 8, 1863, in the presence of dignitaries of the state and a great gathering of citizens. Two wagons filled with earth and adorned with flags were drawn up near the rostrum. On one of these wagons was a large banner bearing a representation of hands clasped across the continent from the Atlantic to the Pacific with the words: "May the bond be eternal."

Charles Crocker as master of ceremonies first introduced Leland Stanford, Governor of California and President of the railroad company, who made a short address. This was followed by a prayer by the Reverend J. A. Benton at the close of which Mr. Crocker announced, "The Governor of California will now shovel the first earth for the great Pacific Railroad." Stanford seized the shovel and with great vigor deposited the first earth for the embankment, amid the cheers of the assemblage.

The Honorable A. M. Crane of Alameda, president *pro tem* of the Senate made the address, closing with these words:

"Then will be celebrated the completion of this greatest, proudest achievement of man. Our sister city of the Bay will develop rapidly, and by the amazing increase of her commerce and manufactures pass beyond any at present conceived limits and sit proudly the Queen of Cities."

Other talks were made by J. W. Warwick, W. H. Sears, Newton Booth, J. T. Morse, and Charles Crocker. In his brief address, Mr. Crocker said: "This is no idle ceremony; the pile-driver is even now, while I am talking, driving piles for the foundation of the bridge across the American River."[1]

The Central Pacific Railroad Company had been granted the right of way into the City of Sacramento, and the rights to the overflowed land within the city limits known as Sutter's Slough. This slough extended from the levee of the American River to I Street, and from Sixth Street to the American River at its old mouth, a depression forty feet deep in places. The company had offered to fill it if given the deed to the site, and the offer was accepted. The company began the fill in 1863, but it was not completed until many years later.[2]

The road for which Stanford deposited the first earth commenced at the junction of the American and Sacramento rivers, and extended easterly along the southern bank of the American River for three miles. The American is a short river having its source near the summit of the Sierras, and is torrential in character. Several times it had overflowed into the city of Sacramento and threatened destruction.

The railroad was built upon an embankment constructed almost wholly by the company, and was protected against the waters of the river by a riprapping of the most expensive and costly character; so that while the road from the point of commencement to Arcade, seven miles from Sacramento, was built upon comparatively level ground, its construction was a matter of considerable expense. This riprap, or broken stones, used in the foundation of the embankment had to be brought from Folsom on the Sacramento Valley Railroad.

Snow Plow No. 1 on the Central Pacific Railroad

Chinese Cutting a Path for a Track Around "Cape Horn"

From Arcade, the stipulated base of the mountain area, the work of cuts and fills commenced, and the difficulties and cost of construction rapidly increased as the ascent of the Sierras was made. It is impossible to portray but faintly the conditions under which the Central Pacific Railroad was built.[3]

Labor was scarce and only obtainable at great cost. Miners, accustomed to work in the Placer mines or not as it suited them, would not undergo the discipline of railroad work. They were indifferent and independent and their labor high-priced. At the first mining excitement many of them would abandon work. As an illustration, eleven hundred men were transported at one time to work on the eastern sections of the road, and out of the eleven hundred only one hundred remained when new mines opened at Austin, Nevada.[4]

In his testimony before the U. S. Pacific Railway Commission, 1887, p. 2577, L. M. Clement, civil engineer, said:

Labor sufficient for rapid construction of the railroad was not then on the coast and labor as it existed could not be depended upon. The first rumor of a new mine meant a stampede and consequent abandonment of all work. The labor question was serious; every day brought up problems that must be solved without delay, if construction was to advance.

In a letter to Philetus Sawyer, Chairman of the Committee on Pacific Railroads, May, 1874, Collis P. Huntington wrote:

When the work was first commenced, portions of it were let in small sections to different contractors but owing to the scarcity of laborers, the price of labor was increased by the competition between the several contractors; the work of one contractor would delay the others; and it was found that the work, which was very difficult and required a large force, could not be prosecuted as rapidly as the Act of Congress and the State Legislature required, and the plan of contracting the work in small sections was abandoned. Besides, it was vital to the interests of the company to be able to reach Salt Lake Valley by the time the Union Pacific reached there in order to compete for the trade of that valley, hence the extreme necessity of pushing construction with all possible dispatch. The work to the eastern line of the state was let to the firm of Charles Crocker & Company. This plan worked much better and the work progressed more rapidly.

In December, 1862, Charles Crocker resigned from the directorate of the company and on December 26, 1862, the board voted to award to Charles Crocker & Company the construction contract for that portion of the work between the foot of K Street, Sacramento, and the California Central Railroad at Girder's comprising Sections 1 to 18 inclusive. The Sacramento *Union* for December 29, carried the following advertisement:

Central Pacific Railroad of California. Notice to contractors. Sealed proposals will be received by the undersigned at 56 K Street, Sacramento, until Friday, January 2, 1863, at 12 M. for the grading and masonry upon Sections 4 to 18 inclusive of the Central Pacific Railroad. Plans and specifications can be seen at the Engineer's office, 56 K Street, Sacramento, California. December 28, 1862.

(Signed) C. CROCKER & COMPANY

The rates of contract were not by the mile, but according to the class of work—clearing, grubbing, rock excavation, etc. Payments were made to Crocker partly in cash and partly in stock valued at thirty cents on the dollar. Crocker let the following contracts:

From the 6th levee to end of levee work, about three miles, and sections 5 to 10, about six miles, to S. D. Smith; sections 11 to 18, about eight miles, to White & Gay.

Sections 7 to 10 were sublet by S. D. Smith to Charles Bates; White & Gay sublet sections 11 and 12 to John Coffee, and parts of sections 17 and 18 to Cyrus Collins.

The piling, trestling, and bridging across the American River was let by Crocker to Baker & Hubbard. There were, therefore, three contractors and three sub-contractors working for Crocker on the first eighteen sections. These eighteen miles proved more formidable and costly than expected due to the heavy riprapping along the American River and the expensive bridge across it.[5]

Judah, the chief engineer was opposed to the Crocker contracts, and according to his report, July 1, 1863, he himself let the contracts for Sections 19 to 31, from the line of the California Central to Newcastle, "to responsible contractors" who would begin work immediately. He reported, also, that twenty-three bids had been received for the remainder of the First division of fifty miles, "a number of which were from responsible parties, and would range within his estimate of costs."[6]

Judah's estimate of the total cost of the First Division of fifty miles as given in his report was as follows:

Sections 1-18, grading, masonry, bridging, ties and track as per existing contracts	$ 400,000
Sections 19-50, for same, as per proposals received from contractors	1,835,896
Iron rails, locomotives, passenger, baggage and freight cars, turn tables, switches and frogs, machinery for machine shops	721,000
Buildings, machinery, right of way and engineering	175,000
Contingencies	89,600
TOTAL	$3,221,496

These estimates did not take into consideration the enormous rise in prices of materials, freights and insurance, and proved to be less than half the real cost. Blasting powder alone for the one hundred forty miles cost $900,000 in gold. Portions to grade cost upwards of $300,000 per mile, and the average mountain section, $100,000 per mile.[7]

When Charles Crocker was awarded his first construction contract he did so under the name of Charles Crocker & Company with the intention of attracting outside men with capital to join him in a partnership. No men could be found, however, willing to join the firm although he continued his contracts under that name until he reached the eastern state line.

During his interview with the Senate Committee on Pacific Railroads in March, 1896, Mr. Huntington told of his efforts to procure partners for the firm of C. Crocker & Company:

Mr. Crocker did not complete that contract, he could not get any partners. I worked very hard myself to get them in California, New York, and Boston, but the capitalists that I spoke to would not go into an open co-partnership and be responsible as individuals for large amounts. I am very certain that Crocker did not finish his contract. That contract was to build from Newcastle to Camp 127 or 128, some one hundred miles of the most expensive part of the road. The Contract and Finance Company took the work up, and he turned the contract over to that company.

From the state line, Charles Crocker worked as the chief supervisor of construction instead of as a contracting firm. As a railroad builder, he proved to be most successful. He embodied great physical strength, cheerfulness of disposition, energy, determination, and a driving power to get things done. He said himself that he was hard to live with during the construction period because he kept himself in a critical, fault-finding frame of mind contrary to his usual amiable nature.

The contracts of C. Crocker & Company and his subsequent work as supervisor of construction brought the usual malicious criticism of the company from opponents. This, like other criticisms, has been handed down from generation to generation, and is thus expressed by a recent writer:

> The resourceful four had already hit on the money-making device . . . their control of the company gave them power to grant contracts for the construction of the road. Rather than let profits from construction go to other contractors, the group organized a construction company of their own quite independent of the railroad . . . and, as directors, to award contracts to themselves as builders on terms liberal enough to assure very large profits.[8]

It was impossible to obtain contracts from responsible people for building over the mountains. It was new work; nothing like it had been seen before in this country or in any other. The great railroad over the Cenis route in Switzerland, or over the Tyrol in Austria, great feats of engineering, sink into insignificance in comparison. It was not contemplated that any profits should be made out of the work of construction. The idea was to get the road through in the shortest time so as to give the Government its use as early as possible. The firm of Charles Crocker & Company was formed with the intention of having others to join in partnership but his financial position was not sufficiently inviting to attract partners with capital.

During the work on the mountains, Crocker found he had assumed a task beyond his financial strength. He was then told to go on with the work without regard for his terms of contract and the directors would see him through. Thus he worked to the state line, knowing he would receive his pay when the corporation could raise it. No solvent contractor could have been obtained to accept the contract that Mr. Crocker undertook. Many years later, the stock, which was at first worthless, did realize some value after years of most difficult work.[9]

While Mr. Huntington, henceforth, spent most of his time in the East, he made at first frequent trips back to Sacramento and the scene of the construction of the railroad, such was the great responsibility he felt for its success. He tells of an incident that happened upon his first visit after work had commenced:

> It had been understood that the Central Pacific Railroad was to run up I Street in Sacramento and I had given orders that it was to go up that street to Fifth and thence to B Street and out to the levee. Work had commenced, however, in running it by a point on the American River, where water overflowed every year, and would require more of the expensive rip-rap to be brought down from Folsom to protect the embankment. Work had been going on for several days when I walked out to see how affairs were progressing. I found over a hundred teams at work and gave orders that they be stopped at once.
>
> Mr. Judah came up and said that the board of directors had given orders to have the work done that way. "But," I replied, "it will cost $200,000 more at least to put the road here; it must go up I Street." I then sent for Mr. Cody and ordered him to move the road to I Street.[10]

On October 8, 1863, the ship *Herald-of-the-Morning* arrived at Sacramento with one hundred tons of railroad iron, the first shipment for the Central Pacific Railroad. The first rails were laid October 26, 1863, beginning at Front Street between J and K Streets. On November 9, 1863, two miles of track had been laid, and the first locomotive, which had arrived in Sacramento, October 7, on the schooner *Anna R. Forbes,* was given its trial run.[11]

"It had been intended," writes Mr. Heath, "that prominent citizens be given the first ride, but the small boys of Sacramento beat the dignitaries to it, and when the locomotive puffed into view, it was covered with a wriggling mass of cheering youngsters."

The Sacramento *Union* for November 7, 1863, sums up to that date the year's work on construction of the Central Pacific Railroad:

The means for building the first fifty miles have been provided. The first contract was entered upon in January, 1863. The agent to buy the iron and rolling stock did not leave California until the December preceding. It is, therefore, less than ten months since active preparations began. Within these months iron and rolling stock was purchased for seventy miles and paid for; eighteen miles have been graded and prepared for the rails and cars; a bridge over the American River has been built which, with the trestle, cost over $100,000; twelve miles more are under contract to be finished for the iron the first of January; the twenty miles more needed to make up the first section of fifty miles has been prepared for letting; and the line has been surveyed and located to Dutch Flat. Rolling stock and iron for over seventy miles have been purchased and some eight hundred tons have arrived. A locomotive is in Sacramento ready for the track. And all this has been accomplished without failing in any instance to meet every obligation incurred to the contractors and without creating any indebtedness. No other railroad on the Pacific side has ever been managed so successfully.

The large amount of supplies required and the foresight which brought them to the railroad as needed is commented upon by a contemporary writer as follows:

A day's delay in receiving material would have caused immense loss to the company yet such were their foresight and calculation that the supplies always came at the proper time and the great work never stopped, though much of the material had to traverse more than half the length of two oceans . . . Fifty vessels sailed up the Sacramento River each month laden with iron and other materials for the railroad.[12]

Chapter XXIV

DIFFICULTIES, NATURAL AND MAN-MADE

MR. HUNTINGTON was in New York and not present at the celebration of the beginning of construction, January 8, 1863, nor did he approve of it. "If you want to jubilate," said he to his associates, "go ahead and do it. I don't. Those mountains look too ugly and I see too much work ahead. We may fail. There are many years of hard work between the beginning and the completion of this road."

Those mountains did indeed look insurmountable by any railroad line, and were so considered by reputable engineers. The Sierras, over one hundred miles wide, reared a snowy crest 12,000 feet and more in height through which the railroad must crawl by a pass more than 7,000 feet above the Sacramento Valley. To reach this pass required an army of workmen and teams to be sheltered and fed; an incalculable amount of grading, filling, trestle building, cutting and tunneling, much of it through solid rock. A number of saw mills must be established in the mountains to produce timber and cross-ties. All the iron to be used had to be shipped around Cape Horn, one of the longest voyages for commercial purposes on the face of the earth; or across the Isthmus of Panama, necessitating two expensive transfers.

There had been years of discussion, innumerable articles and many plans made concerning a Pacific Railroad, yet neither Congress, individual states, nor syndicates of capitalists had been willing to engage in so stupendous an enterprise as that of constructing the Pacific Railroad. The action of these Sacramento merchants in attempting to build the most difficult portion of the transcontinental railroad appeared to many as an extreme act of madness.

When before the Senate Committee on Pacific Railroads in March, 1896, Mr. Huntington said:

I suppose that it is a fact, the mercantile credit of my partners in business and myself was positively injured by our connection with this enterprise. There were difficulties from end to end; difficulties from high steep mountains, from snows, from deserts where there was a scarcity of water, from gorges and flats where there was an excess of water; difficulties from cold and from heat; from a scarcity of timber and from obstructions of rock; difficulties in supplying a large force on a long line; from Indians, and from a want of laborers.

In his testimony before the U. S. Pacific Railway Commission, 1887, vol. 1, p. 10, Mr. Huntington said:

It was a very difficult line, to speak of the physical obstructions to be overcome. Probably the worst line that was ever built. We rise 7,042 feet in 105 miles and all but 134 feet of that was overcome in 84 miles with a maximum grade of 105 feet, except for one short piece which required a grade of 116 feet.

L. M. Clement, civil engineer, testifying before the same Commission, vol. 5, p. 2576, said:

Opinions were circulated to the effect that the railroads then constructed in Europe were mere bagatelles compared to the difficulties to be met in constructing the Central Pacific Railroad, and failure was clearly written on the rocky sides of the Sierra Nevada Mountains. Not only was it impossible to construct a railroad via Donner Pass, but owing to the great depth of snow, some years reaching an aggregate of fifty feet, it would be impracticable to operate, should they succeed in building it.

L. L. Robinson, engineer and a stockholder in the Sacramento Valley Railroad Company, wrote in 1864:

I have had some twenty-five years connection with railways as an engineer, have examined personally all the engineering works of importance in Europe and the United States; have seen much heavy work; have constructed railways where the gradation cost over $100,000 per mile for five consecutive miles, and I must confess that all my ideas of physical obstacles in the construction of railways were so completely below the difficulties encountered on the Central Pacific route, that I cannot conceive that any set of men would seriously undertake to construct a road over such country.

My firm conviction is that the Central Pacific Railroad will cost from $250,000 to $300,000 a mile before it is completed to Truckee and equipped as a first class road. From Illinoistown (Colfax) to Dutch Flat, any railway must encounter work so costly, and so long a time required to construct it, as to weaken the hopes of finding capital and patience sufficient to build it. From Dutch Flat to Summit is still heavier; from the Summit to Truckee worse than all.

This same distinguished engineer said also that it would take at least fifteen years to build the road across the Summit, if it could ever be constructed at all.[1]

Confronting the builders also was the discouraging fact that the Surveys of the War Department in 1853 had condemned the Central route as too impracticable and costly. Other discouraging features that thrust themselves upon the notice of the company were: (1) the state of Civil War throughout the country; (2) the preservation of the Union was not assured; (3) the national credit was little better than that of individuals; (4) the route lay through a country occupied by Indians, and through the Great American Desert; (5) the unfavorable labor market due to war conditions and mining interests; (6) the scarcity of raw materials for the manufacture of rails and locomotives; (7) all iron used must be of American manufacture; (8) the enormous increase in the cost of materials, freight rates and insurance due to the war situation.

In his testimony before the U. S. Pacific Railway Commission, 1887, p. 10, Mr. Huntington refers to the increase in prices:

> We had to overcome a great many difficulties when we started. Iron was $62 a ton, and before we got across the mountain, it sold for $150 a ton. Locomotives went from $8,000 to as high as $32,500. We paid 2.5 per cent insurance in the time of peace, and in the time of the rebellion we paid 17 per cent insuring the goods around Cape Horn. Many things went up more than 200 per cent; and, I guess, many things more than 300 per cent advance from the time we commenced the road before we got it completed.

On another occasion Mr. Huntington said that all the material used in the construction of the road, except that bought on the Atlantic Coast was paid for in gold. The material purchased in California included vast quantities of lumber as many of the canyons and arroyos were spanned by timber trestles, later removed and converted into solid banks or steel bridges for trains to pass over. For some of this timber was paid as high a price as $2.20 in currency for each dollar in gold.

As if this were not enough to discourage the most stout-hearted of men, the builders encountered an antagonism founded on jealousy, malice, local and personal grievances that pursued the Pacific Railroad enterprise and its builders with relentless vigilance. It was felt in Congress when the bill was being considered; it followed Huntington, the pur-

"Cape Horn" on the Central Pacific Railroad

Central Pacific Train Rounding "Cape Horn"

chasing agent, when negotiating for iron and rolling stock in the form of representation that the harbor of Sacramento was rapidly filling up. They claimed that a railroad was building to a new city a few miles lower on the Sacramento River which would command the trade, and that the company named in the bill never could build such a road as the managers were only merchants and not railroad men.[2]

The project was caricatured and abused by the newspapers, derided by politicians, discountenanced by capitalists, and the credit of everyone connected with it impaired. It was opposed and ridiculed at every step by the moneyed men of San Francisco.[3]

The Sacramento *Union* for November 6, 1863, had this to say on the subject:

Strange as it may seem, there is undoubtedly a very active opposition in San Francisco to building the Pacific Railroad and, to some extent, in other parts of the state. This opposition in certain sections arises from the selection of Sacramento City as a terminus of that route, and is attributable to local jealousy. Another opposition comes from the Sacramento Valley Railroad which is largely controlled by Pioche, Bayerque & Company of San Francisco. They oppose the enterprise on the ground that the construction of a railroad from Sacramento to Dutch Flat and thence toward Washoe [a mining center] would damage the business of the Valley road, which runs from Sacramento to Folsom, as it would divert the Washoe [stage] travel from that route. Another opposition is the Market Street Railroad [in San Francisco] owned by Pioche, Bayerque & Company.

All these oppositions may be natural enough on the part of the interests affected, but with the public at large no such hostility should be felt. It looks as though the San Francisco Board of Supervisors were too much influenced by the managers and agents of the Valley and Market Street railroads when they refuse to issue bonds voted by the people to the Pacific Railroad.

In a letter dated May, 1874, to the Honorable Philetus
Sawyer, Chairman of the House Committee on Pacific Railroads, Mr. Huntington comments on the origin of this
antagonism:

This crusade against the railroad company had its origin far
back in the history of the company, almost at its very commencement
. . . It first originated with the owners of a railroad running a short
distance easterly from Sacramento who wanted to be bought, but
careful surveys were made of that and various other routes, and it
was determined that it was not on the proper location for a route over
the mountains, and for that reason was rejected, and the company
. . . encountered the opposition of the owners and their friends. The
opposition was not large or very formidable but it was persistent
and malicious. It showed itself on the first and subsequent applications to Congress, but, as it was not then popular, it was secret and
malicious. It showed itself, still secretly, in each application made by
the company to the State of California for legislative aid . . . It
showed itself more openly by endeavoring in Common Councils and
Boards of Supervisors, and also, before the Courts to prevent the
company from realizing the benefit of the subsidies that had been
authorized by legislative enactment and by popular vote. The effect
of this opposition was to cause delay in realizing aid when most
needed, and the expense in finally obtaining it. This opposition has
been manifested in may ways in futile attempts to prevent the building of the road and up to the present time [1874] to retard the
success of the enterprise. It has not always been confined to the
original opposers, but in most cases, it can be traced back to them, or
to their successors, or to their adherents.

One individual stockholder of the Sacramento Valley
Railroad, L. L. Robinson, by name, wrote to Theodore D.
Judah, chief engineer of the Central Pacific Railroad, formerly engineer of the Sacramento Valley Railroad, that
unless the Central Pacific purchased his interest in the Sacra-

mento Valley Railroad upon his own terms, he would throw every obstacle in the way of the Central Pacific that he could; that with the active opposition of his company, wielding a money influence of $30,000 per month, the Central Pacific Railroad could not hope to succeed, and that he, Robinson, would wield that influence with all his power and energy against the Central Pacific both in California and the East unless they complied with his terms.

The company did not purchase his interest and he did his utmost to fulfill his threat, even to the extent of declaring falsely that Judah had confided to him the fact that he had never made a survey of the Dutch Flat and Donner Pass route.[4]

One of the most unjust charges brought against the management of the railroad company in its early stages was that the builders fraudulently assumed that the grants made by Congress to the Pacific Railroad were made to the individual incorporators, and that they had undertaken to sell those rights to the company, receiving therefor capital stock amounting to several million dollars in value.

The board of Supervisors of Placer County appointed a committee composed of A. B. Scott and D. W. Madden to investigate those charges before paying to the company the $250,000 subscription in bonds authorized by the legislature and voted by the citizens. After a full, careful and thorough examination of the books, records, and papers of the company, the committee returned a report in September, 1864, completely exonerating the company in every detail.[5]

There were other interests that manifested a strong opposition to the railroad company as soon as they became convinced that the builders were in earnest. They did everything in their power to obstruct, hinder, even to kill the enterprise. They attacked the integrity of the leaders of the company and their credit. They sent emissaries into the working camps with stories that would delay the work. Men were bribed to wreck trains of supplies; and every conceivable obstacle was set in motion to retard and stop the work.

A railroad line across the continent would abolish existing stage and express companies, hence the opposition of the California Stage Company operating between Sacramento and the mining centers of Nevada; the Overland Stage Company which received $1,800,000 a year for carrying the mail between California and Missouri; and the Wells Fargo Express that had a monopoly of that business on the West Coast.

The Pioneer Stage Road, a toll road that had brought its owners $693,000 in 1862, was concerned about the Dutch Flat and Donner Lake Wagon Road to Carson Valley. The Pacific Mail Steamship Company, operating between San Francisco and the Isthmus of Panama, and the California Steam Navigation Company between San Francisco and Sacramento, feared transportation competition.

Among the chief opponents was the Sitka Ice Company, supplying ice from Alaska to San Francisco at five cents a pound, at a profit of $75 a ton.

Placerville, a prosperous town upon the Nevada-California highway, and a station for several stage coach lines and pack trains between the mines and the market, was apprehensive over the probable loss of traffic. A host of freight contractors employing thousands of men also attempted to block the progress of the railroad.

By these various interests a campaign of interference was started which extended to the money centers of the East, Germany, France, and England, with the purpose of injuring the credit of the associates and preventing their raising the money to build the road.[6]

In his speech on the subject of "The Press" delivered in the Assembly Chamber of the State Capitol at Sacramento, February 28, 1895, Marcus D. Boruck had reference to the malignity of this antagonism:

> The paper that I edit [*California Spirit of the Times*] was the only paper published in San Francisco that advocated and supported construction of the Central Pacific Railroad. All the dailies were purchased to fight the enterprise and prevent its success. In the interest of the people? Not much! but altogether in the interest of the California Steam Navigation Company, the California Stage Company by Henness Pass route, the Placerville Stage Line from that place to Virginia City, the telegraph company, the express company, and other lines of travel. There is no florid word painting in this; *it is history*. The purchased press did everything in the world to prevent the building of that road. They lied by day, they lied by night, they lied for the very lust of lying in regard to that enterprise.

There were two reasons why the Central Pacific Railroad was regarded with such aversion in San Francisco. (1) The conviction that it was doomed to failure. One writer says that it was the joke of the year among the banking fraternity of San Francisco. (2) The enterprise did not originate in that city as had been intended. Some light is thrown on this resentment by a paragraph written April 10, 1854, which appeared in the *Annals of San Francisco*, in 1885, p. 528:

> The people of San Francisco and California, if they study their own interest, will take care that a rival state and city do not arise to overshadow their own greatness. The best way to maintain the

supremacy of the former is to make sure by all and whatever means, that the first great interoceanic railroad terminate at San Francisco. Later through lines may terminate where they will; only let our city have the first one.

The following testimony of Leland Stanford before the U. S. Pacific Railway Commission, 1887, vol. 5, p. 2533, may suggest additional reasons for the antagonism:

When we began to build the railroad, the merchants of San Francisco had absolute control over the other merchants of this coast, and they could, and frequently did, combine to arbitrarily increase the price of provisions and all other articles of commerce. Sometimes they would advance the price of a single article 100 per cent in a single day. They kept a record of all inbound vessels with their cargoes, and whenever they found there was a limited supply of any given commodity, they went out and bought up all in the market and all in transit. No further supplies could be furnished until orders from here could be filled in the East, which would take fully six months.

All this is corroborated in the Reminiscences of William Morris Stewart, Senator from Nevada, New York, 1908, p. 339.

Before the same Commission, p. 3283, S. T. Gage, assistant to the president of the Southern Pacific Company, had this to say:

The hostile legislation in California toward the Central Pacific Railroad was without parallel in the history of the nation. We had to employ everybody who could pull a pound morally; there was necessity for all the strength we could get to avoid hostile legislation. I doubt whether you gentlemen would have been here to investigate the Central Pacific, if the legislation which was pending from time to time had become law. The Central Pacific would have been bankrupt the first year under the operation of any of those bills. You have no idea of the hostility that once existed in this state against the old Central Pacific.

J. C. Stubbs, traffic manager, testified to the same situation, p. 3353:

I have understood that there never has been a session of the California legislature since the road was started, but that there were bills of a hostile character introduced against the railroad . . . resulting from misstatements and misrepresentations on the part of those who thought they had grievances against the railroad company, and the disposition of human nature to hit something.

The company was subjected frequently to protracted litigation and its adversaries used every device available to poison the minds of capitalists against it. The company, however, always employed the best legal talent to be procured in the state, and always fought with vigor and determination, usually winning the cases and thereby causing bitter enemies.[7]

During the inquisition of Collis Potter Huntington by the Senate Committee in March 1896, p. 158, he said:

These fellows in San Francisco charged us with every crime in the catalogue except one, and I told them to put that in, too; that is, Piracy on the High Seas. I told them to add that.

Chapter XXV

DISSENSION IN THE COMPANY

CONSTRUCTION of the railroad began early in the year 1863, and friction soon developed between the chief engineer and the other officials of the company. Judah considered himself the logical leader of the company by "rights." His early explorations in the mountains, his pamphlet and talks to attract attention to a possible route for a railway, arousing the interest of the Huntington group, the organization of the railroad company, the surveys that followed, and finally the Act of Congress, July 1, 1862, were, he felt, all results of his own activities. He considered, consequently, that it was his "little railroad," as he expressed it, and as such he was entitled to supervise and direct it and to control the expenditures.

There were men in the company, however, who would dominate and control any work of which they had a part, and they did not hesitate to assume the management of this railroad. As they provided the funds, they felt themselves obligated to control the use of it and to be responsible for the decisions made.

Judah's resentment was aroused against Huntington early in the proceedings by his refusal to accept Judah's plans for a railway office which Huntington thought was too costly. Then he had corrected an item in Judah's estimate of the surveys, and had changed the route of the railroad at a point on

Locomotive "C. P. Huntington," Central Pacific No. 3, Southern Pacific No. 1

the American River where frequent overflows occurred. Judah felt that Huntington had an undue influence on the rest of the company.

He vigorously opposed the construction contracts that were awarded to Charles Crocker, and at once proceeded to let contracts to another firm, although the work of small contractors had proved very unsatisfactory. His report to the Board of Directors dated July 1, 1863, contained the following item: "Sections 19 to 31 inclusive, or from the line of the California Central Railroad, have been let to responsible contractors and will be commenced immediately."

In his letters to his friend, Dr. Strong of Dutch Flat, he complained bitterly. On July 10, 1863, he wrote:

I have had a big row and fight on the contract question, although I had to fight alone. I carried my point and prevented a certain gentleman from becoming a further contractor on the Central Pacific Railroad at present. Huntington has returned and seems to possess more than usual influence. Stanford, who I told you was all right, is as much under their influence as ever.[1]

As early as May 13 of that year he had written to Dr. Strong:

I had a blowout about two weeks ago and freed my mind, so much so that I looked for instant decapitation. I called things by their right names and invited war; but counsel of peace prevailed, and my head is still on my shoulders. My hands are tied, however. We have no meetings of the board nowadays, except the regular monthly meeting which, however, was not had this month; but there have been a number of private conferences to which I was not invited.[2]

Another cause for contention between Judah and the associates is given by a recent writer who fails to give the source of his information:

Judah was asked to join the others in stating that the foothills began many miles distant from the spot where, in his opinion, they actually did begin. He refused . . . was able to put a temporary check on the group's rapidly growing talent for thinking up ways for reaping extra profits.[3]

According to the records, the "others" did not think up this one. In March, 1863, after a trip for observation, J. D. Whitney, state geologist of California, recommended, that Arcade Creek, 7.18 miles from Sacramento, be established as the western base of the mountains from which the Government aid of $48,000 per mile would begin, as the distance of one hundred fifty miles from that point, he considered, would traverse the most difficult and mountainous portion of the route. The same point was selected by the Surveyor General of the state of California, on the principle that the two extremities of the one hundred fifty miles allowed by Section 11 of the Act of 1862 for the maximum subsidy should rest upon corresponding grades, one to the west, the other to the east of the mountains.[4] This view was accepted by President Lincoln and so proclaimed by him January 12, 1864, saying jocularly, "Here is a case in which Abraham's faith has moved mountains."[5]

Since the company was authorized to receive $48,000 per mile for one hundred fifty miles across the Sierras, the point of beginning this section did not matter so long as the distance did not exceed one hundred fifty miles. Said the same writer:

This clash of interests and viewpoint had of course been inevitable from the beginning . . . It was another skirmish in the traditional battle between the builder and the speculator; between men whose aim was to create and those whose sole purpose was to make a profit —as large a profit as possible as quickly as possible.

This was written, mind you, many years after the associates had established a railroad system second to none, creating most of the funds themselves as the work progressed; and had paid back every farthing of their indebtedness to the Government and to others.

Various and sundry reasons are given by different writers for the final break between Judah and the associates, some of them interesting, others amusing. Another recent writer on the first transcontinental road gives his views of the question as follows:

It soon developed that Judah and the Huntington group viewed the first forty miles from poles apart. Huntington and his crowd considered this section as a deplorable hurdle that must be surmounted before the subsidy would come into the coffers. Judah thought that the first forty miles should be built rapidly but well. The others wanted only speed and the cheapest sort of construction. On this difference the two parties broke, and it was apparent to Judah that he could not work with those men to whom the dollar was everything. The Big Four and their associates were happy to buy him out for $100,000. He took a ship for the East Coast and died one week after landing.[6]

Surely, had the writer of these statements stopped a few moments to consider, he would not have written them. Judah was eliminated from all operations of the Central Pacific Company in less than ten months after construction began, and before the first rail was laid. Why then did the group not proceed at once to build the "cheapest sort of construction," if that were their desire? Judah was not there to prevent them. What is the record?

In 1873, a writer said:

The projectors of the Central Pacific Railroad . . . did their work so well that, in the opinion of the best engineers, their road is today one of the most thoroughly built and best managed in the United States.[7]

A traveler from London in 1871 says:

As an achievement of engineering skill it [Central Pacific Railroad] surpasses anything [else] on this continent, and competes successfully with any work of the same kind in Europe. Anyone who imagines the Pacific Railways carelessly because quickly built, will find himself disappointed. The great national highway will never cease to be a wonder both in the rapidity and perfection of its construction at the outset.[8]

A visitor to California from Illinois writes back home:

A most noticeable thing about this company is that all it does is done well. There is nothing slipshod anywhere. Its cars, locomotives, shops, houses, wharves, boats, docks—everything—are all first class.[9]

With reference to Judah another writer makes the erroneous statement that in October, 1863, Judah set out for Washington to ask for further benefits, but was stricken with a fever and died in New York, when Huntington succeeded him in his work before Congressional committees.[10] Judah left California for an entirely different purpose; and, in appearing before Congressional committees, Huntington never succeeded anyone. He had been recognized as a legislative agent of the railroad company since the fall of 1861 when he worked with the 37th Congress over the Pacific Railroad Bill.

An executive of the Southern Pacific Company gives the following plausible account of Judah's break with the company:

Money was getting scarcer and scarcer. The State Legislature had authorized the counties of Placer, San Francisco and Sacramento to subscribe to the capital stock of the company. Before this help became available, however, the work of construction came almost to a stop. The money raised by Huntington in New York had been exhausted. A meeting was called to discuss the emergency. Judah and James Bailey wanted to raise money by mortgaging such of the road as had been graded and the equipment. Huntington, Stanford, Hopkins, and Crocker opposed this on the ground that such borrowing would harm their credit; that to mortgage the property at this stage would prevent future loans except at ruinous rates. The suggestion of the four was that the directors provide money from their own means until Government aid should become available. They would then have enough of the road in operation to give it standing as a borrower. "Buy us out, sell out to us, pay your share of what is necessary to keep the work going, or let's quit." was the ultimatum of the four to the others. They elected to sell out. Judah is said to have received $100,000 for his holdings.[11]

In his biography of Leland Stanford, George T. Clark says that Judah secured options on the stock of those in the directorate whom he considered hostile, and engaged in correspondence with Eastern capitalists for the purpose of obtaining funds with which to purchase it, thus placing himself in control. He arranged for a meeting in New York and sailed on the S. S. *St. Louis* from San Francisco early in October 1863.[12] On the steamer he wrote to Dr. Strong as follows:

If the parties who now manage [the Central Pacific] hold to the same opinion three months hence that they do now, there will be a radical change in the management of Pacific Railroad. . . . If they do not, they will rue the day they ever embarked on the Pacific Railroad. . . . If I succeed in inducing the parties I expect to see to return with me to California, I shall likely return the latter part of December; if not, I shall stay later.[13]

While on this voyage Judah was stricken with tropical fever the day after leaving Aspinwall, and on November 2, 1863, one week after his arrival in New York, he was dead. He had not been dismissed from his position with the Central Pacific Company, as has been sometimes stated, nor had he disposed of his interests therein. At the time of his death he was still chief engineer of the company.[14]

Years later Judah's widow wrote:

> He had secured the right and power to buy out the men who opposed him and the true interests of the Pacific Railroad at that time. Every thing was arranged for a meeting in New York City upon his arrival. Gentlemen from New York and Boston were ready to take their places.[15]

There must have existed in Judah's mind some doubt about his return to the Central Pacific Railroad Company, since, on the 28th day of September, before his departure in October, he sold to Charles Crocker all of his holdings in the Nevada Railroad Company for the sum of $10,000.

At the same time, James Bailey, who had withdrawn from the Central Pacific, sold his shares in the Nevada Railroad Company to Asa Philip Stanford, Leland Stanford's younger brother.[16]

Samuel S. Montague succeeded Mr. Judah as chief Engineer of the Central Pacific Railroad. Relocation of several surveys were made under his direction, authorized by the state legislature. From Sacramento to Colfax, the road was located on the line run by Mr. Judah in 1861; from Colfax to Long Ravine, the line was changed materially; from Long Ravine to Alta, on Mr. Judah's survey; and from Alta to Summit on an entirely new line located by Mr. L. M. Clement, engineer in charge of the 2nd Division. This final location gave a better grade line and less snow in winter, two very desirable improvements.[17]

The value of these changes was plainly shown by the report of George E. Gray, formerly chief engineer of the New York Central Railroad. He was requested by Leland Stanford in a letter dated July 10, 1865, to inspect the road and surveys then made and report to the board of directors his opinion of the quality of the work and the economical location of that portion yet to be built.

Mr. Gray's report gave as his opinion that the road already completed would compare favorably with any road in the United States. That the altered line caused a saving in distance of nearly 5,000 feet, and reduced the aggregate length of tunnels about 5,000 feet, thus saving in cost of construction over $400,000 at least.

Chapter XXVI

PACIFIC RAILROAD PROGRESS IN 1864

THE FIRST RAILS of the Central Pacific Railroad were laid October 26, 1863, and early in March 1864, the track had reached Brigham's quarries on the line twenty-two miles from Sacramento.

On Saturday, March 19, the first excursion on the Central Pacific Railroad was given in honor of the members of the State Legislature, then in session at the Capitol, and their friends. The guests enjoyed the outing, including a bountiful luncheon, and returned to Sacramento at dusk loud in their praises of the railroad.[1]

A few days later on March 25, the locomotive "Governor Stanford" arrived at Sacramento with three carloads of granite, about thirty tons, taken from Brigham's quarries, the first installment on a contract of one hundred tons which Brigham was to furnish to P. Cadus of San Francisco. This was the first paying freight to pass over the line.[2]

Daily passenger service was inaugurated on April 25, 1864, between Sacramento and Roseville, a distance of eighteen miles. There it connected with the California Central Railroad for transfer of passengers for Folsom or Lincoln. The first train left the foot of J Street at 6:15 A.M. with a number of passengers. From April 25 to April 30, two hundred

Central Pacific Drawing Room Carriage

Central Pacific Saloon Carriage

ninety-eight passengers had passed over the line whose fares amounted to $354.25. This was the first money earned by passenger service on the Central Pacific.[3]

By July the railroad was open for service to Newcastle, thirty-one miles from Sacramento. By November 30, 48,941 passengers had been carried on the line, the revenue amounting to $63,403.15; for freight, $38,666.89 had been received; for express and messenger, $1,487.50. The total operating expenses for that period was $56,289.17, leaving net earnings of $47,265.37.[4] As fast as the line was open for business it produced a revenue to aid the company's needs. Newcastle was the eastern terminus of the line for nearly a year.

The thirty-one miles to Newcastle were built under the Act of 1862 and entirely with means provided by the company. A sufficient number of stocks had been sold to comply with the law and enable the company to start, but a number of the original stockholders had become alarmed and withdrew from the company. None of the county subscriptions authorized in 1863 by the State Legislature had been received, and the company was not entitled to Government bonds until forty consecutive miles of the road had been built. Of this period Charles Crocker said:

We actually spent our own money building that road up to Newcastle, thirty-one miles. Mr. Huntington bought the iron and gave our personal obligation for it, and put up the bonds of the company besides as security; and we entered into an agreement to be personally responsible for the interest on those bonds for ten years. Those were the responsibilities we took, and had we not done so there would have been no road.

When we had thirty miles of that road built, I would have been glad to have got a clean shirt and absolution of my debts . . . and to have gone into the world and started anew.[5]

The ship *Success* from New York arrived on March 19, bringing a large quantity of iron and rolling stock for the Central Pacific Railroad. Among the rolling stock was a first class locomotive named "C. P. Huntington."[6]

This locomotive was built by Danforth, Cook & Company at Paterson, New Jersey in 1863. It was 29.5 feet long with cylinders 11′ x 15,′ the diameter of drivers 54″; weight on drivers, 18,500 pounds; weight on trucks, 20,500 pounds; total weight, 39,000 pounds. It could haul four cars weighing twenty-two tons each, at thirty-five miles an hour up a grade of twenty-six feet to the mile.

The "C. P. Huntington" locomotive went into service in April 1864, as the Central Pacific's No. 3. Later it became the Southern Pacific's No. 1, and made its last run in 1898. It is carefully preserved in a small park in front of the Southern Pacific Station in Sacramento, being taken out only for exhibition purposes, such as the San Diego Exposition. In 1930 it puffed proudly across the Southern Pacific's new Martinez-Benicia bridge as a part of the dedication ceremonies. The early locomotives were picturesque in appearance. Their large, diamond-shaped smoke stacks, brass fittings, and gay paint made them very ornate.[7]

Early in 1864, the Central Pacific was subjected to one of its numerous investigations. As has been stated, San Francisco had been authorized to subscribe $1,000,000 in bonds for the Pacific Railroad. The Opposition, however, led by Mayor Teschemacher, whom the periodical *Argonaut* called a "foreign accident," and the firm Pioche, Bayerque & Co. were doing everything possible to delay if not to prevent the $600,000 from being paid to the Central Pacific. Legal proceedings were instituted by the company in the District Court which decided in favor of the plaintiff. The Supervisors carried the case to the Supreme Court, and while awaiting its decision, appointed a committee to investigate the railroad company, which resulted only in delaying the progress of the road.[8]

On July 1, William Shaw and George P. Kimball of San Francisco applied for an injunction from the Fourth District Court against the Mayor, Board of Supervisors, City Auditor, Treasurer, etc., to restrain them from issuing $400,000 to the railroad company, another delaying action. Again in December resolutions were drawn up by McCoppin, a member of the investigating committee and his adherents against the payment of the $400,000 to the railroad company.[9]

Of the enmity of *The Alta Californian,* toward the Central Pacific, the Sacramento *Union* said in the issue of December 3, 1864:

> *The Alta* is the organ of the enemies of the Pacific Railroad. It pretends to favor the road, but opposes the administration of it. It supports the idea of having a road, but opposes every effort made to build it. It labors with all its vigor and with intensely bitter feeling to deprive the managers of the road of the means to accomplish the work, to deny them the "sinews of war" which the people of San Francisco have voted them; and by all the strategy which cunning and recklessness can suggest, it endeavors to embarrass and delay the execution of the work with a view to its final defeat.

The Territory of Nevada felt the need of a railroad more acutely, perhaps, than did any other section. Without sea coast and surrounded by mountains, the people had to rely upon other sections for the necessities of life. The cost of transportation over the Sierras by wagon was enormous. Hauling, at from $120 to $150 per ton, amounted at times to nearly a million dollars per month. A railroad, they considered, would reduce this cost at least three-fourths and the cost of living fully one-half. It was important, therefore, that they have a railroad at the earliest possible moment.[10]

The Nevada Legislature on November 21, 1861, authorized the incorporation of the Nevada Railroad Company to construct a railroad and telegraph line across the state in conformity with the charter and on the same terms as provided for the main line, the Central Pacific.[11]

Nevada held a convention at Carson City, in July 1864, for the purpose of framing a State Constitution. It was proposed to include a clause in the document permitting the people of Nevada, when it became a state, to vote $3,000,000 to the first railroad company that would connect Nevada with navigable waters. Leland Stanford was on hand to protest the resolution and to explain that the delay of the Central Pacific was due largely to the action of San Francisco in the delivery of the bonds voted by the people. The clause was finally stricken out.

Nevada was admitted to the Union, October 31, 1864, and during the first session of the State Legislature, on December 21, 1864, a resolution was offered by State Representative Epstein that their representatives and senators in Congress be instructed to use their utmost endeavors to secure the passage of an Act by Congress giving the sum of $10,000,000 in United States, six per cent, thirty-year bonds, to the corporation that should first construct a railway line from navigable waters to Carson City.

This resolution was the result of the information that a "large and wholly responsible body of respectable capitalists"

[English] were prepared to push forward a railroad to Carson City on a route direct and feasible, the San Francisco & Washoe Railroad Company.

A letter from L. L. Robinson, a large stockholder of the Sacramento Valley Railroad, dated February 3, 1865, was read in the Assembly. In this he stated, among other inaccuracies, that Judah had never made a survey over the Dutch Flat and Donner Pass route, and that the Central Pacific Company gave Judah $100,000 in bonds not to reveal that "fact," and that no railroad could ever be built over that route.

To this Stanford replied in a letter dated February 14, 1865, defending Judah and his surveys and showing that Robinson's false statements were motivated by personal spite. Crocker, too, made a statement in which he revealed that Robinson in a letter to Judah had threatened to do his utmost against the Central Pacific unless the company purchased his holdings in the Sacramento Valley Railroad upon his own terms.[12]

During the debate, the Speaker of the Assembly, C. W. Tozier, left the chair, February 6, to make a speech against the resolution. Here follow a few pertinent extracts from this speech:

It will be remembered that the San Francisco & Washoe Railroad Company was only organized by that "large and wholly responsible body of respectable capitalists"—ten Placerville millionaires whose aggregate wealth would not buy a whistle—on the sixth of January, 1865, and yet in a few days appears this elaborate report prepared evidently for this market.

The resolution asks Congress for a donation of $10,000,000 in U. S. bonds and the repudiation of the action already made by them. This the Congress could not comply with if we make the request.

Since the organization of the Central Pacific Railroad Company and the selection of their route, the owners of stage lines, toll roads, and other projected but impossible railroad lines across the mountains, have notoriously resisted in every possible way the building of this road. They have sent their agents to Washington, to the legislative halls of California, to our Constitutional Convention, before the people of the counties of California who proposed to aid in the work, before the courts of those counties after the people had voted to subscribe to the capital stock of the Central Pacific Company, and being beaten there, before the Supreme Court of California.

And, gentlemen, we meet them here urging the passage before this Legislature of identically the same proposition argued so long, but happily, so unsuccessfully before the Legislature and courts of our sister state. Those agents are numerous, popular, and powerful, and no effort of theirs has been or will be spared to carry these resolutions through this Legislature. The Central Pacific has had many obstacles to overcome but chiefest among them all has been these opponents. The capital of our state would be fifty miles nearer the eastern terminus of the Central Pacific today, had it not been for the machinations with which these designing men have surrounded every effort of the company.

In spite of the warnings, however, the resolution was passed in the General Assembly on February 20, and in the Senate on February 27. The progress of the Central Pacific Railroad was not affected thereby, however. Financial conditions had greatly improved, and with the beginning of the year construction on the road had been resumed vigorously.

The proposed San Francisco & Washoe Railroad backed by "millionaires" never materialized. Its proponents were only, as Mr. Huntington expressed it on a similar occasion, "throwing words into the air" in an effort to embarrass and delay construction on the Central Pacific Railroad.

Chapter XXVII

ACT OF CONGRESS, JULY 2, 1864

ALTHOUGH the Central Pacific Railroad Company had accepted the Act of 1862, it was found very difficult to operate under some of its provisions. The Government's first mortgage on the road prevented the company's bonds, having second place, from being sold or used as security for loans without the personal guarantee of Mr. Huntington in New York, and some of the other members in Sacramento. Fifty miles of the road had to be completed in two years, and forty consecutive miles completed before any Government bonds became available. In a letter to James W. Throckmorton, Chairman of the Committee on Pacific Railroads, dated January 25, 1886, Mr. Huntington wrote:

> The Act of 1862 served, however, only to show that so stupendous a task could not be successfully carried out under its provisions in the then critical state of the nation's finances.

In spite of all the difficulties, however, the company had made substantial progress by the close of 1863.

When the 38th Congress convened in Washington, Mr. Huntington decided to make an effort to secure more favorable conditions in order to advance the work more rapidly, if not to save it from utter failure. During the first half of the year 1864, Mr. Huntington's time was divided among the financiers and merchants of New York and Boston, his visits to Washington, and an occasional trip to California.

He must have spent considerable time in Washington, as testified by two members of Congress. Representative Holman remarked on one occasion: "We see here every day figuring in this business, a gentleman from New York."[1] Representative Cole of California wrote that during the pending of this legislation, C. P. Huntington spent much of his time in Washington, and many of the amendments were suggested by him.[2]

On March 6, 1864, Representative Price introduced a bill for an Act to amend the Act that had been approved July 1, 1862. (H.R. No. 438)[3]

During a discussion of the bill June 16, Thomas B. Shannon, representative from California said:

For every dollar the nation invests in the construction of this railroad, it will receive a hundred in return. The advantages accruing from the construction of this road will be equivalent in a few years of $1,000,000 to $1.00.[4]

Representative John B. Steele of New York, a member of the Pacific Railroad Committee, whom Mr. Huntington had known before he left New York for California, and a warm personal friend, said of the action of Congress:

It was considered that all they could give, provided the road was built, would be repaid in a thousand ways to this great country.[5]

The Act to amend the Act of July 1, 1862, was passed by Congress and became a law on July 2, 1864, when signed by the President. The chief amendments made by this act were as follows:

1. The width of the right of way reduced to two hundred feet.

Central Pacific Depot at Sacramento, 1868

2. Land grant of ten sections on each side of track for each mile of track, the land selected to be within twenty miles of the track. Cost of surveying the land to be paid by the railroad company.

3. The exemption of mineral land should not apply to coal and iron.

4. Only one-half of the compensation for services to the Government required to be applied to the payment of bonds.

5. Bonds and land grants to become available after each twenty consecutive miles of construction.

6. Repeal of the twenty-five per cent reservation of Government bonds.

7. The company may issue their own first mortgage bonds to an amount not exceeding the amount of Government bonds. The lien of Government bonds to be subordinate to the bonds of the company issued on their roads, property, and equipment.

8. Time for building the first fifty miles extended to three years, twenty-five miles to be completed each year thereafter.

9. The statement of the three Commissioners and the verified statement of the President of the Company to be filed in the Office of the U. S. Surveyor General instead of the Office of the President of the United States.

10. The Central Pacific may extend its line one hundred fifty miles from the eastern boundary of the State of California.[6]

On the day the Act of 1864 became a law, the Central Pacific was operating a daily schedule of service on thirty-one miles of road, from Sacramento to Newcastle. On that same day greenbacks were selling in San Francisco at forty-eight cents on the dollar.[7]

Mr. Huntington and his associates regarded as the most important change in the Act of 1862, the provision whereby the company could issue first mortgage bonds, Government bonds being relegated to second place. This amendment alone probably saved the company from disaster.

The amendment restricting to one hundred fifty miles the distance eastward from the state boundary that the Central Pacific was permitted to build, did not please Mr. Huntington, who said:

That one hundred fifty miles ought not to have gone into that bill. I said to Mr. Union Pacific, I would take that out when I wanted it out.

It was very important that the Central Pacific should have the right to build as far as it could, to the Salt Lake and beyond, so as to control, or at least have some part in the business of that region; one hundred fifty miles from the boundary line would end the road in the arid and unproductive region of the Great American Desert. Two years later on July 3, 1866, Huntington's efforts were rewarded by an amendment passed by Congress authorizing the Central Pacific to continue construction of the road eastward, until met by the Union Pacific. This with the approval of the Secretary of the Interior.

On March 3, 1865, the companies had been authorized to issue their bonds to one hundred miles in advance of a continuous completed line. And another amendment permitted each company to locate its line three hundred miles in advance of actual construction. This provision gave rise later to considerable friction between the two companies. The gauge for the road had been established March 3, 1863, by Congress at four feet eight and one-half inches, instead of the five feet recommended by President Lincoln.

On January 3, 1865, the Supreme Court announced a decision affirming the constitutionality of the Act of the State Legislature which provided for the payment by the State of interest on $1,500,000 bonds of the Central Pacific at the rate of seven per cent for twenty years. This gave the bonds a value equal to the state bonds and made them immediately available.[8] As a result, the following advertisement appeared in the Sacramento *Union* for January 7:

Wanted, 5,000 laborers for constant and permanent work, also experienced foremen.

Apply to J. H. Stobridge, Superintendent.

On the work, near Auburn.

Soon after, construction was being pushed forward with great vigor, and by June, 1865, the track had reached Clipper Gap, forty-two miles from Sacramento.

Another decision of the Supreme Court favorable to the railroad company was handed down on April 5, 1865, after two years of strife and litigation. The San Francisco Board of Supervisors was ordered to pay to the Central Pacific Company the $400,000 stock bonds compromised as a gift instead of the $600,000 stock subscription authorized by the State Legislature and voted by the citizens in 1863; and $200,000 in bonds to the Western Pacific Railroad Company, instead of the $400,000 bonds voted to them. On April 12, the bonds were delivered to the President of the company. The two years delay resulted in a serious loss to the company. With those bonds available in 1864 the company could have pushed on more rapidly and would probably have ended the road some distance beyond Salt Lake.[9]

About this time Government bonds were received for the first forty miles of constructed road. On May 13, 1865, Mr. Huntington sent the following telegram to President Stanford:

I received yesterday twelve hundred and fifty-eight thousand dollars ($1,258,000) United States bonds for account of Central Pacific Railroad of California.[10]

The Union Pacific Railroad Company soon after organization found that it could not operate under the provisions of the Act of 1862. Books were opened for subscriptions in all the prominent cities of the North, and for the stock that afterward became so valuable, only $2,200 was subscribed. The company did not commence the work of grading until after the Act of 1864, and the first rails were laid in July 1865, two months after the Central Pacific had received its first allotment of Government bonds and had a daily train service to Clipper Gap, forty-two miles from Sacramento.[11]

Chapter XXVIII

TUNNELS AND SNOWSHEDS

THE IMPROVEMENT in the financial situation of the Central Pacific Railroad Company was followed immediately by an expansion in the activities of the company. At Sacramento, upon lands granted by the city, were erected suitable freight and passenger depots, and a wharf with a steam engine and derricks for the transaction of business. Commodious depot buildings were constructed at all stations on the line as fast as the road opened for traffic.

Workshops were erected at E and Sixth Streets where the various kinds of cars used by the company were constructed. The woodwork of the cars which was at first shipped from the East, was made of California lumber and put together in the shops of the company. As early as August 1865, there were in use sixty-five flat cars, thirty-nine box cars, six passenger cars, and two baggage cars. Wheels and iron work for one hundred more had been ordered by Mr. Huntington in the East. There were also in use six locomotives, two more on the way, and four others ordered.[1] There was never any delay for lack of materials. Mr. Huntington kept a supply on hand ample for all needs, purchasing them from six to twelve months in advance.

On September 1, 1865, the line was operating to Colfax, a distance of sixty-five miles from Sacramento. The road from Colfax to Summit included the most difficult and expensive section of the whole line, and the directors were deeply concerned as to the progress of the work. Reliable workmen were scarce and advertisements had brought comparatively few responses. Only about five hundred workmen had beeen employed during the winter of 1864-65.

In discussing the alarming situation, Charles Crocker and his superintendent, J. T. Stobridge, decided to employ a few Chinese on trial. Crocker thought that the race that built the Great Wall of China could build a railroad. They employed fifty Chinese on the road near Auburn with such satisfactory results that fifty more were engaged, and soon the majority of workmen were Chinese. As they increased in numbers and skill, construction toward the Summit became more rapid in spite of the more difficult terrain. Before the road was completed to Promontory Point, there were 12,000 or more Chinese on the payroll.

The Chinese were trained to all sorts of labor, driving horses and mules, using the pick and shovel, cutting and blasting rock, etc. In some places they literally hewed out of the mountain paths for the track. At a point on the line called "Cape Horn," the road was cut out of the almost perpendicular mountain side about fifteen hundred feet above the American River. To enable the Chinese to drill and blast out a foothold, they were lowered over the cliff in "bosun's chairs" supported by ropes to do the preliminary cutting. The track around "Cape Horn" has been abandoned and trains now go through a tunnel to which the railroad men have given the name of "Panama Canal."[2]

Mr. Huntington strongly approved the employment of the Chinese on the railroad. In several of his letters and addresses we find him deploring the policy of the people of California, particularly San Francisco, in not employing the cheap labor of the Chinese in manufactures:

I would like to see California take her rightful place as a great manufacturing center instead of accepting a tithe for her raw materials and paying the other nine-tenths to have it fashioned and brought back for the use of the people. So long as the policy of California is to drive out the cheap labor of the world, the state cannot compete successfully with the East or outside countries. . . . Certainly San Francisco can never grow up to be a great city by merely trading or exchanging commodities made outside the state. She must have manufactories of her own so as to give employment to her people. They tell you this cannot be done because labor is high, yet they do not utilize the cheap labor they can get.

To cross the Sierra Nevada Mountains by the railroad, fifteen tunnels were required. These varied in length from the eighty-five feet of Red Spur to the 1659 feet of Summit tunnel. The winter of 1865-66 was so severe with such heavy snowfalls that the work on the tunnels had to be abandoned altogether. During the summer of 1866 three shifts of men were kept at work at night and day at the approaches to the tunnels, so that when winter came the work was underground and could be carried on uninterruptedly. It was necessary, however, to dig long tunnels *under the snow* to reach the entrances to the rock tunnels, and through these snow tunnels the rock was removed. Shafts were sunk in the snow, domes excavated under it and in these domes the masonry necessary to be used in construction was laid, the stones being lowered through the shafts.[3]

The rock through which the tunnels were driven was penetrated with great difficulty by the only tools they possessed, drills and black powder. Neither nitroglycerine nor dynamite were available. An attempt to manufacture nitroglycerine at the tunnel was a failure, and after a disastrous explosion, Crocker ordered all the materials to be buried.

Early in 1866, it was decided to work the Summit tunnel in four faces, the east and west portals and from the center in both directions. To start from the center it was necessary to sink a shaft in rock so hard it was almost impossible to penetrate it with a drill. A small Hinkey hoisting engine was procured and, with great difficulty, hauled up the mountain without road or trails, the trip requiring six weeks. By August the shaft was down ninety feet, and in December the shaft was deep enough to begin the laterals. It took one year from August to complete the tunnel.[4] All tunnels were constructed wide enough for a double track which it was believed would be required in a few years to do the business of the road.[5]

The company at this time had about ten thousand laborers and thirteen hundred teams engaged in the work, and the year 1866, saw the company pressing on vigorously. In October the road reached Cisco, ninety-four miles from Sacramento. When the heavy snowfall of that winter stopped outside work on the mountain, it was decided to build a section on the eastern side in the Truckee Valley. Materials for forty miles of track were hauled on sleds over the company's wagon road, steep and difficult in many places, from Cisco to Donner Lake. There it was reloaded on wagons drawn by oxen and hauled over the road to Truckee. There followed three locomotives and forty cars. All supplies had to

*Snow Sheds
Across the Sierras*

Gallery in the Snow Sheds

be shipped over the same route, a distance of twenty-three miles.

A forty-mile section of road was built on the east side of the mountain, including an eight hundred-foot tunnel nine miles east of Summit. In August 1867, the Summit tunnel was completed and the first locomotive crossed the divide. Late in December, the track had reached a point two miles east of the Summit. The Truckee section was being built both eastward and westward, and on December 13, 1867, the Central Pacific construction engine crossed the Nevada line. Only a seven-mile gap separated the two sections over which stage coaches carried freight and passengers.[6]

The greatest difficulty in the construction of the railroad through the Sierras was undoubtedly the snow. The snowfalls were so frequent and so heavy that as soon as the grading line and tracks were uncovered after a storm, another would bury them deeper than before. In addition to the shoveling by an army of workmen, every known appliance had been used including the largest and strongest snow plow, weighing nineteen tons, and requiring sixteen engines to operate.

In 1867, after many discussions on the subject, the directors decided that the only positive means of protecting the road was by snow sheds, literally houses built over the tracks. The work was put in charge of Arthur Brown, superintendent of the company's buildings and bridges, who had this to say on the subject:

The expense of building a snow shed nearly forty miles in length was appalling and unprecedented in railroad construction. In the summer of 1867 we built some experimental sheds which we had to modify considerably. We commenced in earnest in the spring of 1868. We had to gather men from all quarters and pay high wages—

carpenters, $4.00 a day, and suitable laborers from $2.50 to $3.00. We employed about twenty-five hundred men and had six trains with locomotives to distribute material. There were not enough sawmills to furnish the lumber required and the builders had to use round timbers for a large part of the work. This was more costly and more difficult because axmen in those days were very scarce, and the timbers had to be brought over the snow at great expense.

Two types of construction were adopted: the shed for localities where the weight of the snow had to be supported, and the gallery for such places as were exposed to the terrible avalanches of snow and ice from the steep and rocky slopes. Some of these galleries extend back up the slope of the mountain several hundred feet from the center line of the road, and in other places massive masonry walls were built across ravines to prevent the snow from striking the sheds at right angles. It was necessary to build the sheds and galleries of enormous strength by bracing them against the mountain side, framing them and interlacing them with beams and cross beams. The expense was considerably increased by the necessity of keeping the road clear for traffic and to forward large amounts of building material to the front. The sheds and galleries were finished in the fall of 1869. In them were used 65,000,000 board feet of timber and nine hundred tons of bolts and spikes. The total length was about thirty-seven miles and the cost was over $2,000,000.[7]

The railroad had become the main thoroughfare for transportation between Sacramento and the great mining regions of California and Nevada. The earnings of the road showed a very satisfactory increase from year to year. In 1865, the road operating to Colfax, the net earnings were $280,272.47. For the first nine months of 1866, the road operating to Alta, the net earnings were $449,056.52.

The rates received by the company was very remunerative, being at the rate of ten cents per mile for passengers and fifteen cents per ton per mile for freight in gold. High as these rates may seem, they were less than one-third of the rates that had been paid for transportation by teams over the same region. In 1863, no less than $13,000,000 was paid for transportation over the Placerville road. In 1864, seven thousand teams passed over this road carrying freight at the rates of five cents to ten cents per pound.[8]

In 1865, the Central Pacific Railroad Company acquired the Sacramento Valley Railroad. The purchase was made by George E. Bragg on behalf of himself and others of the entire stock held by L. L. Robinson and Pioche, Bayerque & Company at the price of $800,000. Soon after coming into possession of the stock, Bragg transferred it to the owners of the Central Pacific. The five-foot gauge of the track was changed to four-feet eight and one-half inches to correspond with the track of the Central Pacific.[9]

The motive for the purchase of this road was more in an endeavor to silence a clamorous opposition than for the use of the railroad. This was the first application of that business principle adopted by the company to remove opposition and prevent competition whenever possible at not too great a price.

The franchise of the Western Pacific Railroad Company was acquired June 8, 1867. The promoters of the road became involved in a difficulty with some of the contractors, and asked the Central Pacific directors to take it over. They received twenty miles of completed road, rolling stock worth $50,000 and the rest of the Government subsidy, but did not buy the land grants which later became valuable. The Central Pacific built one hundred twenty-three miles of the Western Pacific through toward San José.[10]

The Sacramento *Union* for March 7, 1868, carried the following item:

The Central Pacific Railroad Company have bought the following railroads: (1) San Francisco & San José, (2) Southern Pacific, (3) Western Pacific, (4) Vallejo & Sacramento, (5) Sacramento Valley, (6) California Central, and (7) the franchise of Northern Pacific & Oregon. The Central Pacific is now a single railroad that has swallowed up all other railroads in the State. This insures the construction and vigorous operation of these roads which have heretofore existed mostly on paper, and some of which would have remained in that condition for years to come.

Chapter XXIX

CONTRACT AND FINANCE COMPANY

THE SUMMIT RIDGE had been crossed at an altitude of 7,042 feet, the Sierras conquered, and on December 13, 1867, the boundary line between California and Nevada was reached.

The construction work to the easterly line of the state had been let to Charles Crocker & Company with the expectation of inducing moneyed men to become partners in the contract without success. When the road was completed to the state line, the company had expended all the United States bonds it had received, all the proceeds of the county bonds, and all of its own bonds it was authorized to issue up to that point, and had a flowing debt of $5,000,000. This was a very serious position to be in when the company was laying its tracks along the Truckee River with its available assets entirely exhausted. The financial pressure was so great that Crocker, foreseeing the situation, had asked for relief.[1]

Since capitalists would not come in under the unlimited partnership of Crocker and Company, it was thought that a corporation would offer greater inducements. Accordingly, on October 28, 1867, the Contract & Finance Company was formed under the laws of the state of California with a capital stock of $5,000,000, for the purpose of constructing the railroad from the eastern boundary to its junction with the

Union Pacific Railroad. The stock of this company was offered to owners of capital everywhere hoping they might become stockholders and in this way insure the completion of the road, but there was no favorable response. The feeling of the capitalists was expressed by A. E. Davis, himself a railroad builder: "We thought they were a little off; yes, sir, that is what we thought."

The company had to take up the stock themselves: "By endorsing paper individually which we did pretty largely, we managed to get through," said Mr. Huntington. "There never was a work done so closely as that. We had to work to get the money to pay for it, selling Government bonds and taking the currency and buying gold."[2]

The stock was nearly all held by the four associates with a few small stockholders. When Mr. Hopkins asked Mr. Huntington how much stock they together should take, the latter replied, "Take as little as we can, and as much as we must." The contract was to take $64,000 in Government and company bonds, and $36,000 in stock per mile and build the road. The Contract & Finance Company was bound to return value within the terms of the contract to the Central Pacific for what was paid for it. Whenever the Government accepted a section, the business on that section was closed as between the Central Pacific and the Contract & Finance companies. Said Mr. Huntington when before the Senate Railroad Committee, 1896, p. 158:

When the Contract & Finance Company had completed the road to Promontory, there was not enough by several millions to pay the debts created by building the road, and a cleaner piece of work was never done. We paid the debts by borrowing money; we paid the borrowed money by selling the stock after it had appreciated.

The Contract & Finance Company became one of the most controversial subjects in the history of the Central Pacific Railroad. The Opposition avidly seized upon it as fraudulent, and even the Government investigations, as we shall see later, probed into its validity. The associates were charged with violating a rule of equity in dealing with themselves. As Trustees, it was unethical to represent both sides of the contract. The answer to that is that they could not find anybody else to deal with. They could not find anyone who would take the chances of building a railroad through an almost uninhabited country and accept the bonds and stock of the company in payment.[3]

Many years later two writers on the subject of the Contract & Finance Company and its promoters expressed the following opinion:

We may conclude that Stanford, Crocker, Huntington, and Hopkins were typical of their time. Rapid business expansion, the growth of great corporations, low standards of economic and political morality, and a philosophy of individualism and laissez-faire characterized the age in which they lived. Their methods were not different from those practiced by others of their day. If they let contracts to themselves, so did others. It was an age of every man for himself, and nowhere was this better typified than in the construction of the Central Pacific Railroad.[4]

"The men who at the risk of their fortunes and by great personal sacrifices opened California to the world, and gave transcontinental construction its first practical demonstration, spent a large part of riper years defending their names and their property from attacks either from jealousy or a complete misunderstanding of the truth," said one writer.[5]

In a letter to members of Congress and published in the Southern Pacific annual report, 1894, Mr. Huntington said:

I have been at work for myself more than fifty-four years with an honesty of purpose and, I believe, an intelligent economy, but in all the work I have ever done, and all the money I have ever made, none ever has cost me the mental or physical strain that the work done on the Central Pacific Railroad has cost me; and in all this work, I can truly say that I have done no injustice to my conscience or to my country.

Chapter XXX

YERBA BUENA
OR GOAT ISLAND

EARLY IN 1867, while yet struggling to overcome the Sierras, the Central Pacific Company were planning a more direct route for the railroad and telegraph line from Sacramento to San Francisco Bay than that of the Western Pacific Railroad. They realized the commercial importance of the metropolis of San Francisco and the necessity of having on the harbor a deep water terminal where ships could be loaded direct from the cars, and from where ferry boats could be used to transport entire freight trains as well as passengers to San Francisco.

They had in mind for the terminal an island situated in San Francisco Bay, five or six miles from the city of San Francisco and about two miles from the eastern shore, known as Yerba Buena or Goat Island. This island was a mile in length with an area of about three hundred acres, mostly rocky with some arable land on the east side, the highest point being an elevation of about three hundred feet. A terminal on this island would bring the Central Pacific Railroad a mile nearer the proposed terminal of the Southern Pacific Railroad at Mission Bay than any other location.

At that time the island belonged to the United States and was used as a military reservation with a half company of troops garrisoned there. A lease could be obtained only by an Act of Congress. The company considered that a right-of-way around the base of the island and a lease of one-half its area for depots, wharves, turntables, etc. would furnish them with a satisfactory terminal without disturbing the troops.

Accordingly on March 21, 1867, the Board of Directors of the Central Pacific Company filed in the Office of the Secretary of State certified papers accompanied by a map showing the proposed extension of the railroad by the shortest route as follows: from the city of Sacramento through the counties of Sacramento, San Joaquin, and Contra Costa, crossing the San Joaquin River at Antioch, and thence to the shore opposite Goat Island, a distance of ninety miles. The bridge or causeway to the island would be wide enough to accommodate two tracks.[1]

About a month before the railroad company had filed their papers in the office of the Secretary of State, Articles of Association of the Terminal Central Pacific Railroad Company had been filed in that office. This company, with a capital of $4,000,000, was organized, ostensibly for the purpose of constructing a railroad between Goat Island and Vallejo, a distance of thirty-two miles. This company had no connection with the Central Pacific Railroad and was composed of the following citizens of San Francisco: J. P. Flint, president; H. E. Bacon, treasurer; Edwin P. Flint, secretary; Alpheus Bull, R. B. Swain, R. E. Cole, J. Mora Moss, W. H. L. Barnes, R. W. Kirkham, John Bensley, Alfred L. Tubbs, and Wm. B. Hyde, chief engineer. Several of these men had long been strong antagonists of the Central Pacific Company.[2]

Later in the year, by an Act of the State Legislature, the Terminal Company obtained a grant of one hundred fifty acres of submerged land immediately north and east of Goat Island. This company then made overtures to Congress in 1868 for an Act granting them the right to take two million square yards of earth from Goat Island to fill up their one hundred fifty acres of submerged land along the Contra Costa shore.[3]

When it became known that there were applicants for the use of Goat Island, a protest against the passage of any law of Congress granting permission to the Western Pacific Railroad Company to use the island for depot purposes was sent to Congress by one David S. Turner, attorney-at-law, acting for Benjamin S. Brooks, John Center and Egbert Judson of San Francisco, who claimed to own the title to Yerba Buena Island and that the rights of the United States to the island were limited to such portions as may be required for military purposes only. This claim of ownership seems to have been ignored.[4]

Letters from Collis Potter Huntington to Mark Hopkins on the subject of Goat Island:

November 7, 1867.

I had a long talk with Cole[5] about two weeks ago about this Goat Island matter. He said he would do all he could for us. . . . I think now I shall have a bill granting Goat Island to the Western Pacific introduced in Congress soon after it meets, as I have no doubt but what these other interests will ask it of Congress early in the session and it will be well to keep ahead of them.

November 19, 1867.

While I was in Washington, I called on the California members. Conness, Cole, and Higby are all right, but Axtell said we had a princely franchise and he was for giving the other fellows a chance. I answered that he must remember that he had great public interests to look after, and he could ill afford to ask that Goat Island be given to individuals for speculative purposes when it was wanted for a terminus for the great Pacific Railroad, as that was the nearest practicable point that the road could come to San Francisco.

June 6, 1868.

Flint, Hyde & Company that had got a grant from the State of one hundred fifty acres of land back of Goat Island, were in Washington and had been working with the Land Committee until they had got them, all but two, to agree to report a bill giving them the right to go to Goat Island and take two million yards of earth to fill up their one hundred acres of land; but I went before the Committee and gave them a little talk, and three minutes after I had left the room, the Committee put the whole matter off indefinitely.

The newspapers of California and the public generally were, at first, in favor of the Goat Island terminal, and when the bill was first introduced in the Senate it came within one vote of passing. Little more was done about the bill, however, until the Congress of 1872. By that time considerable opposition had developed, originating from the usual sources. An explanation is offered by Leland Stanford in his testimony before the U. S. Pacific Railway Commission in 1887:

There was no objection here in the newspapers, there was no objection of any kind until one morning six gentlemen met, three of whom happened to own an interest near Ravenswood where it was supposed we might cross, and the other three had interests over in Saucelito where it was also supposed we might cross. They got to talking and joking each other about being left out in the cold and then the question was raised whether they could not do something to prevent it, and they did. They stirred up the bitter feeling here by saying that if we had Goat Island, the city was going to be ruined.

Treasure Island

S.P. Gen. Offices

S.F. Terminal

Goat Island and Southern Pacific Offices

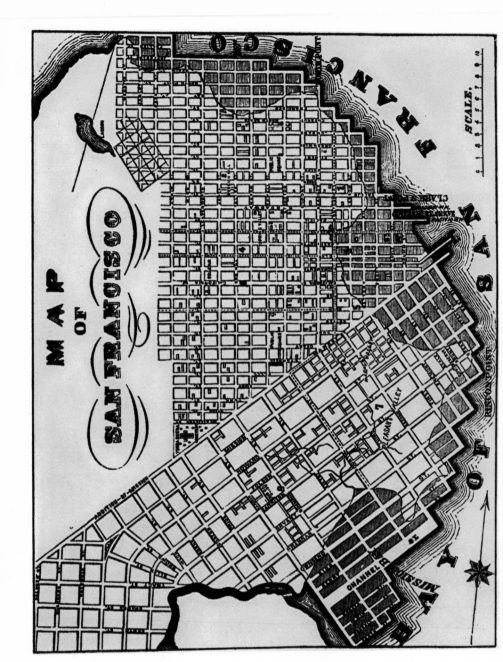

That was why we did not obtain Goat Island. It was worth nothing for defensive purposes. One member of Congress told me himself that $10,000 would get the necessary votes.

The newspapers took up the cry and fiercely denounced the use of Goat Island for railroad purposes, and charged, incredible as it may seem, that the main object of the promoters was to create a new port, a new city on the east side of the Bay in competition with San Francisco. As one writer put it: "The discussion was more notable for the extreme hostility to the managers of the railroad than sober consideration of the case."

When the Coast Survey engineers were asked for an opinion, they said that any bridge or causeway from the Oakland shore to Goat Island would check the currents along the eastern shore of the Bay, cause deposits of sand and mud, diminish the tidal area, reduce the amount of tide water flowing out of the Golden Gate with the ebb and lead to a shallowing of water on the bar, thus injuring the value of the harbor.[6] Later uses of the island show this to be an extremely erroneous decision.

Extracts of some letters of Mr. Huntington to Mr. Hopkins when the bill was before the House:

March 11, 1872:

We have had Goat Island bill up to-day in the House and there was a very sharp fight on it. It was recommitted to the Railroad Committee but in such shape it can be called up at any time. The telegrams that are being sent from California are very damaging to us here, and it does seem to me that you ought to take care of them there.

March 16, 1872:

The reason why the San Francisco Ring oppose the bill is so they can tax all merchandise that goes through the city from one to two dollars per ton. If the Central Pacific were now in Mission Bay with the depot away from the water front the 700,000 tons of surplus wheat in the State would be taxed at least one dollar per ton, which is so much taken from the producer.

March 19, 1872:

I wish you would attend to this Goat Island matter. For God's sake, attend to it at once. It would hurt us three times the value of the island to get beat at this time.

April 20, 1872:

It does seem to me we are working for what is the true interest of the people of San Francisco, and that if you would go to that city and explain to them what we propose to do, then the people would all be for our going to Goat Island. Of course excepting those few that have got up this howl for the sake of making money out of some part of the city around the particular spot that they hope to compel the road to locate.

April 26, 1872, to Leland Stanford:

I received from you yesterday a clipping from *The Alta*. It does seem to me so strange that San Francisco should be so much opposed to the Central Pacific having a landing at Goat Island. When I was in San Francisco I talked with many on the subject, and I think every one was pleased except MacCrellish [editor and proprietor of *The Alta*]; he thought we should bring everything to South Saucelito where, I understand, he and his friends have property. . . . Now if we wanted to build up another city there are several places that would be much better than Goat Island, as you and I well know.

On April 24, 1872, Mark Hopkins received a telegram from George C. Gorham that the House had passed the Goat

Island bill, 105 to 85. Mr. Huntington's efforts were then centered in the Senate, aided by the Senators from Nevada and Oregon, and from other states east of the Rocky Mountains. Both Senators Cole and Cassidy of California were now in the ranks of the Opposition.

The opposing interests, through the influence of the *Press* of San Francisco, held a mass meeting in Platts' Hall on March 16, 1872, one James Otis presiding. At this meeting, the Committee of One Hundred was organized for the express purpose of looking after the welfare of San Francisco and its railway connections; and Caleb T. Fay was appointed to oppose the passage of the Goat Island bill in Congress.[7]

A few days before this meeting, a memorial opposing the Goat Island grant to the railroad and signed by "thousands of leading citizens in San Francisco" had been sent to Congress. This memorial was laid before the Senate in May by Senator Cole of California accompanied by a vigorous protest of his own.[8]

After an examination of the books containing the names of the petitioners, the Washington correspondent of the Sacramento *Record* wrote:

The petition is a fraud. I can affirm that hundreds of the names belong to men long since dead or departed from the city; that dozens of pages are signed by the same hand; and fully one-half do not appear in the last San Francisco directory which may be seen in the Congressional Library.[9]

In the meantime the Central Pacific Company had purchased the Terminal Company outright for the sum of $250,000, in order to acquire the route from Goat Island to Vallejo where they intended to construct a short line to the Straits of Carquinez. In a letter to Mark Hopkins, dated

May 11, 1872, Mr. Huntington comments rather bitterly: "Directors of the Terminal Company now oppose the Goat Island after selling out to us."

The bill was not brought up again that session at the request of President Grant, who wished to have it held over until after the November elections. The next session expired March 3, 1873, and the bill was accorded a hearing before the Committee on Military Affairs, February 17, 1873, and was there dropped.

The following extracts are from an interesting letter dated March 19, 1872, addressed to Ellis H. Roberts, member of Congress from the state of New York, 1871-75, and written by Samuel Williams, an editorial writer on the San Francisco *Bulletin*, "the newspaper that raised most of the Goat Island rumpus:"

This howl against cession of Goat Island is gotten up for factions and selfish purposes to carry the measure of bad men. The Bank of California who control nearly all the organs of public opinion, have had a difference with Stanford & Company. With their measures are carried the Chamber of Commerce and Board of Supervisors cliques, and all the men creatures of Ralston & Company [bankers]. ... During the six years I have lived here, I have never heard a word against the railroad having the island, and the present furor is simply manufactured to order. I thought you might like to know from one who is disinterested and never asked a favor of the railroad.[10]

Previous to this letter, on March 9, Mr. Williams had either written or wired a Mr. Merriman:

House against Goat Island concession to railroad all bosh. Not one man in twenty here cares a cuss whether the railroad has it or not. A desert, no utility to any one else, will not hurt the harbor or commerce.

Apparently this gentleman did not approve the hostile attitude of his employer, nor the stand he himself was forced to take.

Senator Cornelius Cole, mentioned above, who was an advocate of the Goat Island bill in the House, and an opponent in the Senate, said in his Memoirs of 1908:

Whether the determination of the Goat Island matter was wise or not has been much questioned, and upon this point I have my doubts. Not because the affair contributed to my defeat in re-election, but because of its effect commercially upon the city. San Francisco failed to gain the advantage looked forward to. The energies of the company were carried further away to Port Costa on the Straits of Carquinez.

Incredible as it may seem, in 1911, forty years later, the San Francisco *Examiner*, one of the most virulent opponents of the Central Pacific Railroad Company, in a series of articles and editorials, strongly advocated the use of Goat Island as a Union Passenger Terminal! On March 11 of that year, there was an editorial of which the following are extracts:

Goat Island is meant to aid big growth; it is the most suitable site in the Bay region for a terminal station for all railroads. . . . There is no other spot in the Bay region so suitable for a Union depot for the travelling public as the island, because the site and the location make it a natural terminal. The Government should give it up for this more important public use. . . . You must realize that any big improvement in freight and passenger facilities in San Francisco redounds to the benefit of all the interior cities and towns . . . because this city is the center. Nature has done much for this city. She should constantly strive to supplement nature by the best of transportation agencies.

These articles must have produced a favorable impression upon the California delegation in Washington. Senate Joint Resolution No. 26 was produced asking Congress to cede the island to the state of California to be used solely for general railroad purposes. Here are some of the reasons given for this request: (1) Shorter time lessens dangers to passengers in a fog. (2) Time from slip to slip reduced to less than one-third. (3) Great benefits to suburban communities and the traveling public. (4) Island is useless for any other purpose. (5) Opens up an avenue for competing railroad lines. (6) Shows the Central Pacific Company they have no right to enjoy special privileges. (7) Our people should have the benefit of the advantageous feature nature has provided for us and which nature intended we should have; etc., etc.

Goat Island was never assigned to the state of California for use as a railroad terminal. It became the meeting place for the two sections of the Bay Bridge which opened January 15, 1939.

Chapter XXXI

MISSION BAY

AFTER the Western Pacific and Southern Pacific lines had come under their control, the Central Pacific Company applied to the State Legislature for a grant of five hundred acres in the tidelands belonging to the State and known as Mission Bay, a tract of submerged lands near San Francisco. They desired a right of way requiring two hundred acres and three hundred acres for depot purposes which they would purchase at a fair price and fill in at their own expense, the whole amounting to several million dollars. Also, they would construct upon a system approved by the proper authorities, bulkheads, docks, wharves, etc., which would belong to the State.

A bill to that effect was introduced in the Senate on March 5, 1868, which was referred to the Senate Committee on Commerce and Navigation for consideration.[1] The Committee made its report a few days later. After a reference to lands in this tract already sold to homesteaders and corporations at $1.25 to $100.00 per acre which still remained unreclaimed, and to the high cost of filling in the lands by the State before selling them, the report went on to say:

We believe that the interests of the State are best promoted by the sale of these lands to the railroad companies for depots, warehouses, machine shops, and other purposes connected with the railroads, at a price to be fixed by the Governor, the Surveyor General, and the Mayor of San Francisco. Of the sum found to be their value, not less than $100 per acre shall be paid into the State Treasury. If in five years, the railroads shall have expended $100,- 000 (over and above the price paid for the land) in reclaiming these lands, and terminating their railroads thereon, they will then receive a patent. . . . The system adopted must be approved by the Governor, the Mayor of San Francisco, and the Harbor Commissioners, and must provide a basin and a seawall and provisions for drainage. . . . This disposition of the lands will give the State their full value.[2]

A warning was included in the Committee's Report that if for any reason their recommendation could not be carried out, the railroads would undoubtedly reach the nearest practicable point on the opposite side of the Bay.

When the bill was made public, followed by the report of the committee, the vociferous cries of the Opposition resounded throughout the State: "It would be an outrage to pass this bill. It was conceived in the interest of parties whose schemes are all in conflict with the healthy growth of the State."[3] "This bill would confer power upon the company to purchase the State's property at less than one-hundredth part of its value. The whole thing is a mere land speculation."[4]

"The scheme is outrageous. The property will eventually be worth as much as the Pacific Railroad itself."[5] And so on, *ad nauseam.*

The debate in the Assembly waged loud and bitter. A San Francisco member said the lands were worth $50,000 per acre, and at this price, the railroad company would receive a gift worth $15,000,000.

It was in vain that a member reminded the Assembly that the bill did not ask for a square rod of land or one dollar in money; they were only asking the privilege of buying it at full cash value.

Another member insisted that no such amount of land was required, and if the company went to Oakland instead, it would not injure San Francisco half as much as it would injure the State to give away all that land in Mission Bay.

A letter from General Rosecrans was read stating that the companies would need 800 locomotives, 3,200 passenger cars, and 9,500 freight cars. The land necessary for a terminal depot would be 385 acres for depots and shops and 125 acres for yards for cattle, sheep, and hogs. The concession would be but a drop in the bucket compared to the vast benefits the State would enjoy in consequence of the completion and working of these roads.

"Ten acres will more than suffice for their uses for the next quarter of a century. The balance they would sell at market prices, putting the money in their pockets."[6]

An amendment was accepted and the bill passed the Assembly on Friday, March 27, 1868, and was approved on March 30. This Act granted to the Southern Pacific and the Western Pacific Companies, thirty acres each of tide lands in Mission Bay for depot purposes on condition that the companies expend $200,000 thereon within two years, and *not to extend their tracks nearer than three hundred feet of the water front.* The depot grounds were subdivided by the authorities into lots, streets, alleys, canals, and reservations.[7]

It was in vain that the railroad company endeavored to convince the people of San Francisco that the space granted was insufficient for their purpose, and that it was necessary to bring the tracks to the water front to avoid the expense of unnecessary drayage and loss of time in trans-shipment between cars and ships, which would tend to drive business from the San Francisco side of the Bay.

Although the Opposition in San Francisco fought the purchase of three hundred acres of submerged lands by the Central Pacific, it is quite evident that they desired to have the terminal on that side of the Bay. To insure this and to prevent the company from seeking a terminal elsewhere, the gift of thirty acres was made to each line. They considered that the railroad company would not purchase the reduced acreage, hence the donation.

The company accepted the donation for future use and carried out all the requirements stipulated, but they went to Oakland for such a terminus as they desired.

In a letter to Philetus Sawyer in May 1874, Mr. Huntington mentioned the amount of work done by the company upon the Mission Bay grant:

The land included in the grant was under water and of uncertain value at the time it was granted and could not be made of value until filled up and reclaimed. . . . The expenditure of the two companies in the improvement of the property and immediate surroundings exceed in the aggregate $1,000,000. Besides to make the submerged lands available for terminal purposes within the time and under the conditions of the grant, the company were compelled to expend more than $1,200,000 in the purchase of adjacent dry land for use in connection with the submerged land donated. At the time they were donated these acres were not worth more than $350,000, and could not have been sold for that sum. Independently of the value attached to the land by reason of its being the terminus of the railroads, it would not bring that sum now, but the terminus of the Southern Pacific and Western Pacific being located on that property will make it very valuable.

In May 1869, an auction sale of the salt marsh and tide lands of the State was advertised, to continue until the lands were disposed of, one hundred forty-five blocks of twenty-five lots, each 50 x 100 feet.[8] In 1872, it was disclosed that the lands sought by the company had been sold to individuals in small parcels, the aggregate sum amounting to about $500,-000. At that time they were unimproved, and there were no bulkheads, docks, or wharves, such as the railroad company would have built had they been permitted to purchase the lands.[9]

On December 18, 1871, a letter addressed to Leland Stanford, president of the Central Pacific, and signed by five prominent citizens of San Francisco, with the approval of Mayor Alvord, proposed that the city grant the railroad company bonds to the amount of $3,000,000, in return for which the company would build a bridge over the narrow strip of the bay between the points of Niles Station on the eastern side and Ravenswood on the western side, and make the terminus of both the Central Pacific and Southern Pacific within the city limits at Mission Bay.

In his reply, Mr. Stanford stated that the Pacific Railroad was designed not merely for local and state convenience, but as a great commercial highway of nations between the East and the West. He reminded the writers that the companies received in the Mission Bay grant only a fraction of the necessary space for the terminal of a great railroad system and the track could come only within three hundred feet of the waterfront. As a result the company was compelled to go to the other side of the Bay for sufficient space for a terminal, and for such waterfront privileges as would enable transfers from cars and warehouses to ships to be made without delay.

Mr. Stanford continued his letter by saying that in view of the great commercial interest that should exist between the overland railroads and the city of San Francisco, and desiring to promote these interests, the Directors of the two companies would enter into the agreement as requested, provided the Mission Bay grant was so changed as to have the best possible facilities for the accommodation of commerce.[10]

This change required the closing of all intersecting streets and alleys in the sixty acres, and a grant of land between the sixty acres and the waterfront together with the portion of the waterfront known as the China and Central Basins. As that city did not own the streets or the market blocks, it required an Act of the Legislature, known as the Railroad Compromise Bill, to donate these reserved portions to the city which in turn was to grant them to the railroad company on condition that they should relinquish all claim to Goat Island as a terminal. The city was required by the State to build a bulkhead along the waterfront and to fill it in. Should the railroad company fail to use the land so granted for the terminal purposes, it would revert to the State. The Act passed the Legislature but was vetoed by the Governor.

The company offered to build the bridge and maintain a line of road on each side of the Bay. The San Francisco Committee was told, however, that the company proposed to build later a short line of eighty-five miles by the Straits of Carquinez, to which they all agreed. An ordinance was introduced in the Board of Supervisors and printed, but when the Central Pacific Company found in it a clause prohibiting the company from building this short line, a notice was sent to the Mayor that the company would accept no such agreement, and the matter was closed.[11]

In a speech at San Francisco on September 23, 1872, on pending railroad questions, a supposed friend of the Central Pacific Company had this to say about the Ravenswood bridge project:

Consider the effrontry of this last demand in addition to the un-bounded privileges in Mission Bay. . . . Earnings of the company's roads for but a single month would be amply sufficient to make an excellent bridge across the Bay of Ravenswood. . . . The people of California who have supplied the means to build her railroads have no share in any of them. Their rights are wholly ignored.[12]

Twenty years later, many of the streets in the 60-acre tract had not been closed, and on October 31, 1892, Collis Potter Huntington, as president of the Southern Pacific Company, sent to the San Francisco Board of Supervisors a request for the vacating and closing of about twenty-five streets lying within the company's tract in Mission Bay, so that the company might use the 30-acre grant for the railroad purposes for which it was intended. This request was accompanied by a tracing showing the streets desired to be closed. It was stated that the city had reserved two or three blocks within the tract, and there was some property belonging to private individuals which the company would have to lease or purchase.

Upon the receipt of this petition, without debate, nine out of the ten members present voted in the affirmative. One member only voted no, and the other member was absent.[13]

A few days after this request of Mr. Huntington's was made public, a man by the name of J. M. Basset published an open letter to Mr. Huntington in which he displayed more than the usual amount of venom shown by the Opposition, as well as the usual disregard for the truth:

You are asking permission to close some twenty-five streets where will some day be a great business center of San Francisco. Closing the streets means giving you the land of the streets. It means that you will appropriate to your own use the blocks of land owned by the city inclosed in the streets. It means that you will make it so uncomfortable for the private owners of the other blocks that they will sell them to you for a song. These blocks are worth a quarter million dollars each, to say nothing of the streets. In all seriousness, my friend, can you think of any reason besides your own covetousness why this city property worth millions of dollars should be given to you? Is San Francisco under any obligations to you? Does the city owe you anything? . . .

Since you built your railroad, the city's trade has decreased forty to fifty per cent. You have closed house after house. You have driven business after business out of existence. You have made a forced contribution on every man, woman, and child. . . . And for these courtesies you ask the donation of millions of dollars of the muncipality's real estate, the disfigurement of the city and the destruction of millions of dollars worth of private property. . . .[14]

It was proposed later by the Opposition to oust the Southern Pacific Company from the possession of its tract in the Mission Bay tidelands, which, it was asserted, they held under an illegal tenure to the injury of the State and City. "Doubtless Mr. Huntington could devise some plan for restoring these valuable lands to their rightful owners, the people," they taunted. "Abandonment and surrender of claim would probably be the cheapest, saving the expense of litigation."

Chapter XXXII

THE SACRAMENTO UNION

DURING FEBRUARY 1868, the Central Pacific Company received a severe blow which both grieved and angered them; grieved because of the loss of a hitherto strong advocate, and angered because of the injustice of the unprovoked, virulent attacks.

The Sacramento *Union*, the most powerful and influential newspaper in California, that had been a staunch supporter of the railroad company since its organization, suddenly and without warning changed to the ranks of the Opposition and became one of the bitterest foes of the builders.

The breach seems to have occurred in February 1868. On the 7th of that month the *Union* published an editorial defending the maximum rates charged by the railroad because of the "uncommonly expensive road to run." On February 17, however, an editorial denounced the Central Pacific Company and approved the bill to reduce railway charges. The completeness of the change-over is shown by the following derisive item that appeared in the issue of March 10:

The Central Pacific—poor, starving, frozen thing which the credulous public warmed into life by its charities—is about to prove a very Egyptian asp and sting the hand that nourished it with a more deadly venom than slave lords ever possessed.

Various reasons have been given for this remarkable change of attitude, some of them too absurd to mention. One view generally held by friends of the railroad, and expressed by one member of the company, Mark Hopkins, was that the journal was in the pay of the Union Pacific Company, who at that time were doing everything in their power to keep the Central Pacific from reaching Salt Lake. They had failed to agree with Mr. Huntington on a point of meeting at Ogden, and were trying to work it so as to control the whole line to San Francisco. Anything damaging to the Central Pacific that the paper could say—and they said about everything—would discredit their bonds, and injure them financially, and promote the plans of the Union Pacific.[1]

Another cause given for the hostility of the newspaper was that the publishing business they had expected to get from the railroad company was given instead to H. S. Crocker & Company, a firm in which Charles Crocker was interested. Years later, Mr. Huntington expressed regret for this action, and said that had he been consulted, he would have recommended giving the job to the newspaper.[2]

Resentment increased when one day, Mr. Anthony, one of the proprietors of the Sacramento *Union*, boarded the train with his gun and dog, and was taken by the conductor to the baggage room, according to a ruling by the railroad company that no dogs or guns be allowed in the passenger coach.[3]

Writers have commented repeatedly on the injustice of the railroad in forbidding the *Union* newspapers to be sold on the train. According to the news agent, Denison, however, the *Union* refused to follow the custom to take back unsold papers; so, in self-defense, Denison bought only as many

Monument Point at Great Salt Lake

1863 C. P. R. R. 1869

GRAND

RAILROAD CELEBRATION

IN HONOR OF THE COMPLETION OF THE

GREAT NATIONAL RAILWAY

ACROSS THE CONTINENT.

The Completion of this Great Work will be Celebrated in Sacramento, on the

EIGHTH DAY OF MAY, 1869,

Under the Direction of the COMMITTEE of CITIZENS

Chosen for that Purpose.

H. S. Crocker & Co's Print, Sac.

Facsimile of Announcement

Union papers as he thought he could sell. Consequently, the *Union* broadcast the story that the railroad company had ordered Denison not to buy their newspapers, while the company claimed they had no more to do with giving orders to news agents on the trains than to news boys on the streets.[4]

For seven years the *Union* waged war upon the associates. As the California *Mail Bag* for February 1873, expressed it:

> The war has been waged with a bitterness and personal vindictiveness that has no equal in this state for severity and duration. It has poured out its malice upon the railroad enterprise without stint . . . assailed its management, denounced its solvency, its credit in foreign markets, and vilified the promoters with personal abuse. Its columns have become a vehicle for the vilest slanders and most offensive lies.

One of the attacks was carried to Washington and was taken up by the President himself. He appointed a special committee to investigate the charges that twenty-five miles of the railroad were unsafe and dangerous to travel over. The investigation was carefully made and the charges proved to be false.

Another charge against the company was that the Government had been cheated in the measurement of a section of the railroad, thus drawing a larger amount of bonds than was their due. Congress took action on this, directing that a group of engineers be employed to re-measure it. The result showed that the section in question was found to be one-third of a mile longer than the length required.[5]

When rumors became current that the railroad company intended to retaliate by moving its shops to Oakland and its general business to offices in San Francisco, a delegation of men waited upon the Directors of the Central Pacific on July 31, 1871, to assure them that the course pursued by the

Sacramento *Union* did not represent the views of the people of Sacramento generally and of business men particularly; that they were deeply impressed with the good results of the railroad and hoped nothing would occur to disturb the good relations existing between them.[6]

This was followed on August 19, 1871, by an open letter in *The Bee*, another Sacramento journal, signed by nearly six hundred persons, repudiating the course of the *Union*, expressing warm regard for the managers of the Central Pacific and appreciation for what they had done toward the devolopment of the city.

The Sacramento *Union* assumed a dictatorship in politics wherever the railroad was concerned. No candidate for any office was eligible unless he was against the railroad. On January 11, 1871, the *Union* warned:

Candidates must be above suspicion. The least taint of railway influence will be fatal to them; for, be assured, this is the issue of this campaign.

The *Union* picked Newton Booth as its candidate for Governor in 1871. Booth had served a term in the California senate, was a resident of Sacramento, and a vociferous opponent of the Central Pacific Railroad Company, hence he was the natural candidate for the *Union*. With that journal's vigorous backing, he was nominated by the Republican Party and won the election.[7]

On March 16, 1872, Mr. Huntington wrote to Mark Hopkins as follows:

I am sorry that Booth should show so much hostility to us, but let us treat him well. We cannot make anything out of a bitter fight with him. At least I would exhaust all mild means first. I think if you should see him and give him one of your old-fashioned talks, it would do good. Why not try it?

Mr. Huntington seemed to have great confidence in the efficacy of Mr. Hopkins' talks, old-fashioned or otherwise; he recommends them repeatedly for smoothing out difficulties. It is interesting, also, to note the conciliatory attitude of Mr. Huntington toward those that would injure the railroad or members of the company. Again and again we find in his letters to his associates, Mr. Hopkins particularly, the admonition: "Let us not quarrel with him; let us treat him well."

The associates finally decided that some means must be found to counteract the spreading hostility caused by the continuous attacks of the Sacramento *Union,* and the resulting depreciation of the railroad securities in the markets. They therefore acquired control of the Sacramento *Record,* a newspaper that had been started by a company of printers in 1867, and placed William H. Mills in charge. On March 16, 1872, Mr. Huntington in a letter to Mr. Hopkins offered some advice on the subject:

The Sacramento *Record* has improved, but it is not quite up yet. I would advise that we put a first class business man in the office to attend to its financial matters, then an A-1 editor. Then publish a first class daily and weekly and put it into every home that has ever taken the *Union,* if we did not get more than 10 cents per year for it. I hear much talk that Anthony and Morrill are both hard up for money, but I doubt it.

On March 15, 1872, soon after *The Record* had been acquired, a request came from George C. Gorham, a California delegate to Congress, and a friend of the railroad, to publish both a speech made by Sargent in favor of the Goat Island bill, and the remonstrance of the San Francisco Chamber of Commerce. Thereafter, the Sacramento *Record* became the Voice of the Central Pacific Company, defending their policies, emphatically confirming their solvency, and exposing the personal malice behind the attacks of the Opposition.

The people discovered at last that the *Union* had ceased to be a public journal and was but a private weapon in personal conflict, hence the falling off of the subscription list and the withdrawal of columns of advertising. In September 1874, the proprietors of the *Union*, James Anthony, Paul Morrill, and H. W. Larkin announced that Larkin wished to retire on account of poor health. On December 28, the property was sold at auction and bid in by one of the proprietors for $65,000.

The last issue of the *Union* was on February 20, 1875, in which it gave this parting shot at the railroad: "There is no other instance known to us where a single journal ... has been able like the *Union* to defeat the worst schemes of a corporation as powerful as the Central Pacific Railroad."[8]

The paper was sold to H. O. Beatty, an attorney of Sacramento, who sold it to the Sacramento *Record* Company. The two papers were consolidated under the name of the Sacramento *Record-Union*. A letter from Mr. Huntington to Mark Hopkins, March 18, 1875, said:

> Yours of the 5th instant is received in relation to the purchase of the Sacramento *Union*. I think that was well done.

On February 25, 1875, Mark Hopkins received the following letter of congratulation from F. C. Hall of Ione, California:

> It is a matter of rejoicing to know that the fountain that has so long fed the public mind with poison fatal to the interest of communities and general prosperity, has ceased to flow. A foe is vanquished! A foe to friends, to public interests, to public improvements, and to universal prosperity.[9]

Chapter XXXIII

FROM TRUCKEE TO OGDEN

WHEN THE CONSTRUCTION forces of the Central Pacific reached the Nevada boundary line, December 13, 1867, the most difficult part of construction work had been accomplished. Five years had been spent in building the railroad from Sacramento through the Sierras, five years of heartbreaking toil and incredible expenditures.

While the worst was over, building the rest of the line was anything but easy, and the distance had to be covered as quickly as possible. Although the Union Pacific company had begun construction on their part of the line about a year later than the Central Pacific, they had built a greater mileage owing to the advantage of a much easier grade averaging only thirteen and one-half feet to the mile, and having a comparatively near base of supplies. While the Central Pacific was getting through the Sierras, the Union Pacific had built four hundred miles across the plains. At the beginning of the year 1868, the two companies were about eleven hundred miles apart.

Early in January, 1868, Mr. Huntington entered into negotiations with the directors of the Union Pacific Company to establish a point for the meeting of the two railroads, but without success. The Union Pacific directors hoped to shut the Central Pacific out on the American Desert somewhere between California and Utah which would practically give the former control of the whole line and be worth millions of dollars to them.[1]

Echo Canyon, eighty miles east of Ogden, was selected by Mr. Huntington as the objective of the Central Pacific. Then there began a construction race between the two companies which is still regarded as a classic in the annals of railroad building. "A mile a day for every working day," was Charles Crocker's New Year resolution, but the days came when he greatly exceeded that estimate.

The Central Pacific forces were at a great disadvantage in having to transport supplies by long sea voyages. But Mr. Huntington kept a steady supply moving; at one time he sent thirty vessels on the long voyage around the Horn. Some supplies were hauled in wagons from the end of the Union Pacific line when five hundred miles away by teams costing from $12.00 to $14.00 each. Mr. Huntington tells of meeting some teams hauling railroad ties in the Wasatch Mountains when inspecting the road:

I asked what the price was and they said $1.75 each. They had seven ties on each wagon, which the driver said came from a certain canyon. They said it took three days to get a load up to the top of the Wasatch Mountains and get back again. I asked them what they had a day for their teams and they said $10.00. That would make the cost of each tie more than $6.00. I passed back that way in the night in January, 1869, and saw a large fire burning near the Wasatch summit, and I stopped to look at it. They had, I think, from twenty to twenty-five ties burning. They said it was so fearfully cold they could not stand it without a fire to warm themselves.

Lumber was furnished chiefly by twenty-five saw mills around Truckee, while mills in the Black Hills and the

Rockies supplied the Union Pacific. The Central Pacific employed between ten and twelve thousand men and several thousand teams. Wages were $35.00 per month and board for white employees, and $35.00 for the Chinese who boarded themselves. The company were compelled to pay gold coin for all wages, supplies, fuel, materials and contracts, gold having been always the currency of the Pacific Coast region. The Central Pacific had no such aids as steam shovels, steam derricks, or high explosives.

On April 3, the Central Pacific line was above the Truckee River; on June 19, Reno was reached; and on July 22, it had arrived at Wadsworth and the desert where there was no water, wood, coal, population, or anything to help. Huntington said later that when they began to build the road there was only one white man living between the Big Bend of the Truckee and Bear River, a distance of nearly six hundred miles.

Thousands of dollars were spent boring for water in the nearby hills with but little success. When water was thus obtained, it was piped over miles of desert to the workmen and animals. Most of the water to supply the large force of men and teams was hauled on water trains to the end of the track, and from there on wagons for the use of graders forty miles or more away.[2]

Some three thousand men, and four hundred horses with wagons and materials were sent over the desert, three hundred miles in advance of the track to Palisade Canyon on the Humboldt River for grading.[3] A carload of tools and materials were transported by wagons over the long distance from Wadsworth in order that there would be no delay when that point was reached, and the expenses for the teams alone were $5,400.00.[4]

The Indians resented the intrusion of the white man and his iron horse in the part of the country they considered their territory, and they proved so troublesome to the Union Pacific that the United States troops had to be employed to guard the railroad and the workmen.

The Central Pacific, however, obtained peace by a treaty. When the Indians started warfare with that company by setting a building on fire, Crocker engaged an old man who could speak the Indian language to negotiate a treaty with them. He was armed with two large sheets of white paper impressively decorated with bright red ribbons. The Indians were not to attack any of the company's property, shoot the Chinese or other workmen, or molest the people riding on the trains. In return, the company would give free rides to the Indians, their squaws and their papooses. The treaty was duly ratified, signed and witnessed in duplicate, and thereafter all was peace. The Indians would come in, light their pipes, solemnly mount the construction train, ride thirty or forty miles, wait for the train to load up, and then ride back.[5]

Many times after the construction of the road was completed, these Indian tribes were at war with the United States, but in no single instance did they violate that treaty or injure a man connected with the road or a passenger on the trains.[6]

On August 21, the road was operating to Browns, Nevada; Argenta was reached November 19; and on March 5, 1869, the road was operating to Carlin, about two hundred miles from Promontory Point; the graders, however, were three hundred miles east of Carlin.

In October, 1868, Mr. Huntington had filed with the Secretary of the Interior, O. A. Browning, maps and profiles

Meeting of the Central Pacific and Union Pacific Railroads, May 10, 1869

"Driving the Last Spike"
(From a Painting by Thomas Hill in the State House at Sacramento)

of their proposed route from Monument Point to Echo Summit, eighty miles east of Ogden, the points between which the decisive contest with the Union Pacific would be fought. This line was formally approved and accepted by the Secretary.

While on an inspection tour of the line in January, Leland Stanford wrote to Mark Hopkins as follows:

We are working substantially along our whole line between Ogden and Monument Point . . . Our work here goes very slowly, the contractors have many excuses . . . But I have started Brigham [Young] after them and they give indications of doing better. We must rely upon Stobridge's forces to finish up the work and have the grade ready.

On January 14, 1869, President Johnson appointed a special commission consisting of Major General G. K. Warren, Lieutenant Colonel R. G. Williamson, and Jacob Blickensdorfer, Jr., to examine the ends of the completed tracks and the ground between them, and send a map and profile of the route selected as the most advantgeous, and to designate a point at which the two roads would probably meet.

The Union Pacific had sent its surveyors as far west as Humboldt Wells in Nevada, while the Central Pacific had surveyed to Echo Canyon in Utah, the two construction companies working on parallel lines for two hundred miles, from two hundred to five hundred feet apart. It is estimated that at least $1,000,000 was wasted by the two companies, each endeavoring to gain the greater mileage. One day the Union Pacific broke all records by building six miles of track in one day, and the Central Pacific responded with seven miles. The Union Pacific met this with seven and one half miles, whereupon, the Central Pacific laid in one day ten miles of track, a record for all time.

After the commissioners had acquainted themselves with the situation, and made their report, the two companies were notified by the Secretary of the Interior to decide upon a place of meeting. Mr. Huntington notified the directors of the Union Pacific that Promontory Point, fifty-four miles west of Ogden would suit the Central Pacific, and that they would like to buy enough of the Union Pacific completed road to enable them to enter the Salt Lake Valley; intimating at the same time that if the Union Pacific would not agree to sell, the Central Pacific would build their own line to the valley.

The Union Pacific offered to sell forty-five miles of their road from Promontory Point east for $4,000,224.96. The Government interposed and they reduced the price to $3,-000,000 for forty-seven and one half miles of road. The remaining part of the track to Ogden, which was to be the terminal for both roads, was leased to the Central Pacific for 999 years. As late as 1927, the company was still paying for this leased road, though using only a small part of it. In 1903, the road was shortened forty-six miles by extending a line from Lucien directly across the Salt Lake to Ogden, cutting off Promontory Point with its grades and curves.[7]

The junction of the two roads was made at Promontory Point, ten hundred eighty-six miles west from Omaha, and about seven hundred miles east from Sacramento. There on May 10, 1869, at 12:45 P.M., the last tie was laid and the last spike driven by Leland Stanford, president of the Central Pacific, seven years earlier than the time allowed by the Government. Of this ceremony, a writer had this to say:

American history in its triumphs of skill, labor, and genius, knows of no event of greater thrilling interest than the scene which attended the driving of the last spike which united the East and West with bands of iron.[8]

In the Capitol building at Sacramento is a large painting of this event by Thomas Hill, a landscape artist; and in the Southern Pacific passenger station in the same city is a large painting by J. A. MacQuarrie, San Francisco artist, which portrays Stanford lifting the first spadeful of earth at the beginning of construction. Mr. Huntington was not present at either of these ceremonies, his manifold duties keeping him at his post.

The ceremony had been scheduled to take place on the 8th of May, but the Union Pacific train carrying the officials was captured by some unpaid contractors and held until payments were forthcoming, and the ceremony was delayed until the 10th. The cities of Sacramento and San Francisco had made preparations for celebrating on the 8th, and as special trains had come from outlying sections for the purpose they went ahead with their parades, bonfires and fireworks.

Two days after the junction was made, the first train passed over the roads from Omaha to Sacramento, and on May 15, trains began to run regularly. From that date to September 8, through passengers made the trip from Sacramento to San Francisco by steamer. The company operated twenty-seven steamers of all sizes and a score of freight barges. The first carload of freight through from the East was received in San Francisco August 23, loaded with three hundred twenty-eight cases of boots and shoes for H. M. Newhall & Company. It had left Boston on August 7, and was the first car of goods on any road or line from the Atlantic to the Pacific.[9]

The first railway passenger train ever operated from the Atlantic to the Pacific was the transcontinental excursion sponsored by the Boston Board of Trade in May, 1870. The trip from Boston to San Francisco required eight days and was made in "Pullman hotel cars." A daily newspaper, *The Transcontinental*, was published en route.

When the junction of the two roads was made and the trains in operation, the association had expended all their means, all the aids granted and were more than $3,000,000 in debt for which they were personally liable. They had given eight years of their time and labor, all their fortune, and all their credit to the undertaking. They had a road to Ogden subject to Government liens and first mortgage bonds. They had acquired, also, several additional railroad lines and the control of others, units in what was to become a vast railroad system. They held most of the Central Pacific stock which at that time was not worth more than ten cents on the dollar. Credit alone, largely established by Mr. Huntington, kept them from bankruptcy.

Many enthusiastic and highly complimentary remarks were made about the transcontinental railroad.

I regard the building of these roads as the most important event of modern times.[10]

Search the whole history of railroad building through and we shall find nothing to equal it in scope and arrangement, in brilliancy of plan and execution.[11]

Building this railroad across the country ranks among the greatest of human achievements.[12]

The great national highway will never cease to be a wonder both in the rapidity and perfection of its construction.[13]

The work done upon this road is of a character never before attempted or excelled.[14]

The Opposition, too, had plenty to say:

Long ago the public have regarded the much lauded transcontinental enterprise as merely a private affair to be used for the enrichment of a few individuals.[15]

This road is nearly altogether a free gift. It cost the company less than any equal number of miles on any road in New York or Pennsylvania has cost its builders.[16]

The 1,171 miles of road cost $27,217,000, but they charged three times as much. Here was looting of $50,000,000 in one grand haul.[17]

The rapid building of the Central Pacific through the mountains was, for the times, a great exploit. Abating nothing of admiration for the physical performance, it is now time to reflect that it was also a monstrous triumph of greed, fraud, and corruption; that it might have been had for a fraction of its cost to the public; and that it might easily have been a blessing instead of a blight.[18]

Some comments both for and against the railroad made by the same person reveal curious workings of the human mind:

1. Not only was the road and equipment entirely a gift, but in addition thereto they found themselves at the completion of the road the owners of fortunes which would have satisfied the ambition of any ordinary man.

2. When this road was finished everyone of these directors was mortgaged up to all his credit would carry. Their notes were out everywhere. They had to sell stock to redeem their personal obligations incurred for the benefit of this road.

Again:

1. The aid afforded was more than sufficient to build the road from Sacramento to Promontory. The Government issued $27,000,-000; the company issued as much more, making about $55,000,000. I say without fear of successful contradiction, the road was built at a cost not exceeding $35,000,000.

2. It cost as much money to build one mile of road then as three miles could have been built five years before. Very little was realized from Government bonds . . . The country through which it was built made necessary its *great cost.*[19]

A complimentary dinner to the officers and directors of the Central Pacific Company was given by the business men and firms of Sacramento, September 28, 1869, at the Golden Eagle Hotel. The following are extracts from the invitation:

We have watched your progress and noted the many difficulties you have had to encounter. You have met the jealousy of rival undertakings; you have been annoyed in the courts by causeless and expensive litigation . . . your efforts have been retarded with an unscrupulous tenacity of purpose. A portion of the newspaper press of the state have misjudged your actions, and misrepresented the work you had in charge. With all these obstacles you have preserved the even tenor of your way with a business persistency that has deserved, commanded and created success . . . We desire to meet you and as citizens of Sacramento to express our high esteem and the appreciation of the people of this city for the great enterprise which you inaugurated and carried through to a triumphant completion.[20]

On September 25, 1869, was announced the completion of the Great Overland Road from the Atlantic to the Pacific, the Western Pacific having been completed and in good running order. The following lines gave an unbroken connection between Omaha and San Francisco: Union Pacific, from Omaha to Ogden, 1,032 miles; Central Pacific, from Ogden to Sacramento, 754 miles; Western Pacific from Sacramento to San Francisco, 139 miles; total distance, 1,925 miles.[21]

The rolling stock of the Central Pacific on October 30, 1869 was reported as follows:

166 locomotives
13 Silver Palace sleeping cars
62 passenger cars, first class
35 passenger cars, second class
23 baggage, mail and express cars
648 box, fruit and stock cars
1,293 platform cars

In 1869, the managers of the Central Pacific erected a hospital in Sacramento for their sick employees. It was built of stone at a cost of $64,000, and occupied an open square at C and 13th Streets. It was maintained by a monthly assessment of fifty cents each from officers and men. The surgeon in charge was Dr. Thomas Waterman Huntington, a cousin of Mr. C. P. Huntington. This institution, like everything else connected with the Central Pacific, was a target for the Opposition. The San Francisco *Chronicle* on April 1, 1884, published an article with the heading, "Profitable Philanthropy—How the Railroad Has Made Half a Million," in which it was charged that the assessments amounted to much more than the expenditures, and the difference was divided among the directors. This charge was ably defended by A. N. Towne, general manager, in a letter to the editor of the *Chronicle*, April 2, 1884.

From the first it was understood between the Government and the Railroad Companies that the early operation of the transcontinental road was of such vital importance that many portions of the line would be hurriedly built and would require additional work after the junction was made. The Government commissioners who inspected every section of twenty miles understood this, and the Government bonds were never held up for minor deficiencies.

However, in order that the Government might not advance all the subsidies to the Central Pacific and to secure a first class road, President Johnson on September 25, 1868, appointed a commission of civil engineers to examine the entire road so far constructed and report upon it in accordance with instructions furnished by the Secretary of the Interior, which were in part as follows:

The rapid construction of this great national thoroughfare being deemed wholly important, it was not originally considered that in the early stages of the enterprise the standard of absolute completeness of each section should be exacted as a condition precedent to the payment of the subsidy . . . It becomes the duty of the executive to require that all past omissions shall now be supplied, that in lieu of temporary structures, those which are permanent and substantial shall be erected.

The Commissioners made their report on May 14, 1869. They estimated that to supply the deficiencies on five hundred fifty-six miles of road eastward from Sacramento would require a further expenditure of $4,493,380. As security for the improvements on this road, the Secretary of the Interior ordered the Commissioner of the General Land Office to withhold all patents for land from the Central Pacific Company until further notice. He also ordered the directors of the company to deposit with the Secretary of the Treasury $4,-000,000 of their first mortgage bonds, which order the Central Pacific complied with in May and June, 1869, together with a written agreement that the bonds and lands should be held by the Government as security for the completion of the road.[22]

On January 25, 1869, the Secretary of the Interior appointed the following persons as another Special Board of

Commissioners to examine the Central Pacific and Western Pacific Railroads: R. S. Williams, Lieutenant Colonel, USA, Lloyd Tevis, Sherman Day and Calvin Brown. Their report estimated for deficiencies, a total of $310,000: $200,000 for the road, $110,000 for new cars. The report concludes as follows:

We recognize with pleasure, the energy, liberality, and good faith manifested by the company in the construction and equipment of the road. Such deficiencies and defects as we have noticed seem not to result from niggardly and false economy, but from the haste in the construction demanded by the public, stimulated by a wholesome rivalry with the Union Pacific Company.[23]

The great difference in the estimated cost of supplying the deficiencies given in this report from that of the report of the civil engineers precluded any action upon it by the Government.

On April 10, 1869, a new Administration in charge, Congress passed a joint resolution by which President Grant was authorized to appoint a "Board of Eminent Citizens," not to exceed five in number, to examine and report upon the condition of the road, and what sum, if any, would be required to complete it for the entire length as a first class road. The President was also "authorized and required" to withhold from the company an amount of subsidy bonds to secure its full completion as a first class road, and for such sections where subsidy bonds had been issued, an equal amount of the company's first mortgage bonds should be deposited.

The board was composed of the following "eminent citizens": General Hiram Walbridge, General C. B. Comstock, General Winslow, Ben Wade, and Mat Carpenter. "A very good commission," wrote Mr. Huntington to Mark Hopkins. This commission was furnished with a copy of the instructions given to the Board of Engineers, and a copy of their report, and directed to be governed thereby in their examinations. They began examination of the Central Pacific and the Union Pacific in September, 1869, and made their report on October 30, 1869, giving a detailed estimate of the cost of the work necessary on the Central Pacific from Sacramento eastward in order to complete it amounting to the sum of $576,650.

On November 3, 1869, the Board of Eminent Citizens having reported that the amount required to complete the work had been reduced from the $4,493,380, as reported by the civil engineers, to $570,650, the Secretary of the Interior so modified his order to the Commissioner of the Land Office as to allow patents to one-half of the lands, the other half being retained. Also, the company was permitted to withdraw from the Treasury their first mortgage and Government bonds, amounting to $4,498,380, that were being held as security.[24]

On August 2, 1874, Mr. Huntington addressed a communication to the Secretary of the Interior, stating that the Central Pacific railroad was completed and in successful operation, and requested a re-examination to determine whether it had been completed as required by law and the report of the commissioners.

On September 21, 1874, a board of commissioners composed of Eugene Sullivan, Calvin Brown, and J. W. Dwyer, was appointed to re-examine the roads. They made their report on November 2, 1874, in which they stated that the

Central Pacific had completed its road in conformity with the law by October 1, 1874, and had expended in improvements $5,121,073.23.

Of this amount, $1,014,681.34 was for wharves and depot building at Oakland, $241,490.87 was for improvements of grounds at Mission Bay, and $105,906.60 for the ferryboat *Thoroughfare*. The greatly detailed improvements enumerated in bringing the road up to standard included relocation of sections of the road, stone culverts, heavier ballast, bridges, masonry, sidings, machinery, repairs to snow sheds including a fire alarm, new rolling stock, increased water supply, and many others.

The commission reported that up to the date of completion, October 1, 1874, the Central Pacific Railroad had cost the sum of $140,895,887.30 as shown by the company's accounts. The cost of the Union Pacific line for the same time was given as $115,214,587.79. The following are extracts from this report:

> The commissioners are of the opinion that the company has manifested a disposition not to limit the improvement of the road to the mere letter of the recommendation of the eminent citizens, but with a commendable policy and liberality has shown a desire to render the work what it ought to be . . . They have expended on these improvements $4,338,387.23 more than the amount estimated as necessary by the former commission . . .

> In closing . . . we cannot forbear an expression of profound approval of the establishment of the company's hospital for the sick and disabled in its service . . . a large and commodious edifice of good architectural proportions and finish . . . and containing accommodations for eighty-four patients at one time . . . It appears that a total of 7,255 cases have been treated since its first establishment.

A brief mention of such a noble institution maintained by a railroad corporation seems to the commissioners to be required from them as illustrating the humane spirit by which the company has been guided, and which, they think, should in all similar cases be adopted.

On November 12, the Secretary of the Interior transmitted the report to the President, and on November 18, the Commissioner of the Land Office was directed to issue patents to the remaining lands that had been held as security.[25]

The date of the completion of the Central Pacific railroad, whether in 1869 or in 1874, became a matter of disagreement between the company and the Government which required the Courts of law to settle. The Government regarded the road as incomplete until all improvements had been made, and withheld as security land patents due the company until the commissioners had pronounced the road completed on October 1, 1874.

Yet, the Government demanded payment from July 1869, of the five per cent of the net earnings of the company which, according to the contract, was to start only upon completion of the road. The Government in 1877 lost its case in the U.S. Circuit Court, for the district of California, but the Court of Claims in 1878 reversed that decision.

Since March, 1873, Congress had been retaining the whole amount due the railroad companies for services to the Government instead of the half, in violation of the contract. This disposition to take unfair advantage of the companies by the Government was shown by many harsh and unjust claims until the final settlement in 1899, and resulted in much expensive litigation. The virus of the Opposition had spread even to the Halls of Congress.

Chapter XXXIV

UNREMITTING TOIL
AND ANXIETY

THE FAILURE of the Central Pacific to complete the line to
Echo Canyon as planned was a bitter disappointment to Mr.
Huntington. That he attached great importance to reaching
this point in order to compete with the Union Pacific for the
trade in the Salt Lake Valley is shown by his letters to his
associates during the race with the Union Pacific, urging
greater haste in pushing the road forward. These letters dis-
close also much of the weariness and strain under which he
labored. The following are extracts from some of those
letters:

To Charles Crocker, January 26, 1868:

I consider it of the most vital importance that we build to the
Wasatch Mountains for many reasons which I have given before.
I would build the road in the cheapest possible manner then go back
and improve it at once, because the Union Pacific have built the
cheapest kind of road.

To Charles Crocker, April 15, 1868:

Keep right on laying rails just as though you did not care a d—
for the snow, but were bound to get to Weber Canyon before the
Union Company, and if you do that I will forever pray that you will
have your reward.

To Mark Hopkins, June 8, 1868:

I told General Thomas Ewing that if he could compel the Union Pacific to build as good a road as we were building that we could build to Weber Canyon before they did. He said he thought he could do it.

To Mark Hopkins, June 10, 1868:

I telegraphed you yesterday not to take possession of the line more than 300 miles in advance, as they no doubt have possession, and therefore I thought we had better take high ground and confine ourselves to the law.

To Leland Stanford, June 15, 1868:

It is all important we build to Weber Canyon, we all understand that, but I have been sorely troubled about iron. It sometimes seems as though the fates were against us from the mills that have burned and broke, hands striking, etc. But all great enterprises of this kind must have their mishaps. I only hope the Union may have as many as we do.

To Charles Crocker, July 1, 1868:

There has left this port in all up to this time, 60,146 tons of rails. I shall continue to ship on fast ships until I have on the way 90,000 to 100,000 tons. I think all the iron that we lay on the Central Pacific (except for repairs) will be laid between this and the first of next February. So work on as though Heaven were before you and Hell behind you.

To Mark Hopkins, July 6, 1868:

I think all these roads being built under the Railroad Act of 1862 will have a terrible overhauling. I hope they will show as clean hands as we can, but I doubt it.

To E. B. Crocker, July 9, 1868:

The Union Company are in a quarrel again, but I think nothing will delay them pushing their track forward. It is a pity other railroad companies do not take high ground as we do.

To Leland Stanford, July 17, 1868:

Hurry up with all possible speed to reach within 300 miles of Echo Canyon, as it is all important that we make that point.

To Charles Crocker, October 21, 1868:

I do hope you will push the work from this on as work was never pushed before, for the interest at stake is immense. Why doesn't Stanford go to Salt Lake and stay until the roads meet?

To Charles Crocker, October 22, 1868:

I have got the new line to Echo Summit approved [by the Secretary of the Interior]. You must lay the track to the tunnel. By God, Charley, you must work as man never worked before. Our salvation is you.

To Leland Stanford, November 13, 1868:

If it is the power of God, man, or the devil to get our rail laid to within 300 miles of Echo by, say the tenth of December, it should be done.

To Mark Hopkins, December 15, 1868:

I think it a terrible mistake that we have made in letting matters run as they have at Salt Lake. I sometimes swear terribly about it, but that doesn't do any good.

To E. B. Crocker, December 16, 1868:

I wrote you and Stanford as soon as our line was approved, to have engineers connect our line as approved from Echo Summit to the Union Pacific line as it was being worked, and I supposed you would see the importance of it, and have attended to it at once. But up to this time I have not heard one word in reply. The Union Pacific have just filed a map that laps us by 30 miles.

To Charles Crocker, December 16, 1868:

I shall leave tomorrow night for Omaha, and if I cannot find out from Stanford what I want to know, I shall go on to Salt Lake.

To Mark Hopkins, January 27, 1869:

I have just received letters from Axtell and Franchot [Central Pacific counsel in Washington] to come over to Washington tonight as the devil is to pay in the Department [of the Interior], all growing out of our miserable failure to build the road as we should have done. They have given the Union Pacific all their bonds, and have not taken any security for completing the road as required by the extra commissioners.

On February 26, 1869, Mr. Huntington addressed a letter "To the President of the United States" asking for an issue of bonds for work performed by the Central Pacific upon four sections of its line which were being withheld without legal or equitable reason. The letter stated a number of reasons for the claim, among them the fact that after a survey of these sections, a map had been filed in the office of the Secretary of the Interior which was approved and accepted. The Secretary had never approved any line for the Union Pacific west of that point.

This claim for bonds was endorsed by the Attorney General, the Solicitor of the Treasury, and in two cabinet meetings the majority voted to give them the bonds, yet McCulloch, the Secretary of the Treasury, refused to relinquish them. Finally on March 2, 1869, he was granted an issue of $1,066,666.66, of which $500,000 was retained as security for the completion of the road; and on March 3, was issued the remaining $1,333,333.34, minus the $500,000 retained for security.

The Palisades on the Humboldt River

Mr. Huntington's own version of the matter showing the unnecessary time and trouble to which he had been subjected was given as follows:

I went to McCulloch and said I, "Here is a report I want you to have." He had had a talk with Ames [of the Union Pacific], and I knew he had agreed not to show me the bonds, but I was determined to have them. I went there nearly a week. I wanted to get them the day the Administration closed, so I called at McCulloch's office and sent in my card. McCulloch would let me know the next morning. I said, "Never mind, I will go in and see him." I wanted those $2,400,000 bonds. "Well," said he, "you seem entitled to them, but I can't let you have them."

I answered, "Give me the reasons, Mr. Secretary, why you won't let me have them." "Well," said he, "you seem entitled to them under the law." Said I, "That is all right; give me the bonds." "Well, no," he replied, "I can't do it." I said, "I want your reasons. I have men in New York who are interested with me; when I go back, if I don't have the bonds, I want the reason why. You can see for yourself." "You do seem entitled to them," said he.

Well, I was nearly a week. I went in there every day and asked him to give me the bonds, and asked for the reasons. One day, there was a score of men right behind me. "Now," said he, "if you do not let these gentlemen see me, I will decide this thing against you." "Now, Mr. Secretary," I replied, "rather than have the Secretary of the Treasury do as foolish a thing as that, I will sit here for a fortnight." For half an hour or so I sat there. He then spoke to Mr. Jordan [Solicitor of the Treasury] who had come in. "Now, Mr. Jordan, Mr. Huntington is worrying me to death. He says he wants those bonds; what do you think of it?" Jordan said, "I have given you a written opinion, Mr. Secretary, that he is entitled to the bonds under the law." "Well," said he, "he shall have the bonds." Later I found the bonds in my room.[1]

It seems to have been the custom for the Government to delay the bonds and to give the company, usually Mr. Huntington, unnecessary trouble in collecting them. On October 26, 1867, Mr. Huntington had written to Mr. Stanford:

I returned from Washington this morning where I have been for the last three days, all of which time it has taken me to get the $320,-000 bonds that were called for by the last report of the commissioners. I was compelled to go to the Interior Department, to the President, and then to the Treasury; and I shall be compelled to take the same course hereafter.

Mr. Huntington prepared an able pamphlet addressed to the Senate Railroad Committee giving reasons why the managers of the Central Pacific thought the point of junction should be at Ogden on account of the trade of the Salt Lake Valley and the coal in the Wasatch Mountains. The Central Pacific were four years crossing the Sierra Nevada Mountains and while building only seventeen miles of road, the Union Pacific had built four hundred miles across the plains. Had the Central Pacific omitted the heavy work as the Union Pacific had done, the two companies might have met many miles east of Ogden. As they had a hard task getting through the Sierras, they should have a larger share of the easier road; and as they had filed their map and received a partial issue of bonds upon the sections reaching to Ogden, they had acquired the legal right to go there.

But the Congress would not assent to Ogden as the point of junction. The commissioners had reported that the completed track of the Union Pacific was twenty-five miles west of Ogden at the time the Central Pacific was seventy miles west of that city.

On September 24, 1867, about two months before the race between the two railroads started, Oliver Ames, a director of the Union Pacific Railroad, went to see Mr. Huntington at his New York office to ask advice as to how Durant could be ousted from the directorate of the Union Pacific. The Durant and Ames factions had been contending several months for control. Ames asked Mr. Huntington to join his Board, but Mr. Huntington answered that he had as much as he could attend to. Then Ames asked that if Durant and his friends beat him and his friends, could they not join the Central Pacific forces and so work together against Durant. Mr. Huntington answered this by saying that while he would like to have the Ames brothers with him, the other members would not consent to any changes on the Central Pacific board.[2]

Later the Central Pacific declined a consolidation with the Union Pacific to form a new company of $100,000,000 capital in which the Central Pacific was offered sixty per cent of the stock, the Union Pacific to have forty per cent.

On January 10, 1872, came another proposition to consolidate with the Union Pacific at two to one, which offer was also declined.

Mr. Huntington left Sacramento in December 1862, to make his home in New York. He and Mrs. Huntington brought with them a baby girl whom they had adopted. She was Mrs. Huntington's niece, Clara Prentice, whose father, Edwin D. Prentice, a grocer in Sacramento, had lost his life in a devastating flood. They established themselves at the Metropolitan Hotel at Broadway and Prince Street where they resided until September, 1867, when Mr. Huntington wrote Mr. Hopkins that he was tired of boarding and had bought a house at 65 Park Avenue.

From the day he arrived in New York, Mr. Huntington's life was one of unceasing toil and anxiety. An interesting account of his activities in the early days of the Central Pacific is given by a fellow guest at the hotel whose identity is unknown:

In the winter of '63 and '64, it was my good fortune to see a great deal of Mr. Huntington and to know much of his work then early in progress. I was on duty in New York in connection with Army matters and we were fellow guests at the old Metropolitan Hotel. Mr. Huntington with his wife and little girl, now the Princess Hatzfeldt, was spending the winter at that hotel. I should say, his family were there for Mr. Huntington travelled fully five nights a week. He would go to Washington one night, labor there with senators and members of Congress during the day, trying to convince them of the feasibility and the national value of his great project; travel back at night to New York, labor with bankers and financiers in Wall Street for funds needed every day in the work that was being pushed under the able supervision of his co-laborer, Charles Crocker. Then go to Boston at night to see other bankers and capitalists, and so on week after week, month after month.

In those days to go to Washington was not a comfortable trip. There were so-called sleeping cars, but travel then was so fatiguing that no man with a less iron constitution and less indomitable will than Mr. Huntington could have worked as he did without breaking down. His physique was magnificient then—I used sometimes to think the finest I had ever seen—and his physique was still magnificent when I last saw him, erect and vigorous, cheery and cordial, in his office on Broad Street. It is true that Mr. Huntington had able associates in the Central Pacific enterprise, but he was the chief. He brought the party together, he led. His perfect faith in himself, his judgment as to the value of the work they had in hand, his cheery zeal under the most depressing conditions kept his associates true to their parts. Mr. Huntington went into the project as a business enterprise, and he conducted it on legitimate business lines.[3]

Harvey Fisk and A. S. Hatch of New York, under the firm name of Fisk & Hatch were dealers in Government bonds.

Mr. Huntington engaged them to handle the company's bonds which they did satisfactorily. They published several pamphlets describing the Central Pacific in their endeavors to sell the bonds. One pamphlet entitled "Railroad Communication Across the Continent," published in 1868, attracted considerable attention.

Mr. Huntington engaged also the services of the well-known bankers, Speyer & Company, who stood by the company loyally in days of financial stress. At an early date in his negotiations for the Central Pacific, Mr. Huntington established a credit and a general business prestige unprecedented in the financial world. An editorial writer said of him:

Mr. Huntington has exhibited in all his transactions for the Central Pacific an ability in business matters that has won him a world-wide reputation. His statements in regard to all matters of finance and standing in connection with the Central Pacific have always been so direct, honorable, and truthful, so entirely devoid of quibbles, that his name and word have been sufficient to secure recognition, not only for himself, but for his company throughout the world; and his characteristics are so upright and high-minded as to win the confidence and esteem of all having association with him.[4]

In the magazine *California Mail Bag* for August 1871, we find another expression of admiration for Mr. Huntington's great ability:

In all the multifold requirements of a great undertaking, his has been the master mind, grasping the whole subject, meeting every difficulty, over-coming every obstacle, guiding, controlling, persuading, advising, and finally conquering and binding all to his will.

When the line had joined with the Union Pacific at Promontory, the Associates were so worn and weary from the continued effort they would gladly have sold out could they have made satisfactory arrangements. E. B. Crocker's health had broken down under the strain, and Charles Crocker's physician had warned him that his health was in danger, so they both decided to withdraw from the company.

On October 16, 1870, Mr. Hopkins sent Mr. Huntington a memorandum of the terms of withdrawal: the Crockers to receive $600,000 in twelve, twenty-four and thirty-six months with interest at ten per cent, and to relinquish and transfer to the remaining associates their joint interest in all things in which there was a common interest, all unpaid debts to be paid by the remaining three associates.

When the Crockers were in New York the next spring, however, the terms were revised. On March 27, 1871, Mr. Huntington wrote to Mr. Hopkins as follows:

We have bought the interests of Charles and E. B. Crocker. We are to pay them twelve and one-half per cent for the Central Pacific stock which carries all their interest in everything that has been made out of Central Pacific, Southern Pacific, Credit & Finance Company except bonds and cash and their Wells, Fargo & Company stock, that is, the first lot of it. We are to pay them for the stock one-half in two years, the other half in three years; no interest in the first year, six per cent for the balance of the time. This is a better trade for us than the one made in California.

On March 30, in a letter to Mr. Hopkins, Mr. Huntington added that he had told Mr. Crocker that they would take his land grant bonds at eighty-five per cent for what he owed them. He knew this was much above their value but there should be no hard feelings between them. On April 10, he wrote Stanford that he had the blues whenever he thought of how much they owed the Crockers. On May 11, Huntington wrote Hopkins that Charles Crocker desired further conditions in his sale to which he could not agree. If agreement as planned did not go through, Huntington would like to sell his interest to Crocker. Crocker finally accepted the agreement and sailed for Europe.

Huntington's letters in 1868 mention the fact that his usual good health had been impaired, that he was nervous and dizzy. He went to see a physician, Dr. Clark, who, upon examination told him that his heart was too large, and that he should move about slowly and stay in the open air as much as possible. Mr. Huntington closed that letter by stating: "There is but one thing to do, that is, send forward railroad materials with all my might."

He complained of the fearful heat when going to Washington and wrote:

This going to Washington one night and coming back the next in such weather as this is too much for poor human nature . . . If I have had any sleep the last three nights, I do not know it . . . I returned from Washington this morning. I have ridden all night for six nights out of the last eight . . . We must make some change for I am losing my grip . . . I get so little sleep, I cannot stand the strain.

The correspondence between Messrs. Huntington and Hopkins from November 20, 1871, to April 21, 1873, reveals the fact that both, with Stanford's consent, wished to dispose of their holdings in the Central Pacific; and that negotiations to that effect were being carried on with D. O. Mills, San Francisco banker, and other capitalists through an agent, Alfred A. Cohen. It was suspected that Cohen, through the California syndicate, had intended a resale to Eastern capitalists, but this was not confirmed since the negotiations failed.

That Huntington regarded the sale of his interests with great reluctance is shown by his letter of December 5, 1871 to Mark Hopkins:

The more I think of it, the more valuable my interests on the Pacific look to me, and if I had some boys growing up to attend to this interest, I hardly think I would sell my interests in the Central Pacific and Southern Pacific at par; but I know of no reason why I should wear myself out as I am doing for the sake of getting more money. I have made up my mind to sell if I do not realize over fifty per cent for my stock.

The Crockers returned from Europe and in September 1873, Charles applied to Mr. Huntington for his money. Mr. Huntington told him that the company had to have a fight with the Government and that he must help them. Crocker said he would come back and take his old position just as if he had not been out, but on a vacation, and because of the increased value of the road, would be willing to give the three associates $100,000 each, E. B. Crocker's part to remain as per agreement.

On October 1, 1873, Mr. Huntington wrote Mr. Hopkins that he had agreed with Mr. Crocker to come back and take his old position in the company the same as though he had never been out.

Mr. Huntington spent many weary and sleepless nights on the way to and from Washington whenever legislation important to the Pacific Railroad was pending. His work there was as he said, "to explain a bill to a Member of Congress and get him to vote for it by giving him all the facts in the case," and to prevent, if possible, legislation that would hamper the work or break the contract between the company and the Government to the detriment of the former, as Congress repeatedly sought to do.

He was said to be an able advocate, eloquent without being wordy, always with a comprehensive knowledge of his subject. "No man was ever more ready with facts, more earnest or concise in stating them, or more convincing to his listeners than Mr. Huntington," said a writer.

To aid him in this important work, Mr. Huntington employed able counsel to reside in Washington for this purpose. The chief counsel was Richard Franchot, who was employed as early as 1862. Mr. Huntington had known him as a boy and had the utmost confidence in his ability and integrity. There were other representatives as Franchot's assistants: Henry Beard, a man named Bliss, and during 1868, a lawyer named Axtell who, in 1867, had been a member of the House from California.

In his "Relations Between the Central Pacific Railroad Company and the United States Government," 1889, Gerrit L. Lansing wrote:

"Influencing legislation" has a wide and diverse meaning. Every citizen who undertakes to perform the duties of citizenship influences legislation when he declares his preference for one candidate for legislative office above another . . . There is no more valid reason why one should not properly employ an agent to promote the passage or defeat a pending measure, than that he should be debarred from counsel to prosecute or defend in a Court of Justice . . .

In England, the business of parliamentary agents is recognized and respected. The parliamentary cost of explaining to committees and obtaining the necessary legislation for the Brighton Railway averaged £4,800 per mile, Manchester & Burlington Railway £5,000 per mile, Blackwell Railway £14,400 per mile, and London & Northwestern a total of $500,000 . . . It is said that the Central Pacific has disbursed a large sum for such service. Their expenditures are insignificant, however, as compared with that of the English roads; and the Government is responsible for the largest portion of such expenditure. Long before the last rail was laid, and continuously since, the company has been subjected to the most ceaseless persecution at the hands of the officers of the various departments and of Congress. And it has been to ward off the effects of such hostile action that the company has been compelled to employ agents and attorneys to explain their true position to these officers and to Members of Congress . . .

It is a gross scandal on the American people to assert that money used to influence legislation finds its way into the pockets of the men representing them in their legislatures.

One of the most virulent and oft-repeated charges brought by the Opposition against Mr. Huntington was that he purchased the votes of members of legislatures and of Congress. It mattered not that when asked the direct question by an investigating committee, Mr. Huntington, under oath, answered, "I never did pay any money to anybody directly to influence his vote," they refused to believe him and the false charges are repeated to this day.

Chapter XXXV

THE CRITICAL YEAR OF 1873

FROM THE BEGINNING of operation in 1865, and as fast as the line was open for business, the Central Pacific Railroad had been a paying concern and of great value to the people and state of California. When, by its junction with the Union Pacific, the transcontinental line was established, it became of inestimable benefit to the country at large as well as to the State of California.

As one writer expressed it: "Their engines have become in fact the lungs of California. They daily and hourly draw in and send out the life blood of this Commonwealth. They have created more wealth, developed more country, and multiplied our privileges more than every other agency combined."[1]

The same writer goes on to say that by the sale of bonds and in loans more than $60,000,000 had been drawn from abroad into California to aid in building the Central Pacific and the additional lines then in progress of construction; one extending north through the Sacramento Valley, the other south through the San Joaquin Valley. Most of this money was expended in California and, outside of the vast benefits of the railroad, that money was a great power that added to the permanent wealth of the State.

To show the growth of prosperity in California in the ten years from 1863, when construction of the Central Pacific

Railroad began, to the year 1873, the following statistics are given: value of agricultural products advanced from $15,000,000 to $75,000,000, five hundred per cent; assessed value of property, from $160,369,091 to $424,821,822; savings bank deposits, from $8,000,000 to $47,000,000.[2]

In 1863, the fare from California to New York was $300 and twenty-four days were required for the journey; in 1873, the fare was by rail $140 and only seven days required. Since the opening of the road across the continent, about seventy-five thousand Western visitors had arrived in California, many of them to stay; and at least fifty thousand persons from California had visited the Eastern states.[3]

The savings in freight charges to producers and consumers in the ten years was not less than $25,000,000. In 1871, the through freight on the Central Pacific and Union Pacific amounted to 161,157,266 tons. Operating expenses of the Railroad amounted to over $22,000,000 during the past nine years paid in wages to men living chiefly in California, and in supplies furnished by merchants, manufacturers and farmers.[4]

New towns and villages sprang up continuously along the railroad lines where men established homes, industries, schools and churches, all of which added immeasurably to the wealth and population of the state. California was a prosperous state in 1873, when the rest of the country was suffering from a great business depression.

The earnings of the Central Pacific had steadily increased in volume, year by year, while the corresponding operating expenses had decreased as shown by the reports of 1871 and 1872. Gross earnings for 1871, were $9,467, 072; operating expenses, $4,292,879; net earnings, $5,171,193. For 1872, gross earnings were $12,793,002; operating expenses, $5,327,-377; net earnings, $7,465,625. The ratio of expenses to earnings was for 1871, 45.38 per cent; for 1872, 41.65 per cent.[5]

In June 1873, the Central Pacific was well equipped, having 184 locomotives, 264 passenger, sleeping, and other special cars; 2,060 box cars, 2,074 platform, section and other work cars, and 7 snowplows. For water transportation, the company owned 7 ferryboats, 29 river steamers, and 20 barques. At the close of 1873, the total liabilities of the company amounted to $135,467,333; while the total assets were listed at $180,257,024, with a sinking fund of $1,063,847.[6]

On January 25, 1873, Mr. Huntington wrote to Mr. Hopkins as follows:

At last they have passed resolutions to investigate our matters and I shall no doubt be called to Washington in a few days. The Committee have power to call for persons and papers and no doubt they will want to know all we know and it is fortunate that there is nothing in any matters that we would keep back, so be prepared with all your papers.

Colonel Franchot and Mr. Huntington were summoned before the Wilson Committee for examination, February 13 and 14, respectively. Mr. Huntington wrote Mr. Hopkins, February 17, as follows:

I send you today by Wells, Fargo & Co. a copy of my testimony before the Wilson Committee. I think they will ask for a roving commission to go to California. I very much doubt whether they have any right, excepting that of might to go into our affairs, and if we could keep them out of our business, I would do so. You will see by the questions that they are disposed to be mean. If I had known more I would have told more. You know what I have, and if it is necessary to tell them, you of course, will do so, but as I have never counted the stock or bonds that are my portion, I could not tell them.

Following the report of the examination, which Mr. Huntington said was incorrect in many particulars, a bill was introduced in the House on March 1, that the Secretary of the Treasury should appoint a commission of three persons to investigate the affairs of the Central Pacific Railroad Company. This bill failed to pass.

On the 3rd of March, 1873, Congress passed a law directing the Secretary of the Treasury to make no payments to the railroad companies for Government transportation, in order that the whole amount (instead of the half as provided for in the Act of 1864) might be applied to payment of the interest on Government bonds.

Suit was brought in the Court of Claims which gave judgment against the Government. From this decision an appeal was made by the Government to the Supreme Court which fully affirmed the action of the lower court. However, all the compensation funds continued to be retained by the Government.

In 1873, an agreement was drawn up by Alfred A. Cohen, lawyer, for the proposed sale of the Central Pacific Railroad to D. Ogden Mills, William Sharon, and Michael Reese. Negotiations for this sale had been going on since 1870. In a letter to Mr. Hopkins, March 7, Mr. Huntington stated that the trade with Cohen must be done at once or not at all. Cohen had offered $20,000,000 for the Central Pacific and other property, except the Southern Pacific. To be paid $2,000,000 down and $2,000,000 every six months, the associates to hold all collateral until all payments were made. Huntington wanted to sell and thought that if Hopkins consented, Stanford would agree. These negotiations like the others came to naught.

A confidential letter of Mark Hopkins to C. P. Huntington written February 6, 1873, confirms the statement made frequently that all the money belonging to them from the railroad had been put back into the business:

A. A. Cohen has called my attention to a note for $150,000 due on the 6th to the Bank of British Columbia given by Stanford. And if this is a personal debt of Stanford's, it is provoking to me when every dollar that has ever come to me from Huntington & Hopkins or any other source since 1862, has been put into the business. In the aggregate, it is a large sum voluntarily (but not wisely, perhaps) kept in the common risk to sink or swim with it . . . for I have never felt that our original Central Pacific undertaking had reached a position that would warrant me, or us, in doing anything individually or collectively that could result in weakening our power to handle it to a successful conclusion.

In 1873, anti-railroad feeling had developed to such an extent that it engrossed the attention of the voters. In the election of September 3, strong efforts were made to elect Newton Booth, then Governor of California, to the Senate of the United States to replace the unexpired term of Eugene Casserly, resigned; but he was defeated. In 1875, however, Booth was elected to that office and served six years. It has been said that Casserly and Booth worked together to keep the California legislature out of the hands of the railroad; but it could be stated more truthfully that their intention was to keep the legislature in the hands of the anti-railroad group.

A letter from Mark Hopkins to Mr. Huntington, February 11, 1783, refers to this group:

I hear the San Francisco *Union, Bulletin,* Casserly crowd have recently procured from the Secretary of State's Office copies of all our railroad documents filed there, such as the Articles of Association of Railroad and Consolidations, Annual Reports, Mortgages, Articles of the Association of the Contract & Finance Co., and everything else of this sort. They are as malicious and vindictive as men can be. Our credit, or any other material of interest to us, it is their purpose to injure or destroy, if they can, and they are moving Heaven and Earth to accomplish it.

On February 20, 1873, Mr. Huntington wrote to Mr. Hopkins in his usual conciliatory manner:

We ought to make the press more friendly. Casserly wrote the *Tribune* an ugly letter against the Central Pacific, but the *Tribune* would not publish it. We must do something to improve press relations.

Throughout the year, during Mr. Huntington's valiant efforts to save the Central Pacific from failure, Simonton of the *Associated News Agency* continued to send to Europe clippings from the *Bulletin, Call*, and *Union* containing false statements and figures against the railroad. These were republished there causing depreciation in securities held by creditors of the railroad and adding greatly to the pressure upon Mr. Huntington to meet their demands.

On March 4, of the following year, Mr. A. Fischel of Amsterdam wrote to Mr. E. H. Miller, Jr., secretary of the railroad company, in reference to reports concerning the condition of the Central Pacific and its securities. This letter was referred to Mr. Huntington who, on April 29, 1874, answered as follows:

The Central Pacific Railroad Company has never pretended to answer the false and malicious charges made against it by a portion of the Newspaper Press of California whose editors with a few other individuals have had personal misunderstandings with some of the officers of the company from its very commencement. For such is the character of these opponents that to have answered their base and

Central Pacific Railroad Hospital

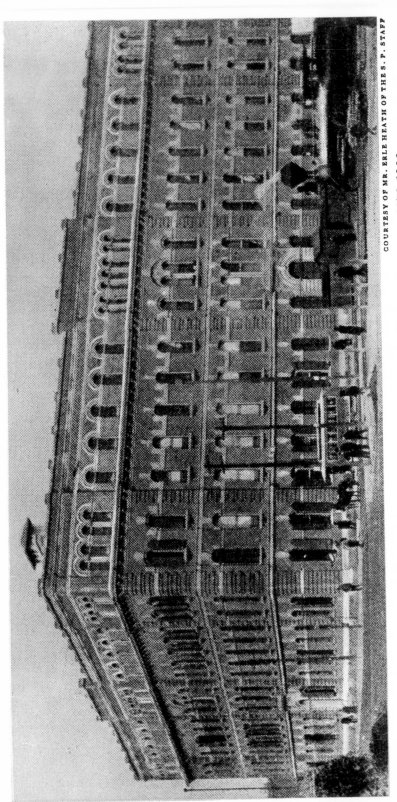

COURTESY OF MR. ERLE HEATH OF THE S. P. STAFF

Central Pacific General Office at 4th and Townsend Streets, San Francisco, 1873-1906

malicious slanders would only have prepared the way for others baser and more malicious, and if possible, more false.

You say that letters received from California bankers and newspapers state that the company owes $6,000,000 in California on which it is paying the highest interest; and also, that private letters have been received stating that bills of the company had been protested in Paris; and that it was with considerable difficulty that money was raised for the bond coupons. In regard to these statements, I would say that the company owed in California the first of April, 1874, $637,887.95 which amount was all it owed there at that time . . . there was nothing on the payrolls on the first inst. No part of the money to pay the last coupons was borrowed, but it was all taken from the earnings of the road. If any bills of the company have ever been protested in Paris, I can only say that your letter gives me the first information . . . I send you the Company's report.

In October 1873, the Central Pacific Railroad offices were moved from 54-56 K Street, Sacramento, to a building at the corner of 4th and Townsend Streets, San Francisco. Of the new location Mr. Hopkins had this to say to Mr. Huntington, November 8, 1873:

Here on the verge of our 60-acre tract of city lands [Mission Bay] we are where we ought to be in the midst of our increasing business at this continental terminus; where with the whole railroad system of the state and coast centered here, the Southern Pacific and Central Pacific freight and passenger depots here, the Oakland ferry running here, we will soon make it the active business center of the city . . . The extension of the railroad up the Salinas Valley to Soledad [the upper section of what was to become the Southern Pacific Coast Line] more than equals our expectations; more than fifty farm houses have been built within sight of the road and population is constantly increasing . . . The tens of thousands of acres of rich lands heretofore used for pasture will this year be sown to grain. Once loaded on the cars it will come to our Mission Bay warehouses, now connected with ship's tackle at a saving of $2.00 or $2.25 to the producer.

When the sixty acres at Mission Bay were acquired by the company in 1868, they were prohibited from extending tracks nearer the water than three hundred feet. These warehouses, therefore, and the right-of-way to them had been procured since by the company in order to save the producer an unnecessary tax of $2.00 per ton.

The Sacramento citizens attributed the removal of the railroad offices from Sacramento to the Sacramento *Union* and its warfare against the railroad. Their indignation was voiced in the November 1873, issue of the *California Mail Bag:*

This warfare has arrested railroad building, has brought dismissal to thousands of industrious laborers in Sacramento; has driven away some sixty families by the removal of railroad offices; has prevented the establishment of foundries and a rolling mill in the town, and has manufactured a public sentiment that should drive every friend of the railroad from the city.

The great business depression which enveloped the country in 1873 was beginning to be felt in the autumn of the previous year. On November 12, 1872, Mr. Huntington wrote to Mr. Hopkins that the money market was very tight, he could not borrow in New York. On February 11, 1873 he wrote:

The money market has not been more sensitive for months than it is today. I think there has been no time when there was less confidence in the immediate future . . . Something must be done soon to get money, cannot raise it in New York.

On March 10, he writes that he is not well, one of the few times in his many letters that he mentions an indisposition:

Things would look better to me if my health were better, but there has a kind of nervous unrest come on me and I cannot sleep. I do not think I have slept any for the last seventy-two hours. My matters on this side, the Chesapeake & Ohio, have given me some trouble of late, but that road has a sure future and someone will see it and be benefited.

The financial situation, and Mr. Huntington's anxiety to meet it successfully, is shown by the following extracts from his letters to Mr. Hopkins during March and April, 1873:

Something must be done soon to get money, cannot raise it in New York . . . Money never so scarce or so high. Our collaterals will not bring money . . . April first is bank settlement day, must send the $175,000 to pay the interest on the San Joaquin Valley bonds . . . Cannot sell bonds or borrow a dollar. Unless times change many will fail . . . A blue day. Danger of a financial smash up. Must have the money telegraphed you for, what we are coming to, the Lord only knows . . . $300,000 due Park Bank, May 3, it must be paid, and the money must come from California . . . The $60,000 currency received. Must have $25,000 per day through the month of May, have $250,000 to raise, God only knows how . . .

In May, Mr. Huntington went to California. His letter to Mr. Hopkins on June 12, was written from San Francisco and enclosed a letter from Speyer & Co., bankers, which contained extracts from the translation of a letter from Amsterdam explaining the decrease in value of the Central Pacific securities in Europe, caused by damaging reports of James de Fremery, Dutch Consul in San Francisco.

While in San Francisco, Mr. Huntington negotiated a loan of $200,000 from the banker, D. O. Mills. From May 19 to July 17, $575,000 in currency and $275,000 coin was shipped to New York from California.

Back in New York on July 31, Mr. Huntington wrote Mr. Hopkins as follows:

Since my return have hardly been outside the office, but there have been several of my friends in who say that there is to be a great effort made this winter to get behind all the Pacific railroad building contracts and rip them up; and all stock that has been issued except that sold for cash at par to be canceled. Then get reports on the line to fix what it should have cost, then on that basis fix the tariff rates so as to pay only ten per cent on what they say the legal stock is, and hold the buildings for the balance of the bonds over what they say the road should cost . . .

We know we are right, but as the whole public seems to have become demoralized, I should suggest that you see Stanford and Crocker and prepare for a wild raid on us next winter, and I do hope you will do all you can to protect our legal right, no other but legal right will be respected, and those not if the public could override the events.

The following extracts are from Mr. Huntington's letters during July and August preceding the panic in September:

Must have $10,000 a day. Curtail all expenses possible at this time. Bonds decline in Germany . . . Southern Pacific bonds cannot be sold now. Spend no unnecessary money, and send me money every week . . . Our credit has suffered in Germany. Get de Fremery to correct his report . . . Memo of bills payable in New York, $4,156,-960.00 . . . Send $10,000,000 to exchange and let me know in advance . . . Extracts from *Sun* and *Tribune* enclosed, very damaging to Central Pacific interests. Next Congress will investigate the Central Pacific, importance of being prepared . . . Railroad bonds cannot be sold now. Must have money from California this fall . . . Think it best to put Central Pacific stock on the market, but declare the dividend first . . . Due in New York in September, $792,796.64 besides daily small cost bills . . . Money must be sent from California.

Mr. Huntington visited Virginia from August 12 to 15 for an inspection of his interests there. Upon his return he answered a letter from the L. Von Hoffman & Co. in Germany, inquiring into the legal connection between the Central Pacific and Southern Pacific Railroads. The Central Pacific Company owed Von Hoffman & Co. a large sum of money and the damaging reports of Simonton and his crowd had caused him to become uneasy over the value of the securities held.

Mr. Huntington's letters for September give a vivid account of the disastrous panic that swept the country that month and his strenuous efforts to save his railroad system.

Extracts from September 4 to 29:

Money market tightened. Kelly & Co. called for the $70,000 gold they let us have to pay the 1873 interest. Must be sent from California . . . Bonds falling in price, 99¼, shall authorize Fisk & Hatch to buy, important that bonds stay above par. Putting stock on the market gives it a borrowing power. Money scarce, must send some every few days as it will give our friends heart to hold their grip on Central Pacific . . . Election in California, September 4, very unfavorable. Simonton will send news to Europe to injure our bonds. To counteract this, bought over $100,000 Central Pacific bonds, and the market closed at 100⅛. This will go by cable to Reuter's News Agency and more than counterbalance the political news from California . . . Several bank failures yesterday and nearly all the papers that went to protest had railroad collateral behind them. Where we are coming out, it is difficult to tell. Must send money from California . . . [Dividend of three per cent declared on Central Pacific stock, announced by Leland Stanford] Important to publish dividend declaration before offering stock on the market . . . I have never known such a time in New York as we have had the past five days, all confidence seems to be lost in railroad bonds . . . It has been rumored that the House of Clark, Dodge & Co. would have to stop, one of the oldest and best houses on Wall Street. If they should go down, I think this would carry failure to three quarters of the railroads in the country . . . Matters look very blue here today, Kinney, Cook & Co. have just failed, one of the oldest and best stock houses in New York . . . You must do all you can to help me out here, there never was just such a time before, and I hope there never will be again. Send some money every day, if possible. I hope to get our Central Pacific stock on the market very soon . . . Have just telegraphed you to send me $25,000 per day for twenty days. It is doubtful if we can get through with that. Fisk & Hatch can do no more. Where we are coming out, the Lord only knows. Kenyon, Cox & Co. suspended on the 13th.

You may well believe that yesterday and today [Sept. 16] were rough days. *Do all you can for me here* . . . Report has just come in that George Updyke and all his system of roads have gone to smash. This carries New York Midland and all its branches and extensions. The three per cent dividend on our stock is having a good effect . . . [Dispatch]—Send half a million dollars, immediately if possible.

Sept. 18—This has been the wildest day on 'Change that I have ever known in this city. The House of Gay, Cook & Co. suspended; House of R. A. Low & Bros. suspended. Newsboys on the streets calling extras over this failure and that. No one is safe in a panic like this. God only knows where we will land. Help me all you can.

Sept. 19—[Telegram] Need $500,000 to-day, send largest amount possible every day from earnings of the Central Pacific. The Central Pacific must be kept up at all events. If we can hold out through this, think we can manage stock so as to come out all right. [Second telegram] Fisk and Hatch suspended payment to-day. *Terrible panic here.*

Fisk & Hatch thought they could go through with the $500,000 I telegraphed you for, and it is possible they could. We owe them over one and a half million but it hasn't got to be paid to-day. Now if it is a possible thing we must sustain the Central Pacific, for everything depends upon that . . . Let us prepare for the worst, but don't let the Central Pacific fall down. There is terrible excitement on the street to-day, but like everything else, it will pass away . . .

Sept. 20—Send all the gold you can.

Sept. 21—The crisis seems to have passed. There is no great excitement on the street to-day. The Chesapeake & Ohio will have to ask for an extension, but it is good and will pay all its arrears sometime . . . It is very important that we keep the Central Pacific on high ground . . . There was of unpaid July coupons $42,058 when Fisk & Hatch suspended that I am paying in this office; and there is $180,000 to pay on San Joaquin Valley bonds the first of October;

and notes for $250,000 due between this and the first of October, and say, $75,000 of other bills. If we can pay these things as they come due in these times, it will help our stock interest, so strain a point to pay the October interest and bills . . .

Matters are looking bad this afternoon, [Sept. 24]. The House of Henry Clows has suspended. They were good folks and their failure will add to the distrust of moneyed institutions . . . The failure of Fisk & Hatch will hurt us here. We owe them, say, $1,700,000; they hold our securities as collateral for $3,373,000 which are liable to be sold. Sept. 24—This has been another blue day. Howes & Macy's, one of the oldest and best private banks in the city, closed to-day. We had a note in the bank for collection and I thought at 2:40 that it was sure to be protested, but I borrowed the money to pay it finally on 15 California & Oregon bonds, five each of yours, Stanford's and mine; but if this lasts much longer we will go to protest.

Sept. 27—No use to go out to borrow money. There never was such a time before and I hope to God there never will be again. Received a telegram from Mills of *The Sun* asking for a telegram that would quiet matters on that side, and I sent him a short one. To-day I sent one to the press in California outside of the *Union*, *Bulletin* and *Call*. Will endeavor to get one off every day until times get better.

Sept. 29—[Dispatch] Send $100,000 gold to pay San Joaquin Valley coupons.

The net earnings of the Central Pacific for the month of September amounted to $1,121,775.65, which enabled Mr. Huntington "to keep our creditors quiet," as he expressed it.

The banking house of L. Von Hoffman & Co. of Germany was a large creditor of the Central Pacific Railroad Company. They owned bonds of both the Central and Southern Pacific and had made large loans to the railroad company. During the panic large amounts became due each month beginning with $170,000 on October 1. The full amount was deposited with Belloc Freres to their credit, and Mr. Huntington wrote Mr. Hopkins that of the $1,000,000 due Von Hoffman that week from his various debtors, the Central Pacific was the only one that paid anything.

While Mr. Huntington could not always pay the full amounts as they became due, he did pay sufficient to keep the securities of the company from being sacrificed. When the false reports of the Opposition were published, causing a depreciation in the value of the securities, Von Hoffman's demands for payments became urgent, even threatening, and as additional security Mr. Huntington gave them 1186 shares of his own Central Pacific stock. The three per cent dividends declared had given the stock greater value. In January 1874, this stock was placed on the market at from 68 to 71.

Other creditors of the company of which there were many, were demanding payment, some of them to keep from failure, and in each case, Mr. Huntington supplied a part if not all of the amount due. On October 29, he wrote that small sums mostly for rails aggregating $100,000 had become due in small notes at different banks and would be protested if not paid. Later he wrote that he had been unable to borrow the money from any moneyed institution to pay the last small batch of notes, amounting to $48,150. To have such small notes protested would have been utter ruin, so he picked up the amount from friends in lots of about $5,000 each, giving his personal obligation, and in addition had to use $14,000 that belonged to Huntington & Hopkins. The last note was taken out of the hands of a notary at 4:20 P.M., just in time so save a protest.

Cascade Bridge and Snow Sheds in the Sierras

Mr. Huntington's letters during the remainder of the year and extending well into the year 1874, were similar in character to those of September, as given above. They reveal his tireless efforts to meet all emergencies as they arose, his adroit handling of difficult situations, his great financial ability and integrity, and his attempts to counteract the malign influence of the Opposition. They show also the great strain under which he labored. "I wouldn't go through another panic like this," said he, "for all the railroads in the world."

All during the time Mr. Huntington was fighting the panic, he was purchasing rails and other materials for the company's railroads then under construction, making frequent overnight trips to Washington, going to Virginia in the interest of the Chesapeake & Ohio Line and, at least once during the year, visiting his associates in California.

He kept in communication with the California office every day, either by telegram or by letter, sometimes both. Frequently he would write several letters in one day, if the matter were urgent, or if different phases of a subject would occur to him at different hours.

On January 1, 1874, Fitch & Hatch issued a "Circular to Holders of the Central Pacific Railroad Bonds" which was, without mentioning it, a tribute to the work of Mr. Huntington. The circular read in part as follows:

Notwithstanding the very general depression in financial affairs, the Central Pacific Railroad Company . . . maintains undiminished its accustomed prosperity in management, resources and revenues. The securities of the company, which in common with all others, suffered a temporary depression in the market from the results of the late panic are rapidly regaining their former values in the chief

money markets of the world. In 1873, the earnings of the company
were $13,871,089; operating expenses, $5,589,440; earnings over
operating expenses, $8,281,649; annual interest liabilities, $3,514,-
357, leaving as surplus earnings $4,767,292 . . .

The company now own and operate in mainline, branches, and
side tracks, a total of 1,329 miles of railroad . . . [which] exhibits a
constantly increasing importance and success in its career as the
great artery of transcontinental travel and traffic, connecting the
Atlantic States with the principal seaport on the Pacific Coast, the
gateway to the commerce of the East.

Mr. Huntington protected his railroads through two other
panics. That of May 8, 1884, when Grant & Ward failed and
President Grant lost all his holdings. The Marine Bank failed,
and for a while pandemonium reigned in the stock market.
Upon this occasion Collis Potter Huntington was said to have
done more to stabilize the stock market than all the others
combined. "His reputation was such that he was able to
throw himself into the breach and almost single-handed avert
a crisis which otherwise would have engulfed almost every
business concern in the United States and brought widespread disaster." A banker in New York paid this tribute to
him:

I consider Collis Potter Huntington was the key to the arch that
held up the people here from May to the close of the year. It seemed
to me that all the imps at one time were trying to break him down,
but he met all calls that were made on him without wavering. Yet
the shrinkage of his properties must have amounted to millions;
still he never asked any special favors and paid up whenever money
was wanted.

The panic of May 3, 1893, in which there were many bank
failures, brought a crisis in the affairs of Mr. Huntington.
He needed a large sum of money to carry his interests

through that epoch; but such was his credit that he found no difficulty in raising the money. He was then a director of the U. S. National Bank which with the Chase First National, and the Fourth National formed a syndicate that supplied the necessary funds. An associate, who had been on especially friendly terms with Mr. Huntington, said:

Taken all in all he was the most remarkable man we ever had in the Wall Street district. He never speculated, always looked ahead and was the greatest planner I ever knew. As a statistician he had no equal in railroad matters and industrials with which he had been associated.

At the time of his death in 1900, the Central Pacific and the Southern Pacific Companies were the only transcontinental roads which had never defaulted in their financial obligations or passed through an enforced reorganization; and which at that time were still in the hands of their original owners or their heirs. Considering all the circumstances this was unquestionably the greatest financial achievement of the age.

Chapter XXXVI

"ALL THE RAILROADS IN THE STATE"

In April 1868, Mr. Hopkins had written to Mr. Huntington commenting rather bitterly about certain attitudes of the people toward railroads, to which Mr. Huntington replied, April 14, 1868:

I notice that you write that everybody is in favor of a railroad until they get it built and then everyone is against it unless the railroad company will carry them and theirs for nothing. In all of which I think you are quite right, but I have about made up my mind that it is about as well to fight them on *all the railroads in the state* as on our road, as it is not much more fight and there is more pay . . . I wish you would send me the names of all the railroads in California, the length of them, and the names of the officers, stating starting point and terminus of each.

And the Central Pacific Railroad Company proceeded to do just that. They had already acquired several lines contingent to the main line. Shortly after the Central Pacific had reached Roseville in February, 1864, the company purchased the California Central or the Marysville & Lincoln Railroad extending from Folsom through Roseville to Marysville. The portion between Roseville and Folsom was abandoned, and the bridge over the Americcn River was condemned in 1868 and sold.[1]

In August, 1865, the company purchased the Sacramento Valley Railroad, from Sacramento to Folsom, twenty-two and one-half miles for which they paid $800,000.[2] The same year the company acquired the Placerville & Sacramento Valley Railroad, an extension of the Sacramento Valley line.[3]

The franchise of the Western Pacific was delivered to the Central Pacific by the builders in 1867. This road had consolidated with the San Francisco Bay Railroad Company which had twenty-two and one-half miles of track.

The California & Oregon Railroad Company was incorporated in San Francisco, June 30, 1865, to extend north from Marysville up the Sacramento Valley to the Oregon boundary line, with a capital stock of $15,000,000 aided by land grants through an Act of Congress, July 25, 1866.[4]

That the Central Pacific had acquired control of this line by November 1867 is shown by a letter of Mr. Huntington to E. B. Crocker, November 11, 1867; which also reveals something of his foresight and method of handling situations:

You say you would not bond the road farther up than Old Fort Redding, but it has always seemed to me that there would sometime be a road from San Francisco to Portland, and that it would be built up the Sacramento Valley, and, as has often been proved, the bonding of a road by no means compels a party to build the road. I had thought it would be well to organize and mortgage the road, say from Folsom to the north line of the State at $30,000, or $40,000 per mile, then get possession of the roads from Folsom to Oroville at a low price, as we are masters of the position, pay in these first mortgage bonds, and fill up the gap between Yuba and the Northern Road.

The company offered to buy the California Northern Railroad, twenty-eight miles in length, between Marysville and Oroville, but the chief owner, Andrew J. Binney, refused to sell for less than $300,000, which the Central Pacific Company refused to pay.[5] In November 1869, Binney petitioned for a writ of *quo warranto* to prevent further work of the California & Oregon, but it was denied on the ground that its construction would be a general benefit. In 1881, the California Northern was sold for $40,000 under a decree of foreclosure.[6]

In August, 1868, the Central Pacific Company purchased from A. A. Cohen a majority of the stock of the Oakland Railroad & Ferry Company, operating a ferry from the foot of Pacific Street in San Francisco to San Antonio.[7]

On August 25, 1869, the company entered into an agreement with A. A. Cohen and others for the purchase of the San Francisco & Alameda Railroad extending from Niles, a point on the Western Pacific, to the eastern shore of the Bay of San Francisco, a distance of 24.31 miles, for the sum of $487,218.72.[8]

The road was brought up to the standard of the main line and extended to a point on the Bay of San Francisco at Oakland opposite the city of San Francisco. A long wharf over two miles in length, extending to a depth of twenty-four feet at low tide and thirty-one feet at high tide, was built out into the Bay in two divisions, one for local traffic where hourly trips to San Francisco were made by ferryboats, and the other for through trains from the overland road.

The main wharf was eight hundred feet wide at the extreme end and had twelve railroad tracks, a wide carriage way, railroad offices, a spacious passenger depot, 75 ft. by 305 ft., two warehouses, one 50 ft. by 500 ft., and the other, 50 ft. by 600 ft., and five large docks providing space for twenty-two vessels. The end of the main wharf was only three miles from the foot of Second Street in San Francisco where freight was landed, and less than two and one-half miles from the foot of Pacific Street where passengers were transferred.

The piles used in constructing the wharf were of the best pine and were driven into the bottom eighteen feet deep and ten feet apart, and six or seven feet apart across the wharf. Where the water deepened, the piles were sixty-five feet in length and fourteen to seventeen inches in diameter, and as heavy as the mainmast of the largest clipper.

Experts in the construction of such work, army and other engineers all agreed that for engineering skill, mechanical execution, and excellence of material employed the work was unsurpassed.[9]

When the transcontinental railroad sought a terminus on the east side of the Bay of San Francisco, Oakland responded generously and with alarcity. The company soon acquired seventy acres fronting on the Bay as a site for machine shops; an area of three hundred fifty acres on the waterfront extending toward Goat Island with a frontage of nearly half a mile; and ninety acres in the proximity of Oakland suitable for car yards, etc. The company acquired also extensive reservations on the southern bank of the estuary of San Antonio, and the right-of-way for tracks leading from the main line. It secured also a large tract of hilly ground which supplied earth and gravel for filling purposes.[10] It is interesting to compare the acquisition at Oakland with the handout of sixty submerged acres at Mission Bay by the State of California.

The Yuba Railroad was purchased from H. W. Rood and C. L. Wilson et al, October 21, 1869.[11]

The San Joaquin Valley Line was begun on December 31, 1869, and constructed from Lathrop, a station on the Western Pacific, south to Goshen. From there, it was continued south under the name of the Southern Pacific Railroad. The main object in building this road, according to Mr. Huntington, was to develop the country.[12] The company thought it would be a good wheat country to develop, as the farmers there could not send wheat far by teams. Nor were the company disappointed. The great region of the San Joaquin Valley was converted into the most productive ranches of grain fields, orchards, and vineyards. Town after town was started and became centers of business and population. Modesto, Merced, Fresno, and Tulare soon grew into prosperous cities, and all the villages and towns between grew right out of treeless and arid plains.

Fresno, the largest city in the valley, was a typical case. Its location was surveyed and staked out in May, 1872, on a barren plain with no water nearer than the San Joaquin River, ten miles away. The first train arrived May 28, 1872, and in March, 1874, it was made the county seat. Today Fresno is a city of nearly 100,000 inhabitants, the center of one of the richest grain and vineyard sections in the country.[13]

In 1874, Mr. Huntington issued a booklet naming the advantages of the great San Joaquin Valley as an agricultural region and calling attention to other important features of California. A. A. Cohen, however, in reply to an inquiry concerning that region, and in a printed letter, took it upon himself to "correct" Mr. Huntington's statements, and referred to the pamphlet in the following terms:

Mr. Huntington's book does not contain that nice discrimination as to facts and accuracy which would jusify its being taken as author-

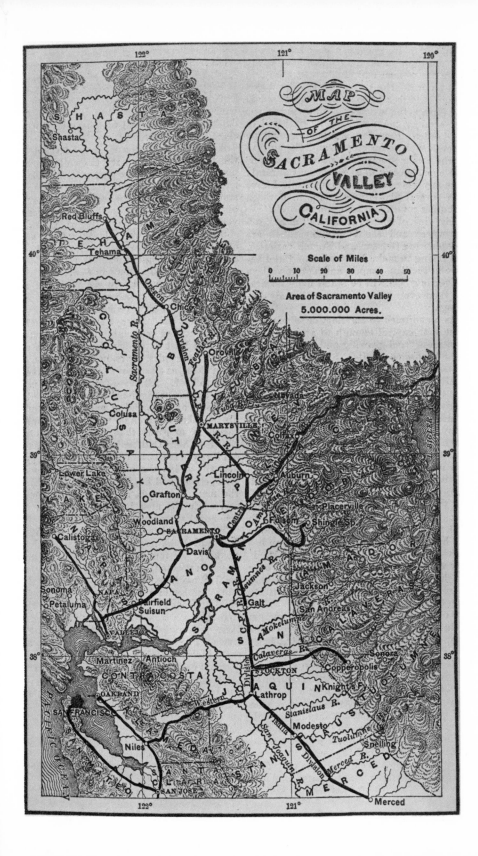

ity by those seeking safe investment for capital; but as a work of fiction, it is entitled to the first rank and may be classed with the travels of Baron Munchausen or Jules Verne.

Events proved that Mr. Huntington's knowledge of the topography and climate of California was both discriminating and accurate, and that Cohen was merely a malicious prevaricator.

On August 22, 1870, the following railroads were consolidated with the Central Pacific and became vital parts of that system: San Francisco & Oakland, San Francisco & Alameda, Western Pacific, San Joaquin Valley, and California & Oregon. The added railroads brought the length of the Central Pacific to 1,206 miles.

The California Pacific Raliroad was incorporated January 10, 1865, with a capital stock of $3,500,000, to extend from Vallejo via Davisville to Sacramento. In June, 1869, it purchased for $500,000 the Napa Valley road extending from Napa to Calistoga, and later the Petaluma Valley road. The company had planned to extend the road to the northern part of the Sacramento Valley and from there to build a line to connect with the Union Pacific.[14] The company's physical and financial position did not measure up to the magnitude of their ambitions, and the spring of 1871 found them in debt to the extent of $8,450,000. When the Central Pacific threatened a branch line from Sacramento via Davisville to Vallejo, the company realized its defeat.

Milton S. Latham, treasurer and director of the California Pacific, and agent for three-fourths of the capital stock, opened negotiations with Mr. Huntington for an adjustment of their difficulties. On September 1, 1871, the Central

Pacific took over the California Pacific, and moved its offices from San Francisco to Sacramento.[15]

The North Pacific Railroad was purchased from Donahoe and his associates in 1871, and resold to Donahoe in January, 1873, for $1,050,000 in gold. Later, however, it became a part of the Southern Pacific System.

The Stockton & Copperopolis Railroad was leased by the Central Pacific, December 30, 1874.

By January 14, 1871, the associates had acquired an interest in the Market Street Railway, and on June 14, 1876, a franchise was granted for a cable railroad on California Street from Kearney to First Avenue in San Francisco, to L. Stanford, M. Hopkins, C. Crocker, and others.[16]

In April 1879, an estimate was made by Henry Root, engineer, for new rails on the Market Street Railway. An effort was made to get property owners to contribute $12,000 toward building an extension from Valencia Street to 17th Street. Double tracks were to be used on McAllister Street from Market to Leguna, a distance of 4,500 feet.

On December 28, 1878, a new line of the Central Pacific from Sacramento to San Francisco via Benecia, a distance of 89.8 miles, was in operation. This shortened the distance to San Francisco by fifty miles.

The Amador Branch of the Central Pacific extended from Galt to Ione, twenty-seven miles, and was built to gain access to some coal mines near Ione.

The Monterey and Salinas Valley Railroad was purchased, January 1880, by the Southern Pacific at foreclosure.

The Watsonville & Santa Cruz line was acquired in October, 1881.

The Oregon & California Railroad was organized in December 1866, to extend from Portland, Oregon, through the Willamette Valley to the California line, and was constructed by Ben Halladay & Company. The Oregon Legislature passed a bill by which the State agreed to pay seven per cent interest on $1,000,000 of the company's bonds for twenty years, secured by a mortgage on the road, the company to issue bonds at the rate of $1,000 per mile.[17] The company procured from Congress a land grant of 1,280 acres for each mile of road to the California border, a distance of three hundred miles.[18]

The progress of the work was hampered by warfare between two factions that had formed, the East-siders and the West-siders. A special meeting of the stock holders was held December 22, 1884, to consider a proposal to lease or sell the road to the Central Pacific. An agreement was made July 31, 1885, by which the 451 miles of road, appurtenances, equipment, rights, franchises, and land grants were to be transferred to the Central Pacific Company, the connecting link between Portland and San Francisco to be completed by the Central Pacific.[19] The railroad connecting Sacramento, California, with Portland, Oregon, was completed Saturday, December 17, 1887. The last spike was driven at Ashland, Oregon, by Charles Crocker during an enthusiastic celebration.[20]

The Los Angeles & San Pedro, a pioneer railroad in Southern California was organized in 1868, to extend from Los Angeles to the harbor. It was completed by October 26, 1869, and in operation on November 1, 1869. The city of Los Angeles had subscribed $75,000 in bonds; the county, $150,-000 in bonds, all bearing a rate of ten per cent interest.

South of the Tehachapi Mountains in Southern California
the country was but slightly developed at that time. The chief
industries were cattle and sheep raising and vineyards. Los
Angeles, the largest center of population in that area, had
in 1870 only 5,729 inhabitants, with an assessed valuation of
something over two million dollars.

Los Angeles was much concerned over the probability of
a southern transcontinental railroad and the location of its
terminal at some point on the coast. That Los Angeles would
be by-passed was intolerable and the leading citizens decided
to do something about it. Harris Newmark, a prominent
business man, and ex-Governor Downey went to San Francisco to see Mr. Huntington during one of his periodic visits
there. A meeting of tax-paying citizens was held in May 1872,
and an executive committee appointed who made a trip to
San Francisco, returning with William B. Hyde who represented the railroad company. The following terms were
agreed upon: The Southern Pacific Raliroad Company were
to receive five per cent of the assessed valuation of the county
which had been set at $10,554,592. To meet this, the county
issued $377,000 in new seven per cent bonds, and added the
$150,000 bonds it owned in the Los Angeles & San Pedro
Railroad. The city gave its $75,000 bonds in the same rail-
road and sixty acres for depot grounds. For its part the
Southern Pacific agreed to build fifty miles of its main trunk
line in Los Angeles County, twenty-five miles northward from
the city and twenty-five miles eastward and to build a branch
line to Anaheim.[21]

Mr. Huntington wrote to Mr. Hyde in regard to the Los
Angeles & San Pedro Railroad and on June 21, 1872, Mr.
Hyde replied to his letter giving details of the road and its

value. On July 1, of the same year an agreement was made with H. B. Tichenor by the Central Pacific Company for the purchase of 2,737 shares of stock in this road, in addition to the $225,000 in bonds already acquired. In 1874 this railroad was consolidated with the Southern Pacific Railroad.[22]

The Los Angeles & Independence Railroad was organized in 1875 by Senator John P. Jones of Nevada, to extend from Los Angeles through Cajon Pass and San Bernadino County to Independence in Inyo County, with a branch line from Los Angeles to Santa Monica, a total distance of 234 miles with a capital stock of $4,000,000. The object of this road was to afford an outlet to certain mines in Inyo County, and to develop property on Santa Monica Bay.[23]

The road cost Senator Jones $716,000 and he sold it to Mr. Huntington for $200,000 and 70 bonds. It was opened for traffic on December 1, 1875. On June 4, 1877, it was leased to the Southern Pacific. During 1892, the famous long wharf was built at Santa Monica, about which there was much controversy and which was later removed.[24]

The Los Angeles & San Diego Railroad Company was incorporated October 10, 1876, to build a road between the two cities. The Southern Pacific had already built twenty miles over the proposed route from Florence on the Los Angeles & San Pedro road to Nietos (now Downey). It opened for traffic to West Anaheim January 14, 1875. The road was extended seven and one-half miles farther to Santa Ana to which the first train ran on December 17, 1877. No other construction work was done by this company, and on May 14, 1888, the road was consolidated with the Southern Pacific. Santa Ana was as far south as the Southern Pacific ever went toward San Diego.[25]

The Southern Pacific Railroad Company was organized November 29, 1865, under the laws of California, to extend from a point on San Francisco Bay through the counties of Santa Clara, Monterey, San Luis Obispo, Tulare, Los Angeles, and San Diego to the eastern boundary line of the State of California at the Colorado River.[26]

In the Act of July 27, 1866, Congress granted the usual right-of-way and ten alternate sections of land per mile, on condition that the company construct a line to connect with a projected railroad known as the Atlantic & Pacific. No money or bond subsidy was granted. Work was to begin in two years and not less than fifty miles annually was to be completed. By the Act of July 25, 1867, Congress extended the time to a completion of thirty miles by July 1, 1870, and a yearly construction of twenty miles.

The evidence indicates that the owners of the Central Pacific gained control of the Southern Pacific Railroad as early as July, 1868. In a letter to E. B. Crocker, dated July 20, 1868, Mr. Huntington enclosed a copy of Secretary Browning's order restoring lands to the Southern Pacific Railroad. On September 28, 1868, Mr. Huntington wrote a letter to the Secretary of the Interior transmitting the annual report of the Southern Pacific Railroad Company as required by Congress.[27]

On October 12, 1870, the Southern Pacific, the San Francisco & San José, the Santa Clara & Pajaro, and the California Southern, a new line on paper only, were consolidated into a corporation known as the Southern Pacific Railroad Company of California, with a capital stock of $50,000,000. The line was extended south from Gilroy to Tres Pinos and was in operation by August 12, 1873. There it stopped. The intended line from Tres Pinos across the Coast Range to Alcade was abandoned owing to the difficult construction across the mountains, and the expense of operating in an uninhabited territory.

The Southern Pacific left the line at Tres Pinos and leaving a gap of one hundred miles, began construction in the San Joaquin Valley to connect at Goshen where the Central Pacific line had ended. The line was extended southward under the name of the Southern Pacific Railroad. It reached Delano on July 14, 1873; Caliente, April 26, 1875; and Mohave, August 9, 1876.

On September 1, 1876, that part of the Southern Pacific Railroad extending south from Goshen to the Colorado River was leased to the Central Pacific Company at a yearly rate of $3,000 for every mile built and in operation, to be continued in force for five years.

Between Caliente and Mohave over the Tehachapi Pass at an elevation of 4,025 feet, was constructed one of the most difficult sections of road on any line in the country. The road loops over itself to climb 2,734 feet in 28 miles, passes around gradual curves on a 2.2 grade through 18 tunnels, the engineering feat of William Hood, chief engineer.

The last spike of the railroad between San Francisco and Los Angeles was driven by Charles Crocker at Lang, where construction from each end met, on September 5, 1876. Regular train service was inaugurated between San Francisco and Los Angeles on September 6, 1876, with the express making the north run in twenty-four hours, forty minutes; and the south run in twenty-three hours, thirty minutes.[28]

No definite route into Southern California had been fixed for the railroad until Congress on March 3, 1871, chartered the Texas Pacific Railroad Company and authorized the Southern Pacific to build south from Mohave by way of Los Angeles to a connection with the Texas Pacific at Yuma on the Colorado River.[29]

The Southern Pacific, moving eastward through the Gargonio Pass, was opened for traffic at Indio, May 29, 1876, and reached the west bank of the Colorado River May 20, 1877. Three days later trains started carrying passengers, mail and freight. By September 30, 1877, a bridge was built across the river at Yuma and the railroad was opened for traffic at that point.[30]

In February, 1882, the Southern Pacific started construction at Mohave toward Needles, 242 miles away. The line was open for traffic in July 1883. The Atlantic & Pacific (later the Santa Fé) had reached the Colorado River about twelve miles below Needles in May 1883. A bridge was built and on August 9, 1883, connection was made with the Southern Pacific at Needles and on August 13, regular train service was in operation over the Atchison, Topeka & Santa Fé transcontinental railroad. The Santa Fé interests acquired this section of the Southern Pacific road from Mohave to Needles and secured trackage rights over the Southern Pacific through the San Joaquin Valley to San Francisco.[31]

In 1886-87, the Southern Pacific Railroad Company built a branch road from Saugus through the Santa Clara Valley and reached Santa Barbara on August 19, 1887. The Coast line of the Southern Pacific was extended from San José via Salinas south, and on March 31, 1901, the first train reached Santa Barbara over this line.[32]

In addition to the California railroads and the Oregon & California mentioned above, which the Central Pacific had

Oakland Long Wharf as Seen from Goat Island

Oakland Long Wharf, 1871, from a Painting

either constructed, leased or purchased outright, there were a number of minor branches, about fifteen "little feeders," Mr. Huntington called them, each running at a loss but profitable to the main line.

On June 7, 1881, General John B. Frisbie, acting for C. P. Huntington, acquired from the Mexican Government in the name of the International Construction Company a concession for a railroad in Mexico. This concession, when approved, was transferred to Mr. Huntington, acting for the construction company which had been organized in Connecticut in March, 1881. On April 26, 1882, the company was reorganized as the International Railroad Company (Ferrocarril International Mexicano) and a charter obtained from the Connecticut Legislature, April 26, 1882. After Mr. Huntington's death in 1900, control passed to the Mexican National Railroad.[33]

How was it possible for the Company to build so many roads and to acquire others? When before the Senate Pacific Railroad Committee in 1896, Mr. Huntington gave an insight into their methods:

As to the roads that we did build our custom was to carry the bonds until the roads had been worked long enough to show earnings sufficient to pay interest on the bonds, after which they were sold as soon as we could find a market for them, and the debts created in the construction of the road, which in the meantime had been carried upon our credit, were then paid.

Chapter XXXVII

SOUTHERN PACIFIC
vs. TEXAS PACIFIC

WHEN THE Southern Pacific Railroad reached Yuma, May 20, 1877, the Texas & Pacific Railroad, which was scheduled to join the Southern Pacific at that point, was still more than 1,200 miles away. On March 3, 1871, Congress had passed an Act chartering the Texas Pacific, a new title for the old Memphis & El Paso Railroad, to build west from Marshall, Texas, along the 32d parallel to San Diego, California. An amendment to the Act, February 28, 1872, changed the "name, style, and title" to "The Texas & Southern Pacific Railway Company." The word Southern in the name appears not to have been used.[1] To aid this road the Government gave double the subsidy in land through Arizona, New Mexico, and California that had been given to the Central Pacific and Union Pacific Railroads, twenty alternate sections on each side of the road. The Memphis & El Paso Company had received heavy grants of land from the State of Texas.

Col. Thomas A. Scott of the Pennsylvania Railroad who had been in charge of railway transportation during the late war and who was considered one of the greatest railroad men in the country, gained control of the Texas & Pacific and undertook to raise capital on the bonds of the company secured by a first mortgage on the lands granted by the Government and the State of Texas. The panic of 1873, however, checked the progress of raising funds when only thirty-five miles of the road had been constructed.

In 1874, Scott had a bill introduced in Congress asking for a subsidy of $100,000,000 in bonds with which to complete the road. Mr. Huntington realized what a formidable competitor to the Southern Pacific and the Central Pacific the Texas & Pacific would be in hostile hands. With the Oregon Short Line and the Northern Pacific, the Central Pacific would soon be deprived of all its through business and its destruction would be certain. From that time there was a bitter conflict between Scott and Huntington, the former, with a large force of his political friends, importuning the members of Congress to pass his bill for a large subsidy; and Huntington, with his agents, striving with even greater force to kill Scott's bill, and to pass one of his own to secure a right-of-way east from Yuma without subsidy bonds, but with the land grants already assigned.

But for the aggressiveness of Mr. Huntington there never would have been a Sunset Route of the Southern Pacific System. The records of the extension of the Southern Pacific east from Fort Yuma portray more vividly perhaps than any other the part assumed and performed by Collis Potter Huntington among his associates. He had not only to fight a rival railroad company and to convince the Congressional railroad committees that he could build without a subsidy, but he had to persuade his associates, all of whom opposed the project, of the great importance of a continuation of the line to save their roads already in operation, and of the feasibility of its construction.

In answer to a letter to Mark Hopkins on the subject, Mr. Huntington wrote, January 10, 1877:

I agree with you that reason and not passion should control us in all our business transactions. I cannot agree as to the policy of building the Southern Pacific road. I believe the Central Pacific could better afford to pay the interest on all costs south of the Mohave and not run it at all than to have had an unfriendly interest control it. You write that it would have been a wiser move to have permitted Tom Scott to build the road with which he wanted to connect the East with San Diego and Los Angeles. Now this would have been as bad a competition on through business to San Francisco as if his road had run direct to that city.

He wrote to Mr. Hopkins on the subject again on February 19, 1877, in answer to a protest:

I do not agree with you about the Los Angeles division of the Southern Pacific. I think for our whole interest we are on the right track. If we had built to Needles, the Texas & Pacific would have got Government aid before this and in a short time Tom Scott would have had a road to San Diego, and when that was done, I have no doubt our road would have lost at least $1,000,000 per year. I think when the S. P. is built to the Colorado River, it will pay much better than it does now. It will settle the Texas & Pacific question as far as the open highway is concerned.

Putting his trust in Mr. Huntington and in conformity with his wishes, Mr. Hopkins then wrote to the Honorable A. P. R. Stafford, Governor of Arizona:

. . . On our behalf there has been presented to your Legislature a bill authorizing the Southern Pacific Railroad Company to go on and build their road through the Territory without waiting for authority from Congress and land grants. If the Legislature will give us such authority, rights, and privileges, then if Congress does not take action on the matter this session, the road need not be delayed.

We believe the passage of our bill by your legislature would more than anything else tend to promote harmony of all interests concerned and to induce Congressional action at this session.

In 1877, Mr. Huntington purchased for the Southern Pacific an interest in the Galveston, Harrison & San Antonio Railway which had reached San Antonio in February. On October 15, 1877, General David D. Colton, who had joined the associates in 1874, wrote to Mr. Huntington as follows:

Crocker, Governor Stanford, and myself had a consultation yesterday (Mr. Hopkins not able to be in his office) and I think we agreed fully. We do not think it wise to buy the Texas & Pacific, it is too much of a load. Nor do we feel like owning the road east of Yuma in common with any of those people on that side. We feel it would be better to agree upon a point, say east of El Paso beyond which neither company should build. It seems to me better for us to have Gould buy Scott out. I think I can speak for all your associates on this side that we do not want to build any more roads east of the Colorado River on the 32d parallel for some time. We want rest. Stop building roads until we can pay our debts. Get strong once again.

Mr. Huntington's reply to this letter is not available, but it is quite evident that the company did not "stop building roads" at that time. On March 10, 1878, Charles Crocker added his protest:

. . . Now as to building the road under the general incorporation Act of the Territory, I can say for myself, that I don't intend to build any road down there under any such law. They would regulate it to such an extent it would be worthless. As I wrote yesterday, none of our people desire to organize a railroad in Arizona or New Mexico, and I for one do not care anything about Mexican railroad projects.

Mr. Huntington's reply is not available, but it must have caused a change of heart for on March 28, 1878, Mr. Crocker wrote:

In relation to building the road between Yuma and Maricopa Wells [in Arizona, nearly 200 miles east of Yuma], I would say that no contractor can build that road as cheaply as we can build it. I will try to find out what some responsible party will undertake that work for you for. As I said before, I want no interest in it, at least not until I am out of debt.

Crocker's later letters, however, show a deep interest in the road. The company had started to build east through Arizona on November 19, 1878, and on May 17, 1879, he wrote that business was increasing rapidly on the Southern Pacific line of Arizona. On the 10th, there were 70 cars at Maricopa Wells loaded with freight waiting for teams to carry it away. An auction sale of town lots by the company had realized $10,000 the "first pop" and prospects were bright.

In a letter of April 13, 1879, Mr. Crocker told Mr. Huntington that he had just completed the organization of the Southern Pacific in New Mexico, using the articles of incorporation that Mr. Huntington had sent. The capital stock was $10,000,000.

Mr. Huntington spent much of his time at Washington during the years 1876 through 1878 and almost every day would write or wire to his colleagues:

Scott's political friends do not expect to pass his T. & P. bill this winter. Has largest lobby in Washington ever known, two hundred men, many of them ex-members of railroad committees of Senate and House . . . Shall endeavor to get a report from the Senate Committee in favor of our bill next Monday . . . Am having a rough time in Washington this winter . . . It looks as though all our enemies from California, and Tom Scott and all his friends here and elsewhere, are united to pass his bill, but I think not . . .

T. Scott's bill laid on the table . . . Scott making an ugly fight and doing more mean things than I had supposed any one man could be guilty of . . .

Returned from Washington Saturday morning nearer used up than I ever was before in my life. Shall return there to-morrow night . . . Being attacked by Scott with all his energy. He has a strong hold on the press, and Cohen sending false telegrams . . . Have against us the worst fight our enemies can make . . . Just returned from Washington. It looks as though the devil, the commissioners, and the Pennsylvania Railroad had united against us . . . Scott at my house last night, may arrange a meeting of the S. P. and T. & P. on the east line of Arizona . . . Have agreed with Scott to meet 100 miles west of El Paso. Arrangements nearly complete . . .

Just had an interview with Job Brown, Scott's man who brought a letter from Scott which I cannot accept. He desires permanent control over the whole line . . .

The Committee [Senate Railroad] met in my rooms last night and worked on a bill until one o'clock this morning, and I expect them here again to-night . . . I am striving very hard to get a bill in such shape that we can accept it . . Returned from Washington last night Mar. 15, 1878, and am about tired out.

In February, 1878, Mr. Huntington appeared before the Senate Railroad Committee in Washington to answer questions and to defend the policy of the Southern Pacific Railroad Company. The proceedings of this discussion are preserved in a 48-page Government document and reveal a masterly exposition of the subject and an almost unanswerable argument.

Mr. Huntington spoke of the physical difficulties in the construction of the Southern Pacific: crossing three mountain ranges, 200 miles of dry desert, excavating twenty tunnels, one of them nearly 7,000 feet in length, and yet the railroad arrived at Yuma, the point of junction, well within the time limit, only to find the Texas & Pacific 1,250 miles away. Said Mr. Huntington:

We should not be asked to wait at the Colorado River indefinitely for an embarrassed and mismanaged connecting company to build 1,250 miles to give us connection when we are ready to construct right along and willing to provide the outlet to the East for ourselves without cost to the Government . . . It is not disputed that a road built without a subsidy will do the Government business, supply those military posts, keep down the Indians, develop the mining interests, and protect our frontier quite as well as one built with a subsidy. The Southern Pacific will agree to the same provision as the Texas & Pacific in regard to Government regulation of rates, will pro-rate everything and assume the same obligation as those named by the Texas Pacific bill.

It was Mr. Huntington's contention that the part of the Texas & Pacific railroad proposed through Southern California, from Yuma to San Diego, was impracticable without entering Mexico, as shown by the survey made by the engineers of both companies:

The Texas & Pacific are asking for $40,000,000 in bonds [reduced from the original request for $100,000,000 in bonds] to build a road two hundred miles of which is needless, and six hundred miles of which we offer to build without Government aid . . . Let Col. Scott build his line across California if he pleases with his own money; we cannot complain if he does. But to give him the use of the national credit to do so would be most unfair and unjust to us; or to aid him to build any other portion of the road we offer to construct without it. At a hearing before the House Railroad Committee, January 19, 1876, Col. Scott himself declared that the line from Yuma to San Diego was impracticable.

Mr. Huntington complained that the agents of the Texas & Pacific had thought best to establish their claim by alleging something of a damaging and scandalous character against the Central Pacific and Union Pacific Companies. Said he:

Col. Scott has had his agents and attorneys rummaging for years, and ransacking everywhere on both sides of the continent for some-

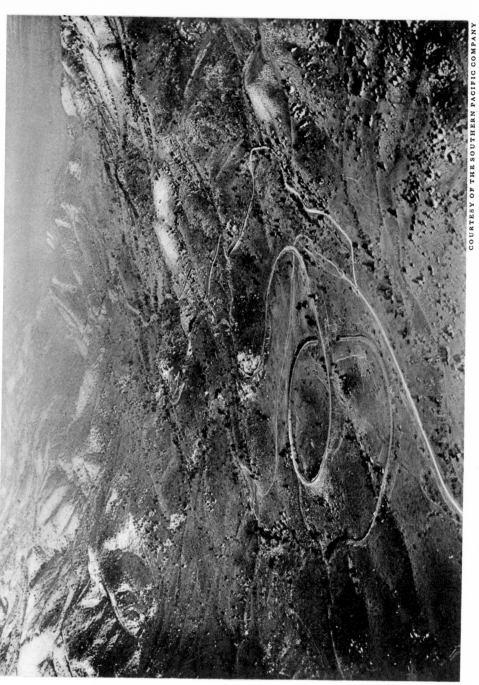

Tehachapi Loop on the Southern Pacific, Engineered by William Hood

J. H. Stobridge,
Superintendent of Construction

William Hood, Engineer

thing or other that would help his case by damaging us. Two of them have dumped in here a mass of petitions and resolutions drawn up by paid attorneys, anonymous letters, *ex parte* statements, and the rubbish of vindictive reports which sound to me preposterous and hardly worth while to follow up and refute in detail. They have come back with two sets of stories, one that we are making ourselves rich out of the Pacific Railroad by its subsidies; and the other that we are virtually bankrupt. "You pays your money, and you takes your choice."

When Mr. Huntington claimed that his company could build the road east for $32,000 per mile, he was reminded that the Central Pacific was said to have cost $116,000 per mile. Mr. Huntington admitted that this was true and described the circumstances of its construction, high mountains, war prices, snow sheds, payment in gold, etc. Then he continued:

I am quite willing to contrast this exhibit with Col. Scott and his Pennsylvania family of railroads . . . The Pennsylvania main line built under the most favorable circumstances over an easy country . . . stands charged to-day at over $400,000 per mile. And yet Col. Scott's agents have the effrontery to complain to you that the Pacific railroads built as I have described, have cost something over $116,000 a mile! Why, his little piece of road over the flat country between here [Washington] and Baltimore stands charged at over $100,000 a mile!

The claim that the bill of the Texas & Pacific would create a railroad from ocean to ocean to compete with the first transcontinental road, while the Southern Pacific would not be a competing road came up for discussion. Of competition as a railroad policy Mr. Huntington had this to say:

It seems to be assumed that competition, which may be called a state of war of capital, is a good thing in itself, and is to be promoted and intensified by Acts of Legislature. This is as much as to say that it is desirable that through traffic on railroads should be done at a loss, which must be made good out of local traffic or the capital embarked in railroads should go without remuneration. Is either of these doctrines desirable, as a matter of fact? And, if it were desirable, is it, I ask, any part of the province and function of Government to set capitalists to warring upon one another's property by stimulated competition engendered by aiding one of the parties out of the public Treasury to injure the other?

Mr. Huntington referred to the charges of Scott's agents against himself in their efforts to convince the Committee that he was not the man to be trusted to build a railroad for the people. Said Mr. Huntington:

This does not much disturb me, but I think it would be unfair and unfortunate for the cause of truth and justice if the Committee were to allow any prejudice to influence its decisions, simply because I happen to represent one corner of the issue . . . I hope the fact that I happen to have an interest in the Southern Pacific, and also an interest in the Central Pacific companies and have been asked to represent the former before this Committee will not be allowed to injure my friends who have put their labors and fortunes into those great works; and I hope it may not be allowed to blind your eyes to the real and only question before you, namely: Can this 32d parallel road be brought to a speedy completion without resort to the pledge of national credit? And if so, how can it best be brought about?

Huntington revealed that the destination was New Orleans if the Southern Pacific constructed a line east from Yuma:

This work in California has cost the Southern Pacific a large amount of money. Now the company asks to build on east . . . Those roads in California pay pretty well, but not as well as they will when the eastern through connection is made . . . If we undertake it, we are satisfied it will be done, and we shall have a first class route between San Francisco and New Orleans.

At that time Fort Yuma was a military post on the west bank of the Colorado River while the population and traffic were centered on the opposite bank in Arizona. This was the natural point for a bridge to cross the river according to all engineers who examined it. Recognizing this, the Texas & Pacific on October 18, 1876, while the west end of their track was still over twelve hundred miles away, was granted permission by the military authorities to break ground on the reservation for the crossing of the Texas & Pacific over the Colorado River. On November 27, this permission was revoked by General McDowell, who commanded the Military Division of the Pacific, until the decision of the War Department had been received.

On April 11, 1877, about a month before the Southern Pacific Railroad had reached Yuma, the company was granted permission by the Secretary of War to carry their road provisionally through a corner of the reservation, as shown by a map, subject to the condition that a right-of-way be granted by Congress; if refused, the track was to be removed from the reservation and the road abandoned. A like permission was granted the Texas & Pacific at the same time. The T. & P. protested this grant to the S. P. and on September 1, 1877, the Secretary of War suspended all authority granted either company until Congress should have determined the controversy.

This order was modified on September 6, to permit the Southern Pacific to continue its work within the limits of the reservation to the extent of preventing waste and injury to their property and opening the way to the passage of steamboats. Under this modification the Southern proceeded to complete its bridge, lay a track, and by September 30, trains were carrying passengers to the Arizona shore. The War Department then ordered the running of trains to be stopped until Congress had decided the controversy.[2]

This action gave rise to a barrage of complaints from citizens in Southern California and Arizona that mails were delayed, business deranged, time was lost, etc. On October 8, 1877, Mr. Huntington called on the President and explained the situation to such good effect that the next day the President authorized the Southern Pacific to run their trains across the bridge into Arizona, and likewise gave his approval to building the Southern Pacific east through Arizona.

Chiefly as a result of Mr. Huntington's strenuous efforts, the Scott bill for subsidy bonds was finally defeated. The Huntington bill for the land grants suffered a similar fate. As soon as this defeat was assured, the construction of the Southern Pacific Railroad was started east across Arizona on November 19, 1878, and was vigorously conducted. Mr. Huntington's foresight had already procured a charter from the Legislature of Arizona for the Southern Pacific Railroad Company of Arizona; and Charles Crocker, early in 1879, organized the Southern Pacific Railroad Company of New Mexico.

The construction forces followed the line as surveyed by the Texas & Pacific Company, and this was the cause of an unique lawsuit instituted by the Texas & Pacific in the U. S. District Court of Santa Fé, New Mexico, in 1881. That company calmly claimed that the Southern Pacific had kindly built for them a road through Arizona and New Mexico upon a right-of-way granted by Congress which they appreciated, and of which they now demanded possession. Each side was represented by a brilliant staff of lawyers, and on November

26, 1881, Jay Gould having succeeded Scott, an agreement was reached by the two executives of the companies, the famous Huntington-Gould agreement which settled the dispute over the right-of-way, and made provision for the joint use of the track to El Paso.[3]

The Southern Pacific reached the Rio Grande May 19, 1881, and El Paso welcomed its first train. The Texas & Pacific never built west of Sierra Blanca, about 200 miles east of El Paso. From that point west all land grants were cancelled.[4]

The Galveston, Harrisburg & San Antonio Railway, in which Huntington had purchased an interest for the Southern Pacific, reached San Antonio on February 6, 1877, continued west and met the Southern Pacific near the Pecos River on January 12, 1883, and a new transcontinental line connected the two oceans.[5]

The Southern Pacific in Texas and Louisiana was composed of a number of separately organized railroad properties, largely inefficient due to lack of capital. One of these was the New Orleans, Opelousas & Great Western which was sold to Charles Morgan on July 31, 1869. Morgan began operation of this line in conjunction with a fleet of steamers, which by the end of 1873, numbered seventeen vessels in active service. This fleet was then one of the most important factors in the commerce of the Gulf of Mexico. Charles Morgan died in 1878, but a year before his death, he consolidated his various railroads into the Louisiana & Texas Railroad and Steamship Company. This company with its fleet was purchased by Mr. Huntington in 1883 for the Southern Pacific, and passenger service was inaugurated between New Orleans and New York in 1885.[6]

The through line from New Orleans to San Francisco was composed of the Central Pacific and its parts, and the various divisions of the Southern Pacific as follows:

I. MAIN LINE

Morgan's Louisiana & Texas Railroad & Steamship Co.	300 miles
Louisiana Western Railroad	141 miles
Texas & New Orleans Railroad	374 miles
Galveston, Harrisburg & San Antonio Railway	917 miles
Southern Pacific Railroad of California	2,711 miles
Southern Pacific Railroad of Arizona	393 miles
Southern Pacific Railroad of New Mexico	167 miles
	5,003 miles

II. DIVISION

Carson & Colorado Railway	300 miles
Galveston, Houston & Northern Railway Co.	56 miles
Gila Valley, Globe & Northern Railway Co.	126 miles
Gulf, Western Texas & Pacific Railway Co.	111 miles
Houston, East & West Texas Railway Co.	191 miles
Houston & Shreveport Railroad Co.	39 miles
Houston & Texas Central Railroad Co.	670 miles
Iberia & Vermilion Railroad Co.	16 miles
New York, Texas & Mexican Railway Co.	122 miles
California & Oregon Railroad Co.	670 miles
Southern Pacific Coast Railway Co.	101 miles
San Antonio & Arkansas Pass Railway Co.	687 miles
	3,089 miles
Central Pacific Railway Co.	1,349 miles
TOTAL MILAGE OF RAILROADS[7]	9,441 miles

Numerous difficulties arose out of these separate units and it became important to have them united under one company. To achieve this end, the State of California and the

U. S. Congress were in turn requested to grant a charter of consolidation of all these roads in one system. The Legislature of California influenced by the cry of "Monopoly!" refused the request and besought the Congress to do likewise.

Not to be outdone, Mr. Huntington went to Kentucky in whose railroads he had interests at that time, and on March 17, 1884, an Act to incorporate the Southern Pacific Company was approved by the Governor of that state. A formal organization was effected August 14, 1884, with the unanimous approval of the stockholders; and on October 6 of that year, the Board of Directors met to raise the capital stock from $1,000,000 to $100,000,000.[8] The new company took over by lease for a term of ninety-nine years all the lines owned by the Central Pacific Company and proceeded to operate the whole as one complete unified system.[9]

The Southern Pacific System then extended from Portland, Oregon, through California and across Arizona, New Mexico and Texas to New Orleans; and from San Francisco to Ogden, Utah, a distance of 9,000 or more miles, with 16,000 miles of water transportation, the greatest system of its kind in the United States. It was said to possess the most complete monopoly, superior to any other railway system in the country. The strength of the position of the company and its prospects is thus described by Sir C. Rivers Wilson in a report of 1884 to stockholders of the Central Pacific in England:

With great skill the promoters of these lines have acquired for their properties a strategical position which almost defies competition . . . It is undeniable that if the S. P. had not fully occupied the ground in California, other companies would have done so. In support of this statement I may add that 277 companies have been incorporated at different times to build railroads in California none of which under-takings have come to maturity on account of the enterprise of the promoters of the Southern Pacific.

The consolidation brought a torrent of criticism and abuse from the Opposition. An anti-monopoly mass meeting was held at Union Hall, but nothing could be done of course. The newspapers were bitter in their protests and denunciations, much of their indignation being due to the fact that Mr. Huntington had circumvented them and gained legal endorsement of his plan. The Opposition stormed:

The Southern Pacific Company is a fraudulent and predacious concern got up to perpetrate the control of the dishonest directors of the Central Pacific Railroad Company, and to absorb the profits of that and other companies by fraudulent leases . . . By their omnibus lease and the lease of the Central Pacific they have practically all the roads in the State under a foreign corporation, the Southern Pacific Company which is under control of an individual whose greed has no limit . . .

To prevent the competition designed by Congress in granting aid to the Texas & Pacific, the managers of the Central Pacific have leased that road for ninety-nine years to the owners of the Southern Pacific Railroad Company and both roads put under common management in direct hostility to the beneficent policy of Congress. It substitutes consolidation and monopoly for competition and freedom of trade . . .

However, from the more discriminating there were many expressions of satisfaction and approval for the new trans-continental line even before consolidation took place. The The *Argonaut* for March 31, 1883, said:

These railroad builders gave us the Central Pacific connection with the eastern system, and at a reduced price enabled us to make the transit of the continent in six days. Now they have builded us another complete and entire national steel highway to connect the Bay of San Francisco with the Gulf of Mexico, and by that accomplishment have brought us the trade of an empire . . . Arizona with its treasures is our suburb, New Mexico and Utah send us their trade. It has breathed the breath of life under the ribs of death in Southern California. It has given the counties of Los Angeles and San Bernadino prosperity, wealth, and population. It has given every grain grower in our great valleys a cheaper mode of transportation to the Liverpool markets than was afforded by God who gave to merchants and their ships free traffic over His unmonopolized billowy highway.

On the same date an item appeared in the *California Spirit of the Times*:

Freight is now being brought from New York to San Francisco in fifteen days via the Morgan Line and the Southern Pacific Railroad from New Orleans . . . The object of the railroad people in their proposed railroad consolidation is for the very purpose of furnishing greater facilities to the people of this coast in the carrying business, cheapening the rates for freight and lessening the time of delivery. But the request was refused in response to fanatics on this coast who are so bigoted in their insane hatred of the railroad they would mulct the people in heavy damages rather than grant the railroad a concession.

In an address at the annual meeting of the American Bankers' Association in 1881, Lloyd Tevis, a loyal friend of the railroad company, said:

Despite all the jealousy that their acquisitions may have excited, there is no doubt that it has been on the whole good for California that the railroad management has been thus concentrated. Railroad development has been more regular and thorough and healthy, and economy in building and operating much greater than it would have been in the hands of a dozen different companies, each working independently and perhaps at cross purposes and each maintaining a separate staff and wasting means in opposition and rivalry, which the public at large must ultimately make up.

Of the enormous sums thus saved by a single intelligent and harmonious management, the portion taken by those men for their own personal purposes amounts to an insignificant percentage. And after all is said of their colossal wealth, it still remains true that they have used this wealth but as trustees for the whole community. The profits of the roads have not merely been larger than they would have been under diverse management, but these profits and credit that have been acquired have been used in building more roads.

At the annual meeting of the Southern Pacific stockholders at San Francisco, April 9, 1890, C. P. Huntington was elected to the presidency to succeed Leland Stanford who had been the president since the organization of the Central Pacific in 1862.

This change in the administration has been attributed by some writers to Huntington's love of power and his desire for vengeance because Stanford failed to support A. A. Sargent in his race for United States Senator in 1884, but accepted the nomination for himself and was elected.

For several years, however, Stanford had been so occupied with private interests, his university, his stables and race track (which Huntington jocularly referred to as "Stanford's Circus"), his vineyards and Senatorial duties that he had paid little attention to the railroad, at the same time to maintain these enterprises, he had drawn more funds from the treasury than the other associates combined.

On March 7, 1883, Charles Crocker had written to Mr. Huntington, "Governor Stanford seems to be withdrawing from the railroad business." On March 23 of the same year, he wrote:

I fully agree with you that Stanford did not do right in selling his bonds the way he did . . . When I see you, I will tell you of a good many things that are occurring constantly which prove to me that we have either got to see our interests differently or gradually separate.

The situation became so serious that on February 28, 1890, representatives of the Hopkins and Crocker interests met with Huntington and Stanford in New York, and an agreement was reached whereby Huntington was to become president of the company at the next annual meeting and a new board of directors was to be appointed.[10]

On May 29, 1922, a decision of the Supreme Court of the United States directed that the control of the Central Pacific Railway Company by the Southern Pacific Company, either by stock ownership or by lease, be terminated in accordance with the Sherman Anti-trust Law of 1890. The people of California opposed this decision and the Southern Pacific filed with the Supreme Court a petition for a rehearing, arguing that the dismemberment of the Southern Pacific System would not only be unjust and inequitable to that company but would be a calamity from the point of view of the people of California. It is most interesting to compare the arguments against consolidation in 1884, with those against dismemberment in 1922. The arguments against the un-merger won and the Supreme Court reversed its decision.[11]

Chapter XXXVIII

WATER TRANSPORTATION

WHEN THE BUILDERS of the Central Pacific and Southern Pacific reached coast lines with their railroads, they were not content to stop there, but extended the service by watercraft to farther ports, even to Yokohama and Hong Kong on the Pacific and to New York on the Atlantic. These extensions were made, (1) by purchase of vessels in connection with purchased railroad lines; (2) by contract with a steamship line already in operation; and (3) by founding a steamship line of their own.

FERRYBOATS

In 1868-1869, the Central Pacific Railroad Company gained control of the San Francisco, Oakland & Alameda Railroads together with their ferryboats that operated across the San Francisco Bay between San Francisco and Oakland. There were six of them at the time, the *Contra Costa, Oakland, Alameda, Washoe, San Antonio,* and *Louise*; the last three had been converted into ferryboats from Sacramento River steamers. The first ferryboat built by the Central Pacific was the *El Capitan* which began the run in 1868.

The first overland passenger train to reach Oakland was on September 8, 1869. It was met at the wharf by the *Ala-*

meda, and the passengers transported to San Francisco. The first ferry that transferred cars from one side of the Bay to the other was the *Thoroughfare*, built in 1871. It was 248 feet in length and 1,012 gross tonnage, with a capacity for eighteen of the small freight cars then in use, and pens for sixteen carloads of stock. The car ferry operated from the Oakland Long Wharf to the foot of Second Street in San Francisco. The largest car ferry ever to operate on San Francisco Bay was the *Sacramento* built many years later by the Southern Pacific Company.

On January 22, 1882, the Oakland Pier, or Mole, as it was usually called, opened with large train sheds to take care of passenger traffic; the Long Wharf being used thereafter exclusively for freight. The Mole was constructed by filling in an embankment to replace the pier trestle. The large passenger ferryboat *Piedmont*, began service on November 28, 1883, from this Mole.[1]

The following "Ferry Tale" was related many years later by a veteran employee of the Southern Pacific Company:

One day there walked into the office of A. N. Towne, General Manager, a young man who presented a letter signed by Collis P. Huntington in which he asked Towne to "put this man to work." Towne gave the youth an examination to find out where he would fit in, and discovered that he was a natural misfit. He knew nothing except that Mr. Huntington was a distant relative of his father and had promised to take care of him.

Mr. Towne told him to call the next day. In the meantime he telegraphed to Mr. Huntington protesting that the lad was not fitted for anything. The reply came back, "Put him to work." When he showed up the next day, Towne told him that he was on the payroll as the official "Seagull Enumerator," and his duties would be to travel on the ferries and count the seagulls that followed the boat, and turn in a report at the end of the month. Other provision was made for him later, but not before he had turned in three monthly reports; at the foot of each he had written: "The birds look so nearly all alike after the first hour, that I may have counted some of them twice."[2]

This is said to be the only occasion known in which C. P. Huntington authorized the spending of money foolishly.

CALIFORNIA STEAM NAVIGATION COMPANY

This company was organized on March 1, 1854, with a capital stock of $2,500,000 and began operations on the Sacramento and San Joaquin rivers with a large number of steamboats. In 1856, two steamers left San Francisco and two left Sacramento each day to carry passengers and freight.[3]

This steamship company was acquired by the California Pacific Railroad Company which had been organized in January 1865, to extend from Vallejo to Sacramento via Davisville. The railroad was purchased April 1, 1871, by the Central Pacific Company and at the same time the steamship company was purchased for $620,000 by the four associates. This is best told by Mr. Huntington himself.

We bought those steamers with the California Pacific. I did that trading myself. I bought the California Pacific, and with it I bought the California Steam Navigation Company's steamers. We used them between Sacramento and San Francisco, and between San Francisco and Stockton on the San Joaquin River. We used some of the steamers between San Francisco and Oakland.

We did not buy the steamers for the Central Pacific, but the four of us owned a large majority of the stock on an individual purchase. The California Pacific had bought the California Steam Navigation Company.[4]

The report of the Central Pacific for 1872 listed twenty-five steamers of which the *Capital*, 1,625 gross tons, and the *Yosemite*, 1,272 gross tons, were the largest. The chief cargo for the river steamers was wheat of which 20,000,000 bushels were grown in the Sacramento and San Joaquin Valleys in 1872.

PACIFIC MAIL STEAMSHIP COMPANY

The Pacific Mail Steamship Company[5] was chartered by a special Act of the Legislature of the State of New York passed in April, 1848, and aided by an United States Government contract for carrying the mail. Mail contracts were made also later with Mexico and the following Central American Republics: Gautemala, Honduras, Costa Rica, Nicaragua, and Salvador.

The company ran their ships on five lines: (1) between New York and Aspinwall; (2) Panama and various Central American ports: (3) Panama and various Mexican ports: (4) Panama and San Francisco, extending later its service to Astoria, Oregon; and (5) San Francisco to Yokohama and Hong Kong. The connection between the Pacific Mail line on the Atlantic with that on the Pacific was made by contract with the Panama Railroad Company.[6]

When the Pacific Railroad opened to the Atlantic in 1869, it offered keen competition to the Pacific Mail which had dominated the East and West transportation by way of the isthmus. Unrestricted competition would have been ruinous for both companies, so a compromise was effected. In 1871, the Central Pacific and the Union Pacific adopted the policy of contracting for a certain amount of freight capacity on the San Francisco steamers. This arrangement not proving satisfactory to the Pacific Mail, the company announced that no longer would it issue bills of lading between the Orient and the Atlantic Coast via the railroads; the steamships from the Orient would thereafter make only a brief call at San Francisco to discharge local freight and would go on to Panama and send their through freight over the Panama Railroad and the Company's Atlantic line to New York.

As a result of this decision by the Pacific Mail, the two railroad companies organized the Occidental and Oriental Steamship Company in 1874. Three steamers were chartered from the White Star Line, the *Oceanic*, *Belgic* and *Gaelic*, to ply between San Francisco and the Far East. This brought the Pacific Mail to terms and in 1875, the company signed a contract with the railroads.[7]

Of this contract Collis Potter Huntington wrote to Mark Hopkins on March 4, 1875:

You will see by the telegrams in the California papers this morning that there has been an arrangement between PMSS and the railroads which I hope will benefit the Central Pacific. Like many other things, this was mostly brought about by Jay Gould in the interest of his stock speculation. He and Dillon have been urging me for several days, and some of the large stockholders of the PMSS for several months, to go in on the PM board, but I have steadily refused, mainly because most of the stock is held by speculators. But we have so long an interest that could be affected by what that company could do, that I have sometimes thought it would be well for us to have someone on that board, and so I telegraphed Stanford yesterday to find out what you all thought of it. Nearly all the newspaper articles here on Pacific Mail and Union Pacific are from Jay Gould and are to help him in his stock speculations, and there have been so many [articles] of late puffing up U. P. stock that I am inclined to think he is preparing to unload that stock and that of the Pacific Mail.

Mr. Huntington wrote another letter to Mark Hopkins on this subject, April 19, 1875:

As to combination freight and passenger control with the Union Pacific and the Pacific Mail, I do not like to have Jay Gould control the Pacific Mail and the Union Pacific, but as such is the fact, I shall endeavor to do the best I can for the Central Pacific, and we must be prepared for his doing almost any outrageous thing that will injure our through business.

Gould had purchased large blocks of Union Pacific stock and became a director of that road in 1874. He remained in control of that company until 1878. He was recognized as a speculator in railroads for the sheer purpose of making money. Huntington was an actual builder of railroads, always striving for the development of the country by railroad construction; hence his reluctance to enter into any combination with Gould.

About a year later Gould urged Mr. Huntington to have the Central Pacific join with the Union Pacific in purchasing the Pacific Mail. In a letter to Mr. Hopkins, April 6, 1876, Mr. Huntington wrote:

Pacific Mail is in trouble, and it would be a good time to take it into camp if we had the right parties to work with. I think the whole concern could be controlled for $1,500,000.

The debts of the Pacific Mail at that time amounted to more than $2,000,000, past due, and among the last acts of the retiring board was the execution of $2,000,000 in bonds secured by a mortgage on all the property of the company, and the delivery of those bonds as security for the company's indebtedness and liabilities.[8]

On April 9, 1876, Mr. Huntington wrote to Mr. Hopkins in regard to those bonds:

I agree with you that it is better that we have nothing to do with Pacific Mail if it can be avoided. I spoke to Dillon about getting other parties to go on bond. He said he had not time, and further, that Pacific Mail had been here since they controlled it in the interest of the Central Pacific and Union Pacific, which is to a certain extent true. They have put into my hands $100,000 security for your going on those bonds. They are a part of 2,000 secured by mortgage of like amount on ten iron steamers said to be all the iron steamers that belong to Pacific Mail.

On April 31, 1876, Mr. Huntington sent the following dispatch to Mr. Hopkins:

Have 100 Pacific Mail bonds as security. They say they will get steamships insured as additional security if you wanted it. [The answer was: Have steamships insured.]

In the spring of 1876 the Panama Railroad Company terminated its contract with the Pacific Mail Company for the reasons given in the Report of B. Mosely, General Superintendent of the Panama Railroad, March 21, 1876:

The irregular running of the Pacific Mail steamers and the delay occurring to through freight in consequence thereof, and the heavy and numerous losses of packages of goods and valuables that were occurring here and there, seriously prejudiced shippers against us and created a bad feeling with the steamship lines connecting here.

The new board of directors for the Pacific Mail in the spring of 1876, were compelled, in order to save the company, to raise the necessary funds by their own personal credit, the property of the company having already been mortgaged. They were aided liberally by the President of the Panama Railroad Company. The directors removed all attachments against the company and resumed the interrupted business between New York and California, by arrangement with the Pacific Transit Company securing thereby the privileges under which the fleets of the two companies operated in harmony.[9]

On August 6, 1877, an agreement was made between the Pacific Mail and the Union Pacific and Central Pacific Railroad Companies whereby the steamship company should run two through lines of steamers per month between New York and San Francisco each way, and furnish room for 1,400 tons of freight from New York to San Francisco, and 1,500 tons of freight from San Francisco to New York. In return the two railroad companies guaranteed the steamship company $27,000 per month upon freight from San Francisco to New York, and $42,000 for freight from New York to San Francisco and points beyond.[10]

Mr. Huntington became a member of the board of directors of the Pacific Mail in 1880, acquiring only a few shares of stock just to qualify him to act as a director in the interest of the railroads. At the same time he disclaimed doing any harm to the steamship company.[11] He was a director from 1880 and became president of the company May 31, 1893. Reports for the year 1894 and later, after Mr. Huntington became president, when compared with earlier reports show a remarkable improvement in the management of the company, its physical condition, and financial standing. The company improved steadily and in 1899, two dividends of one and one-half per cent each amounting to $600,000 were paid June 1, and December 1, on the outstanding stock of the company.[12]

OCCIDENTAL & ORIENTAL STEAMSHIP COMPANY

The Occidental & Oriental Steamship Company[13] was organized in November 1874 by Leland Stanford, Charles Crocker, Mark Hopkins, Lloyd Tevis, and David D. Colton, with a capital stock of $10,000,000. Three steamers, the *Oceanic, Belgic,* and *Gaelic* were chartered from the White Star Line and put on the route between San Francisco and the Orient.

While the opening of the Suez Canal in 1869, had cut off much of the commerce from the Orient that the Pacific Railroads had expected, yet there was sufficient traffic to warrant regular sailings and a through route to the Orient was considered of great importance to both the Central Pacific and the Union Pacific Railroads.

In December, 1873, Charles Crocker, as agent for the Central Pacific Company, and accompanied by Major R. P. Hammond, sailed for India, China, and Japan via the Suez Canal. The object of this trip was, as he expressed it in a telegram to A. A. Sargent, "to ascertain what commerce can be developed for our country and diverted to and over our road from these countries, and also immigration from Europe." Crocker was absent 18 months.

As has been stated, this threat of competition was effective in bringing the Pacific Mail to terms, and a contract was effected between the two steamship companies in June, 1875, whereby each line agreed to perform a monthly service from San Francisco across the Pacific with alternate sailings every fifteen days. Agencies for the two lines were the same at the ports of Yokohama and Hong Kong, and the steamers of the two lines used the same wharf at San Francisco.

While Mr. Huntington was not a director of the Occidental & Oriental Steamship Company, his letters reveal not only his deep interest in the company, but the fact that he exerted great influence in its policies. The letters of his associates to him show, also, that few things were undertaken in connection with this line as well as with the Pacific Mail without first consulting him.

A letter to Mr. Huntington from Charles F. Crocker, vice-president and general manager of the O. & O. on October 18, 1881, told something about the growth of traffic on this line:

We have agents now at Amoy, Singapore, Manila, and Calcutta, as well as Shanghai and local Japanese ports which are taken care of in our interests by the local Japanese Steamship Company . . . I believe our business would be increased by putting on more steamers . . . Mr. Ismay of the White Star Line is so sure of success, in case this line were enlarged and more steamers employed, that his firm would be willing to let us have their steamers on joint account with them instead of chartering them . . .

In November of that same year, Mr. Haswell, agent at Hong Kong, and Mr. Emery, agent at Yokohama, each wrote a letter to emphasize the fact that trade had grown to such an extent as to be beyond their capabilities to grapple with; and they warned that unless the expansion of the line kept pace with the traffic growth, it would soon pass out of their hands.

The company added a vessel to its fleet from time to time as needed. During its period of service from 1875 to 1908, the O. & O. employed nine steamers, eight from the White Star Line and one from the Pacific Improvement Company. The company was successful and profitable beyond expectations.

THE MORGAN LINE

Charles Morgan, in 1835, sent the S.S. *Columbia* into the Gulf waters on the route from New Orleans to Galveston. Other steamers followed and he soon had a regular line plying between these points. From Galveston the line radiated to Vera Cruz and another line from New Orleans ran to Mobile. Morgan with Arnold Harris established the Texas & New Orleans Mail Line.

At the close of the Civil War, Morgan picked up several steamers at auction and started the Morgan Line from New York to New Orleans. On May 25, 1869, he purchased the New Orleans, Opelousas & Great Western Railroad for $2,050,000. He operated this road in conjunction with his fleet of steamers, which, by 1873, numbered seventeen vessels in active service. This fleet was then one of the most important factors in the commerce of the Gulf of Mexico.

Morgan acquired two short Texas railroad lines, and secured control of the Houston & Texas Central Railroad, 505 miles in length. A year before his death in 1878, he organized Morgan's Louisiana & Texas Railroad and Steamship Company as a holding company for his various lines.[14]

In 1883, Mr. Huntington purchased those lines with their steamships for the Southern Pacific Railroad Company from the Morgan heirs for $7,500,000, which Mr. Huntington said was a bargain, and they became an integral part of the Southern Pacific System. In 1885, passenger service was inaugurated between New York and New Orleans, New York and Galveston, and New Orleans and Havana. Four largé vessels were built at Mr. Huntington's own shipyard in Newport News, Virginia, and others at yards in Philadelphia and

Wilmington. Auxiliary to the twenty steamships, the Morgan Line owned barges, tugs and ferryboats which operated exclusively in the harbors of the ports mentioned.

The acquisition of the Morgan Line with its fleet of steamships was the crowning glory of the Sunset Route. With it a new transcontinental route was established between New York and San Francisco, and it was not controlled by a hostile company. Surely Mr. Huntington was entitled to an immense satisfaction from the contemplation of that piece of work, and a keen elation from its success.

It was soon recognized by the country at large that in the carrying trade, the Southern Pacific with its Sunset Route and the Morgan Line offered a more advantageous connection than its rival lines over the Panama Railroad and around Cape Horn.

Chapter XXXIX

FEDERAL LAND GRANTS

By 1850, the United States Government owned approximately one and a half billion acres of land acquired in various ways as follows: (1) ceded by the Indians; (2) from individual states; (3) Louisiana and Florida purchases; and (4) by treaty with Mexico. Portions of this land were used by the Government to aid in the building of wagon roads and canals and in the construction of railroads.[1]

Congress, by the Act of July 2, 1864, amending the Act of July 1, 1862, granted to the Central Pacific Railroad Company, the ten odd-numbered sections of land per mile on each side of the road and within the limits of twenty miles of the track with the exception of mineral lands, not including iron and coal, and not already pre-empted or sold.

To acquire these lands the railroad company was required, as soon as the route of the road had been determined to file a map of the route in the Department of the Interior, the Secretary of the Interior then to withdraw from sale all lands within the railroad grant. Upon the completion of twenty consecutive miles of road, the lands would be surveyed and a patent issued to the railroad company.

In theory, the Central Pacific was granted 12,800 acres per mile for its 742 miles between Sacramento and Ogden, amounting to 9,497,600 acres. By consolidation with the

California & Oregon Railroad the Central Pacific acquired a further right of 291 miles, or 3,742,800 acres, a total of 13,240,400 acres. Could the company have realized even the lowest price $1.25 per acre on that amount of land, the grant would truly have been an aid in the construction of its railroad. However, many thousand acres in the area of the grant were unavailable due to the deductions of mineral lands, private claims, pre-emptions and homesteads, Indian reservations and bordering lakes. Much of the land was arid and without sale value, and hundreds of acres were inaccessible in mountain regions. The Opposition had much to say and frequently as to the immense value of these land grants. In 1876, however, C. P. Huntington had a bill introduced in Congress whereby the Central Pacific Railroad Company proposed to return these lands to the Government if allowed one dollar per acre for them, as a part of a sinking fund to be established toward paying the debt which was not due for fifteen years. Had these lands been so valuable that was a good offer, but Congress rejected the proposal.[2]

A letter from Mr. Huntington to Philetus Sawyer, Chairman of the House Committee on Pacific Railroads in May, 1874, had this to say on the subject:

For some years the expense of these lands exceeded the receipts from sales. Up to January 1, 1868, the entire receipts from sales were, in gold, $44,801.64 and the expenses to the same date were $30,-721.19. It will be seen, therefore, that during the trying time of the company's needs for construction, until 1868, the land grants were an expense rather than an aid. The company were required to pay in advance the expenses of surveying the land, also registers' and receivers' fees for listing. Under the rulings of the Interior Department for the last few years, we have had to pay many thousands of dollars for surveying and listing fees in advance, and await the pleasure of the Department for the issue of patents. Sales, as a general thing, can be made only on long credits (in most cases, five years) for eighty per cent of the purchase money. The lands were not salable at all until reached by a constructed road, so that sales could not be relied upon to realize funds in the building of the road, and the result has been that all the money derived by the railroad company from the sales of the lands up to the present [May, 1874], deducting unavoidable expenses, would not have built that one mile of its railroad in which is comprised the Summit Tunnel.

The great bulk of the lands were of no value to the Government when the grants were made, and could only become valuable by the construction of the road, and the settlement of the country along its line. The government retained one-half of the land (the even sections) within the limits of the grant, and doubled the minimum price of the even sections so that it would realize as much from sales of the half retained as it would have done for the whole if the grant of the odd sections had not been made. As the lands could not be sold to any extent until the road was built, and then only in general on long credits, in order to realize from them for the construction of the road, and to pay debts incurred in its construction in accordance with the purpose of the Act, the company mortgaged them to secure bonds issued amounting to $10,000,000. Of these the company sold and disposed of 9,153 bonds of $1,000 each at a price which averaged in gold, $7,894,345. Add to this the total amount of net cash receipts from sales of land to January 1, 1874, in gold coin, $570,-133.33, and $50,508.42 currency reduced to gold coin, $43,541.76 which equals $613,675.09. This will make the amount from sale of land and land bonds $8,505,020.09.

This is the total gold value realized up to this time from the land subsidy granted by the Government.

An announcement made by the Yreka *Journal* for February 1, 1871, stated as follows:

The document recorded at the Clerk's Office by J. Madden, Land Agent of the Central Pacific Railroad Company, is a Land Trust Mortgage from Central Pacific to Charles Crocker and Silas W.

Sanderson, executed on October 1, 1870, acknowledged before C. H. Torbelt, notary public of this state and Commissioner of Deeds for Nevada and Utah. Its object is to enable the company to raise means toward completing their San Joaquin Valley Railroad and their California & Oregon road.

The land held by the Government had been surveyed into townships six miles square; each township subdivided into 36 sections one mile square and having 640 acres; each section subdivided into four sections having 160 acres each; and again into quarter sections of 40 acres each, which was the smallest quantity sold except fractions on the borders of rivers, lakes, etc.

An applicant for land from the railroad was required to make his own selection from a map of the railroad lands in the company's land office. He then addressed a letter to the land agent requesting a copy of the application form which he was to fill in and sign. No sale of land was made until a patent for that land had been received from the Government, nor any definite contract made, but the settlers were permitted to live on the land they had selected and were given the preference when patents permitted the land to be sold.

Prices varied from $2.50 per acre up according to the land; tall timber land usually sold for $5.00, while pine lands brought $10.00 per acre. If the desired tract contained eighty acres or more, it could be bought on time contract; full payment was required for less than eighty acres or a tract covered by timber.[3]

The enemies of the Central Pacific charged repeatedly that the company refrained from patenting the land in order to avoid the payment of taxes. This the company denied, in most cases the lands listed were held months before the patent was issued and the company deposited money for surveys far in advance of its use by the Government.

An official of the Central Pacific declared in 1887 that the company had received no patent in three years and that they had applications pending for patents on surveyed land covering nearly a million acres. About that time a report was made to Congress in which it was stated that the affairs of the General Land Office had been so maladministered during the past few years that that department of the Government had virtually ceased to exist.[4]

On July 27, 1866, Congress granted the Southern Pacific Railroad Company the odd-numbered sections of land for thirty miles toward the south to meet the Texas & Pacific at Colorado River.

On January 3, 1867, the Southern Pacific filed in the General Land Office a plat designating as its route a line extending from San José through San Bernito Pass to Goshen; thence via Tehachapi Pass to a point on the Colorado River from Mohave.

On July 25, 1868, as no portion of the road had been constructed, the company procured from Congress the passage of an Act extending the time for the completion of the first thirty miles of the road until July 1, 1870, but requiring the line to be completed by July 4, 1878.

On June 28, 1870, the Southern Pacific procured from Congress the passage of a Joint Resolution instructing the Secretary to cause patents to be issued to the Southern Pacific Railroad Company for sections of land coterminous to each section of road constructed "on the route indicated by the map filed by said company in the Department of the Interior,

January 3, 1867." This is said to be the only case where a grant of 7,500,000 acres of land is claimed under a Joint Resolution of Congress.[5]

Report of B. B. Redding, Land Agent of the Southern Pacific Railroad Company for June 30, 1873, stated:

> Route of the road in this state on which the Land Department at Washington ordered the lands to be withdrawn is 480 miles long extending from San José through the San Joaquin Valley and Tehachapi Pass to the Colorado River. Reservation extends to odd-numbered sections thirty miles on each side of the road, twenty miles of which are directly granted if vacant, and where not vacant, amounts to be taken between the twenty and thirty miles to make up deficiency . . . Full amount of land grant 6,144,000 acres, one-third of which is in the San Joaquin, Tulare, and other fertile valleys. 3,000 applications have been received, 1,500 of which have already settled upon the lands enhancing the values of contiguous sections. When the patents are received, land will be graded, prices fixed, and sales ready to begin.[6]

Before the road was built, those lands could have been bought for the most part at from $1.00 to $5.00 an acre. They were worth in 1880 after the railroad had been constructed through the great valley, from $35.00 to $150.00 per acre, according to a writer of that period. Over $200,000,000 had been added to the wealth of California in taxable resources.[7]

Town after town was started and centers of business and population rapidly multiplied in the great valley of the San Joaquin, which a few years before any railroad was in sight was almost wholly given to sheep and cattle ranges. In spite of the new prosperity some of the people who stood to profit materially by the advent of the railroad were its bitterest opponents. This is illustrated by a conversation between a special correspondent to the San Francisco *Bulletin* and a man at Tulare, shingling a new house:

"Friend, what did you pay for your two acres?"

"Hundred dollars an acre," he replied.

"Will you sell for that?"

"No," was the answer.

"What was this land four years ago?"

"Could have got the whole of it for 40 cents an acre."

Something was said about railroads. With very emphatic and forceful adjectives, the man opened on them:

"Yes, sir, I am one of the immortal fourteen who voted against the railroad in San Joaquin County. It is the proudest vote I ever cast. I want my children and grandchildren to glory in it after I am gone. I am down on monopolies forever."

"Did you say you paid $100 an acre for this land?"

"Yes, I did."

"And you could have got it for 40 cents a year or two ago?"

"Yes, I could," answered the man.

"Oh, well, I'd be down on railroads, too. No business to be buying nasty sheep lands."

The man had no more to say. $500.00 an acre would not have bought his land, but he was vehemently opposed to the very instrument of his success.[8]

To the ordinary difficulties of the railroad company with their land grants, there arose from time to time, trouble with the settlers or would-be settlers. When a man settled upon railroad land and refused to conform to the requirements for becoming a settler or acknowledge the ownership of the railroad, he was not considered a settler but a squatter, an invader subject to being dispossessed either peaceably or forcibly.

Soon after the Land Agent of the Southern Pacific Railroad Company had filed a map of its route in the Department of the Interior and in the General Land Office, January 3, 1867, a large number of persons settled in the Mussel Slough district near Hanford in Tulare County. So far as can be learned they did not consult the map in the Land Office at Visalia, and they made no request for application blanks as required by the railroad company to register their selection of tracts in order to become prospective owners, but chose to disregard altogether the fact that they were occupying railroad lands.

According to the testimony of bona fide settlers in the vicinity, those persons did not enter upon the lands through any mistake but to use the land free of rent and taxes, and for speculative purposes. The settlers related that in a number of cases, the lands changed hands several times, some claims selling for as much as from $500 to $1,000, then they would move to another part of railroad land. Occasionally they would move their outfits upon the land of the settlers and order the settlers off "Government" land.[9]

Before the railroad had secured patents for its lands in this region, the squatters had sent agents to Washington to fight the railroad and in an effort to procure the lands at the lowest possible rate. On their behalf some members of Congress from California, opponents of the railroad, introduced some bills in Congress. A letter from Mr. Huntington to Mr. Hopkins, April 10, 1876, refers to these bills:

Some bills have been introduced aimed to getting the lands between Goshen and Los Gatos into the hands of settlers. Booth has introduced one which attempts to give the right on payment to the company of $2.50 per acre for odd sections. Of course, this cannot be done legally, but it is of no use to get a privilege to go into long litigation about it. Wiggington has been induced to put in one such bill; and a petition is here [Washington] from 600 settlers. He is somewhat embarrassed and quite thin-skinned about it. There is moreover a strong pressure here against railroad lands in the hands of companies. It occurs to me that some arrangement might be come to with these squatters as to the amount they shall pay the company when it is decided they are on its lands. If it is possible, get them to agree on something, even less than their value, so as to avoid litigation. Please see what can be done at once and telegraph me. It might relieve two or three California members. Just now we cannot afford to have any more enemies in Congress from the Pacific Coast.

By 1877, the railroad company had received its patent to all lands, some 230,500 acres, along the portion of the road then completed. The court held that their right had attached thereto since 1870, and all persons who had settled on railroad land since that date had no rights other than those in conformity with the railroad.[10]

When the railroad company had secured its title to the land, it offered to sell the occupied lands at Mussel Slough to the squatters who had settled there. The price per acre, however, was in advance of the listed price since the cost of the suits brought against the settlers and a rental for the years the land had been occupied had been added to the list price and the lands regraded accordingly, which brought the prices as high as from $11.00 to $35.00 per acre.[11]

This infuriated the squatters who claimed they were being charged for the improvements that they had made on the lands, their irrigation ditches, canals, etc., in opposition to the company's policy as advertised. From that time they resorted to active and hostile opposition.

Siskiyou Mountains, Shasta Route

The so-called Settlers' Land League was organized at Hanford on April 12, 1878, followed by the formation of a military squadron within the league. This squadron was placed under command of Major McQuiddy from Tennessee, who had been a major in the Confederate Army. Companies of the settlers were formed into cavalry and were drilled at night in the towns of Hanford, Grangeville, and Lemore. They patrolled the roads on horseback wearing masks.[12]

Several acts of lawlessness were perpetrated by members of this league. One dark night between twelve and one o'clock from eighty to one hundred mounted men wearing masks went to the house of Ira Hodge, who had purchased a railroad tract about five miles from Hanford. He and his family were ordered to leave the house, and it was set on fire and burned to the ground. Another newly established settler on railroad lands, Perry Phillips, by name, had his house soaked with oil and burned, leaving him and his young family homeless. There were frequent reports of masked and black-robed men calling at homes in the dead of the night and ordering the occupants to leave the district or county.[13]

That these "leaguers" gave the directors of the railroad much concern is shown by the following letter from Charles Crocker to Mr. Huntington on November 30, 1878:

I enclose herewith an account of an unlawful act performed in the Mussel Slough region, by which you can see that we are likely to have a great deal of difficulty. Mr. Jerone Madden, Land Agent for the Southern Pacific Railroad Company, tells me that sales of land have fallen off very much, and until this matter is settled, we cannot expect to receive much money from that source. I talked it over with the Governor [Stanford] this morning, and we decided that the only thing we could do was to prosecute the suits and get judgment.

A number of ejectment suits were brought in the U. S. Courts against the squatters in 1878. Final judgment was rendered against them December 15, 1879, Judge Sawyer deciding in favor of the railroad company both as to the constitutionality of the change of route, about which there was controversy, and the Joint Resolution of Congress, June 28, 1870. The squatters filed cross complaints in the U. S. District Court and lost; appealed to the U. S. Circuit Court and lost; then appealed to the U. S. Supreme Court.

On May 11, 1880, after three years of negotiation with the squatters and no compromise having been effected, an attempt was made by the United States Marshal, A. W. Poole, to dispossess certain holders of the lands and to place purchasers of the tracts thereon. They were resisted by an armed force and a battle ensued in which eight persons were killed. For this, seven Leaguers were indicted, and in the trial that followed, five men were sentenced to eight months in jail at San José and each to pay a fine of $300.00.[14]

That the Mussel Slough people were deliberate and purposeful law breakers was shown by the evidence at the trial. A feature of this resistance to law was the encouragement given by the Opposition. In April, before the battle mentioned above, the Legislature of California passed a joint resolution asking Congress for aid in behalf of a large number of "innocent settlers" on "Government land" in the Mussel Slough district in Tulare County, California, "in danger of being turned out of their homes"; to afford relief if practicable, or to procure national aid through the Attorney General in having the question of ownership determined in the Supreme Court of the United States.[15]

After the trial the Legislature passed a resolution condemning the Court for its decision and requesting the President of the United States to annul the sentence.

Another encouragement of lawlessness was the visit of Dennis Kearney of San Francisco, the Irishman of sandlot fame, who made a fiery speech in which he told the league to stay with their land and if they needed help he would come to their assistance with 40,000 strong from San Francisco and they would "murder the red-eyed monsters," at which the people applauded wildly.[16]

After the unhappy conflict, the railroad company offered to reduce the price of the land twelve and one-half per cent. Most of the settlers made application to rent hoping the Government would come to their assistance. The contracts sent out by the company contained an agreement to apply the rent for 1880 on a purchase of the land at the reduced price offered. Some of the settlers accepted this while others rejected it and continued to warn away the agents of the company. From time to time, however, they compromised until finally the dispute was settled.[17]

Another disturbing case with settlers similar to that of Mussel Slough happened some years later. Lands reserved on the Southern Pacific Railroad were the odd-numbered sections extended thirty miles on each side of the road, twenty miles of which were directly granted if vacant, and where occupied, sections were to be taken between the twenty and thirty miles to make up the deficiency. Much of the land in the twenty-mile limit was included in the old Spanish grants and others.

In 1886, Commissioner Sparks of the U. S. General Land Office decided that the railroad company had no right to claim indemnity lands in the neighborhood of Fresno County and others—and thereupon opened the disputed lands for settlement. Hundreds of settlers immediately entered upon the lands and proceeded to comply with the requirements of the Government relative to the acquisition of title in fee simple.

The railroad company protested the decision of the Land Commissioner and applied to the Secretary of the Interior for a reconsideration of the rulings, but the application was dismissed and the settlement of the land continued. As a test case the Southern Pacific instituted a suit in the Circuit Court of the United States for the southern district of California, against one of the settlers to obtain a decree declaring the title conveyed to him by the Government void and the lands held in trust by the railroad company. The suit was decided in favor of the company by Judge Ross, the latter part of July, 1893.[18]

Whereupon, the settlers on the 200,000 acres of land in the San Joaquin Valley determined to appeal to Congress for relief. A petition was sent to Washington addressed to the senators and representatives from California in which they asked: (1) a conclusive decision in the controversy between the settlers and the Southern Pacific Company; and, (2) settlers to be indemnified by the United States for their labor and money, if the case should be decided against them.[19]

The story of these settlers can be told clearly in the correspondence on the subject between Collis Potter Huntington, the Secretary of the Interior and members of the Southern Pacific Company.

On October 19, 1893, Mr. Huntington wrote to his nephew, Henry E. Huntington, at that time First Assistant in the Office of the President:

I notice that the U. S. Courts have given to the Southern Pacific Railroad Company certain lands in California that were granted to the company by Congress, and I see no other decision that the Court could have reached as the lands were granted to the company on certain conditions which were compiled with. But this seems to be one of the cases where the Government made a great mistake in allowing, or rather inviting settlers to go on after it had parted with all its rights in the land.

As in this case, the settlers do not seem to be to blame in going on and occupying the lands as they did, and as our own Government rarely, if ever, right a wrong, therefore I hope you will be very careful that the railroad company does not charge them for their improvements, but lets them have the lands at the same price that the company would have sold them for before they were occupied. In the case of the people who went on the lands innocently, I would almost recommend a greater concession, but the lands are mortgaged, and the mortgage bonds have been sold, and are widely scattered, not only in this country, but over Europe. Up to this time the parties who built this road have received nothing from it, but hope to be at some future day when the bonded indebtedness can be reduced, or the volume of business so increased that those who have their money in the share-capital will receive something on their investment.

I hope you will manage this so as not to have it a precedent to those going on the lands with the full knowledge that they belong to the railroad company, as they have done in some cases heretofore. But at the same time be very careful that innocent occupants —that is, those who believe they could get a title from the Government—are not harmed, always keeping in view in these transactions between the railroad and the settlers that it is better to give a little more than we ought to give than to take more than we have any righ to receive.

This is a subject on which there is much I would like to say, but I really have not the time. I have raised the question with you, however, and you, I think, can fully comprehend what I wish done.

Letter from Jerome Madden, Land Agent, to Mr. C. P. Huntington, President, Southern Pacific Company, November 9, 1893:

On receipt of your letter of recent date to Mr. H. E. Huntington, to the effect that settlers on the company's indemnity lands should be treated with as much leniency as the company's interests would permit, the Board of Directors here took up the matter with this office and with the company's law department.

After a very careful consideration of the subject, I was directed to put the result of their conclusions in the form of a circular which was approved by them. I now enclose several copies of it, dated November 10, 1893, for your information. From it you will see that a reduction of twenty five per cent below the graded value of lands will be made except that no land will be sold for less than $2.00 per acre, this concession being limited to ninety days from the date of the circular, and applying only to persons who filed in the U. S. Land Office prior to July 24, 1893, the date upon which the U. S. Circuit Court at Los Angeles rendered a decision in favor of the company in the Juana C. Araiza case. A settlement with adverse claimants made in accordance with the provision of the circular will prevent an appeal to the Courts in their cases, and the uncertainty of a final judicial determination of the matter; and it will also, I believe, have the effect of settling many of the suits that have already been instituted. I think the company will receive an average price of from $2.50 to $3.00 per acre for the lands.

Letter from C. P. Huntington to the Honorable Hoke Smith, Secretary of the Interior, November 14, 1893:

I am in receipt almost daily either of clippings from newspapers or personal letters on the subject of lands lying along the Southern Pacific Railroad of California, now occupied by settlers who have taken possession there in conformity with sales made to them by the U. S. Government. Will the Honorable Secretary excuse an intrusion upon his valuable time and permit me, with great respect, to call his attention to the facts concerning the present state of affairs and to urge upon him in the interest of simple justice some action for the relief of the innocent holders of land?

In 1866, the United States granted certain lands to aid in building a railroad from a point on the Colorado River to San Francisco. . . . In the face of this fact the U. S. Government gave notice to settlers that they could occupy these lands that had already been granted to the railroad company; and in conformity with such notification, the settlers purchased the land and paid their hard-earned money to the Government. This necessitated on the part of the railroad company an appeal to the U. S. Courts, which decided that the land belonged to the railroad company and not to the Government. The railroad company had already mortgaged those lands in order to raise the necessary money to aid in completing the road, as it had a right to do. . . . I have written this letter to the Honorable Secretary more particularly to say that the builders of the Southern Pacific Railroad have made no money out of its construction. If they had, I would be willing and would so advise my associates to give back to the settlers their hard earned money which was wrongfully accepted by the Government in payment for land it had no right to under its own laws. . . .

The writer well knows how hard it is to earn money by farming . . . and it is because I realize this hardship and injustice to innocent settlers that I intercede with the Government for a return of this money to them. It is not merely my duty, but a pleasure to do so; more particularly as I feel sure that the Hon. Secretary of the Interior Department will right the wrong that has been committed by returning to those hard-working farmers the money that is justly due them; or, in case there is no money in the Interior Department that can be used for this purpose, that you will do all you can to induce Congress to make, at the earliest possible moment, an appropriation of money that shall be applied to the reimbursement of settlers for the loss of land to which, through no fault of their own, they never had or could have title from the Government.

The Secretary of the Interior acknowledged the receipt of this letter with the information that it had been referred to the General Land Office for further consideration.

In an interview with Mr. Huntington, February 23, 1894, by a reporter of the San Francisco *Call*, he was asked if there were any further developments regarding the lands which belonged to the railroad company and were sold by the Government, to which Mr. Huntington replied:

There has been no change that I am aware of. I spoke to quite a number of members of Congress when I was in Washington, and there seemed to be a disposition to return to the farmers the money wrongfully withheld by the Government. Of course the railroad company will do what it can as it has always been the policy of the company to sell its lands to actual settlers, the object being to have the land occupied by practical farmers who would be raising produce to transport and buying merchandise to take back to their homes; in short, they would be able to furnish business for the railroad.

Chapter XL

FREIGHT RATES AND FARES

OF ALL THE CHARGES brought against the Central Pacific Railroad Company by the Opposition those connected with its freight rates and fares were the most virulent and widespread. From the beginning of the railroad operation in 1864, the directors were accused of extortion in rates and fares and of unjust discrimination. Bitterness increased with the years; it was charged that the railway policy was "saturated with fraud and dishonesty," and that the railroad itself was a "monopoly that had spread a black cloud over the surface of the State."

From the time the Central Pacific Railroad began to transport passengers and freight from Sacramento to Roseville on April 21, 1864, until it connected with the Union Pacific Railroad at Promontory Point on May 10, 1869, the maximum rates of ten cents per mile for passengers and fifteen cents per ton per mile for freight were charged.[1] These rates were allowed under the State law of 1854. At that time the railroads and steamships were permitted to charge passengers twenty cents per mile and shippers sixty cents per ton per mile for freight. It was pointed out by John Bigler, Governor of California at that time, that at these rates, a passenger on the then-hoped-for transcontinental railroad could be charged $500 for transportation from California to Missouri; and that a ton of freight hauled the same distance would cost the shipper $1,500. An amendment was adopted limiting the maximum fare to ten cents per mile and freight to fifteen cents per ton per mile.[2] As high as these first rates of the Central Pacific were, they were less than one-third of the rates previously paid for transportation by teams over this region. Considering the high cost of building the road and the expense of operating it over the mountains, and the long stretch of non-productive desert country, the rates were considered reasonable by the railroad company.

The records show a steady lowering of freight rates by the Central Pacific, year by year, from 1869, when rates were highest. The average rates thereafter, including the Southern Pacific when it began operating, were for 1872, 3.66 cents; for 1877, 3.14 cents; for 1879, 2.753 cents; for 1881, 2.14 cents; for 1885, 2.04 cents. Passenger fares show a similar reduction.[3]

By an Act of Congress in 1877, the Interstate Commerce Commission began the period of United States Government control of railroads and thereafter, fares and freights were regulated by that body.

The Central Pacific had hardly begun to operate when Placer County, through which the railroad passed, and El Dorado, an adjoining county, began to complain of the high rates. Some citizens of Placer County had been among the first antagonists of the builders of the railroad. In December 1867, petitions from certain citizens of these two counties were presented to the General Assembly in session at Sacramento. These petitions represented that the rates of the Central Pacific Railroad were "exorbitant, oppressive, and out of all proportion to the expenses incurred and the services rendered." Placer wanted the rates reduced by one-third, but El Dorado asked for a reduction to one-third.[4]

The Opposition newspapers of San Francisco, the *Daily Call,* the *Bulletin,* and the *Alta Californian,* and the Sacramento *Daily Union* took up the cry, and soon these newspapers were teeming with communications from disgruntled shippers airing their grievances; and the condemnatory editorials exaggerating situations and crying "monopoly." The Central Pacific and later the Southern Pacific, were subjects of bitter denunciation. Some editors declared that the road built by the money and land of the people, should be so conducted as to carry passengers and freight more cheaply than any other railroad in the world. Others claimed that the generous gifts of the State and counties were sufficient justification to compel the road to submit to legislative action.

To the charge of excessive freight rates, they added the charge of unjust discrimination. The merchants and others of Nevada who supplied the bulk of the way fares and freights were taxed out of all proportion with those who transported through freights, they claimed.[5]

Members of all the political parties joined in the accusations. The cities of San Francisco, Stockton, Vallejo, Placerville, and Los Angeles were, at times, full of indignation against them. Even Sacramento and Oakland which owed so much of their prosperity to the Central Pacific Railroad censured it harshly.[6]

It is no wonder therefore, that Mark Hopkins in a letter to Collis Potter Huntington in April, 1868, commented rather bitterly that everybody was in favor of a railroad until they got it built, and then everyone was against it unless the railroad company would carry them and theirs for nothing.

Some speakers and writers, taking their cue from the opposing newspapers, spoke or wrote bitter, even scurrilous things about the policy of the builders of the railroad. The following extracts are from an address delivered at Broadway Hall, Oakland, November 24, 1873, on "The Political Questions of the Day," by Charles A. Washburn:

For years to come, the Central Pacific will have a complete monopoly of the overland business . . . and hold the material interests of the state in its iron folds. . . . What would not these men do as monopolists and millionaires to carry a point! As railroad kings, they thrust their polluting hands into every ward caucus; they dictate to their followers, their boarding houses, their washerwomen. . . . They discriminate in their charges to the minutest details, giving special rates to friends, or rather subjects, general rates to the public, and excessive rates to their enemies or competitors. . . . They wish it to be understood that it is for every man's interest to bow down and worship them, and to make that plain, they plant their iron heel on those who refuse to do so. . . . They feel that they are above the law and can with impunity defy and insult whom they please.

At Platt's Hall in San Francisco on August 2, 1879, Alfred A. Cohen, a rather notorious lawyer of that city, addressed the people on "The Railroad Evil and Its Remedy." He stated unequivocally that the Central Pacific Railroad was built and equipped solely by the aid furnished by the Government at a cost not exceeding $35,000,000, the builders receiving large fortunes at its completion; that all the large earnings of the road had been made by unreasonable and extortionate charges for freight and fares out of the earnings of the people; that this tariff must cease or the company would become the owner of every foot of land in the State which would soon become involved in total and hopeless bankruptcy.

As a remedy, Cohen recommended that voters should have a fair understanding with all persons seeking office, that they would promise to give the relief required. "Demand of those for whom you vote, whether for Governor, for members of the Legislature, or for Railroad Commissioners, that they will accomplish a reduction in the net earnings of the railroad company of one-third of the present amount," he counseled.

Yet the Associates were condemned for taking an active interest in the candidates for office. As citizens they had the right to express their views both vocally and at the polls. The attitude of the Opposition in grooming candidates opposed to the railroad forced them to take an active interest in candidates who favored the railroad. Whenever such candidates were elected to office however, or the company won a case at court, immediately the Opposition struck below the belt by declaring that success was won by a fraudulent use of money.

In an address delivered before the California State Agricultural Society, September 18, 1873, Aaron A. Sargent, California representative in Congress, said:

> I believe with Mr. Adams [Charles Francis] that railroad companies cannot be kept out of the lobby or out of politics, if the people are continually incited to elect only their "reliable enemies," and projects are discussed and promoted by Legislatures to regulate their business and diminish their revenues, where malice or even well-meaning ignorance may plunge them into bankruptcy. "Self-defense is the first law of nature."

At every session of the Legislature from 1863, some legislation hostile to the Central Pacific was introduced. When the road began to operate in 1864, and while the builders were still struggling up the mountain, the Opposition began strenuous efforts to control the railroad by legislation. Senate bill No. 103, to establish lower rates and fares was introduced, but was vetoed by Governor Frederick F. Low. During the same session, desperate efforts were made by some San Francisco delegates to destroy the credit of the company.[7]

On January 4, 1868, a bill was introduced into the Assembly to amend Section 51 of the Act under which the Central Pacific Railroad Company was incorporated in 1862, in which amendment the maximum rates for the railroad were set at five cents per mile for passengers and ten cents per ton per mile for freight.[8]

During the same year another bill was drafted to regulate fares and freights between Sacramento and the eastern boundary of the State. Passenger fares were graded at seven cents, nine cents, and ten cents per mile according to railroad elevation, and freight rates at ten cents, twelve cents and eighteen cents per ton per mile respectively.[9]

In 1869, a bill was introduced in the Senate for the purpose of establishing certain rates by law. The company had already made a reduction in the rates and they argued that goods and passengers were carried at all seasons of the year without delay at about one-fourth the rates formerly charged by teams, with property greatly enhanced. If the Legislature reduced the rates one-third as asked to do, the company would have to cease to build further.[10]

In 1872-1873, the controversy grew so violent, personal animosities so bitter, and complaints so frequent and exaggerated, that the San Francisco Chamber of Commerce on November 11, 1873, appointed a committee of five persons to prepare a bill for legislative action on the subject of fares and freights of the Central Pacific Railroad. Several members of the committee were known antagonists of the railroad and had been members of the Committee of One Hundred whose avowed purpose was to curb the railroad by efficient opposition.

Two bills were submitted by the Committee: (1) an act to create a Board of Transportation Commissioners prescribing their duties and powers; and (2) an act to prevent extortion in the rates charged for transportation of passengers and freights on railroads and steamboats in the State, and to punish the same.

This committee furthermore propounded eleven questions concerning the policy of the Central Pacific with regard to fares and freights which they requested Leland Stanford to answer. His replies set forth clearly that the policy of the company was based upon standard railroad procedures recognized by students of railway economics, and practiced by railroads throughout the United States and in other countries. Although these questions and replies were published in a brochure, in newspapers and magazines, and made available throughout the State, the Opposition steadfastly refused to accept them and the misrepresentation and abuse continued.

In 1874, a special legislature—dubbed the Dolly Varden— was called by election for the expressed purpose of taking action against the "unjust discrimination in freight and fares" of the Central Pacific. When the Legislature demanded proof of this unjust discrimination before taking action against it, there was none produced; it was, therefore, impossible to frame a law against that which had no existence. The cries of the *Call*, the *Bulletin*, and the *Union* for the action that was to deal out ruin to the Central Pacific were exposed as an imposition, a charge without foundation, and all the expense of the extra session went for naught.[11]

In 1876, the California Legislature passed an Act appointing General Stoneman, John T. Doyle, and Isaac W. Smith as Commissioners of Transportation for two years. They were charged to interfere only with the roads under the control of the Central Pacific Company. They were quite aggressive and commenced an annoying series of investigations in several of the roads with dire threats of penalties attached; but the Act was repealed during the Session of 1877-1878.[12]

In 1879, a new Constitution was framed for the State of California. It was said that one of the chief motives for the adoption of the new constitution was the desire to provide stronger checks on the Central and Southern Pacific Railroads. In addition to other railroad legislation, a Board of Transportation Commissioners was appointed with absolute powers—executive, judicial, and legislative. This board, however, did not fullfill the expectations of the Opposition. One board after another came into power and passed out of existence while the regulation of fares and freights never seemed to be considered as a part of their special duties in spite of the instructions the members had received in advance of their appointment. "The wrath of the press rolled like thunder about their heads."

J. C. Stubbs, Traffic Manager of the Southern Pacific had something to say about these instructions:

> The Commissioners are bound by their oaths to deal with these subjects with judicial fairness. I submit that such a thing as a candidate for a place on the board being pledged in advance of election to a reduction in freight rates and fares before he could have information, knowledge, or experience to qualify him to speak on the question at all, was never contemplated by the framers of the Constitution, much less by the peoples whose votes adopted that instrument.[13]

Southern Pacific Wharf at Port Los Angeles

Pecos River Bridge in Texas on the Sunset Route

A writer in the American Law Review, v. 29, 1895, p. 896, asks this question:

What can be said of the state of public opinion which will justify a political party in nominating a candidate for an office upon a distinct pledge to decide the question in a certain way before he has made any investigation or given anyone a hearing? Could blind and unreasoning ignorance go farther? As well might a candidate for the office of judge agree in advance to decide a pending or prospective local controversy in a certain way.

Comparatively few of the many bills to regulate the affairs of the railroad that were introduced in the Legislature were passed. The railroad company had some friends among the members who were active in its support. When such a bill did succeed in becoming a law and the welfare of the road was endangered, the company had recourse to the Courts. Perhaps the Central and Southern Pacific Railroads have had more law suits than any other railroad in the world; and the records show that most of them were won by the railroad company.

A number of companies were organized at various times to devise ways and means to circumvent the railroad and to promote other methods of handling traffic. Among these were the Traffic Association, the League of Progress, the North American Navigation Company, and the Merchants' Shipping Association. None of these, however, produced any lasting effect and each of them in turn subsided.

A competing railroad was the dream of the Opposition as a sure cure for all their troubles with the Central Pacific. In 1872, a company was organized in San Francisco, under the auspices of the Committee of One Hundred, to construct

a Grand Trunk Line from San Francisco to the Colorado
River to connect with the Atlantic & Pacific, with a capital
stock of $30,000,000.

Another attempt was made in 1892. In May of that year
the San Francisco & Great Salt Lake Railway was incorporated by some citizens of San Francisco. The cost of the
road was estimated at $30,000,000. When subscriptions to
stock failed to reach $1,000,000, and the Legislature refused
to intervene, that project, too, was abandoned.[14]

The San Francisco & San Joaquin Valley Railway from
Stockton was promoted in 1893 as a "peoples railroad." It
was financed largely by Claus Spreckels and became a part
of the Santa Fé System in 1896. This competing road, however, failed to still the clamor of the Opposition.

In a debate in the Senate of the California Legislature,
in 1884, on the subject of fares and freights, a senator declared that it was a very simple thing to regulate fares and
freights. All that was necessary was to resolve that fares
should be 3 cents a mile for passengers and freight 2 cents per
ton per mile! The newspapers and shippers under their
influence were strong advocates of this policy in spite of the
many articles on the subject that had been published.

Ten years earlier, a railroad economist had said in an
article that regulation of the charges for railroad transportation involved intricacies compared with which the Gordian
Knot was susceptible of immediate and easy unravelment.
He went on to say that some of the factors involved were the
physical characteristics of the road—valley, mountain and
desert; density of population; distance of transportation;
classification of freight—bulk, value, and quantity; season
of the year; harvest for each year, whether poor or bountiful;

competition with water rates; aid given to build up production in order to increase traffic for the railroad; and others.[15]

With what unjust discrimination was the Central Pacific Railroad Company charged, and how did those complaints compare with the policies approved by students of railway economics? A few examples will illustrate:

In the Sacramento *Union* for December 23, 1869, appeared the following editorial:

> It will be found upon investigation that our merchants and those of Nevada who supply the great bulk of the way fares and freight are taxed out of all proportion with those who transport through freight. It costs nearly twice as much per mile from here [Sacramento] to Elko and between all intermediate towns as it does per mile from San Francisco to Promontory.

In his "Rates of Railroad Transportation," George A. Hart discussed this point and others:

> Charges on through freight are often proportionately not more than a third of the rates charged on way traffic; through freight has frequently to be taken at the very lowest paying margin or not at all, and if refused, the freights to way stations would have to be raised. Goods going one way, too, are frequently charged one-half the price exacted on goods going in the other direction. On many roads the bulk of the traffic is one way, and rather than bring back empty cars, the return freight is taken at a low rate.

In the Yreka *Journal* for November 15, 1871, appeared the following communication:

> An Outrage! The Central Pacific Railroad ships freight on its steamers intended for Oregon at a lower rate than the merchants of Northern California are obliged to pay, probably on account of competition by coast to Southern Oregon. Our merchants and those

of Trinity, Shasta, and Tehama counties pay from $15.00 to $30.00 per ton, while those of Southern Oregon pay only $12.00 per ton. Oregon gold is no better than California gold, and this matter of favoring one section more than another shows the greediness of the railroad monopoly whose great love for the dear people rests solely in filling their own pockets regardless of justice and fair play.

In his "Natural Principles Regulating Railway Rates," published by the *Railway Age* in 1887, Gerrit L. Lansing said:

Where railroads are in competition with water routes, a discrimination must always exist; it is beyond the power of the railroad, or any person, or any other body to prevent it. The shippers demand that freight on the railroad be low or the traffic will take the water route. The railroad has to take what is can get or go without. That this is a source of no justice to less fortunately located places is shown from their history. Before the construction of the railroad, the non-competitive points were supplied with transportation by the slow and expensive means of animals and wagons. The railroad reduced the time and cost of transportation to a fraction of the former amount.

Along the line new towns sprang up and both the old and new increased in prosperity by the impulse to production and industry furnished by quicker and cheaper transportation. The railroads have been to inland places of immeasurably more benefit than to any others. It is in fact for those that the railroads were constructed. The places on the water routes were already supplied with a cheap and sufficiently rapid means of transportation. As the railroad was built for those places to which the highways of nature did not extend, there seems no injustice in charging the expenses of the railroad to the places for which it was constructed.

An illustration of transportation from competitive point to way station, and from competitive point to competitive point is shown by the following letter from a citizen of

Fresno to the Traffic Association, and published by the San Francisco *Call,* September 2, 1884:

The prosperity, the very life of the people of this valley depends upon our shaking off the grip with which the Southern Pacific now holds us. On ordinary freight we have been paying $15.00 a ton, seven cents per ton per mile. . . . Two carloads of sugar leave San Francisco on the same train. One drops off here after being drawn over a dead level route and that car pays seventy-five cents per one hundred pounds of freight. The other car goes on to Kansas City, over the Tehachapi, 4,000 feet high; and over another range, 7,000 or 8,000 feet high, and at the end of the route in Kansas City pays only sixty-five cents per one hundred pounds of freight. This county with a population of 40,000 has paid the railroad over $2,000,000 in a year. We must have relief or we die!

This writer should have remembered that the 40,000 population of Fresno County was due largely to the construction of the Southern Pacific Railroad through the San Joaquin Valley and the development of the immense grain-growing areas which enabled them to pay the $2,000,000 freight for transportation of their large crops. In 1872, the Central Pacific moved 111,616.5 tons of grain at 3.19 cents a ton per mile, and went for it with empty cars.

One of the practices of the railroad least understood by the public generally and the cause of harsh criticism was expressed by a writer in San Francisco:

This Central Pacific Railroad has invented and put into force more different modes of vexations in transportation than probably any other in the world and WE are the sufferers. At one time goods ordered from Eastern points for the interior of California or Nevada had to be hauled to San Francisco and back to its destination to swell the cost.

This method had been explained countless times by the directors. In the first place no goods ever marked for a destination on the line of the road was ever carried by that station, but the charge was always for way station freight. In the second place, in agreement with the railroad, shippers had their goods sent to the end of the line, then back to the way station; the aggregate cost of the long haul and the short way line aggregating less than shipping direct.

Albert Fink, called the "Father of Railroad Economics" expressed the opinion that the laws governing railroad tariffs were the same as the laws of trade and commerce, of supply and demand, and if disregarded it would soon be discovered that the railroads could not operate at all, or that their usefulness would be immensely curtailed. To charge one shipper more than another for the same kind of goods shipped from the same point to the same destination is not in itself proof of unjust discrimination. The quantity shipped by one man may be comparatively small and the cost of carrying the smaller quantity may be twice as much per 100 pounds as that of carrying the larger quantity.[16]

The historian, John Shertzer Hittell, in his "The Commerce and Industries of the Pacific Coast," 1882, applies the laws of the merchant to the railroad:

It is true that there are differences in the charges for freight between large quantities and small quantities; and between competitive and non-competitive geographical situations; but railroads and business men generally exercise a discriminative judgment in their dealings with the public. The merchant demands more by the pound for his goods if he sells a single pound than if he sells a ton. He demands more when the supply is scant than when it is excessive. If he knows his customer must buy of him, he takes that fact into consideration when fixing his price. If his place of business is accessible to both railway and ship, he will be in a position to undersell his competitor who is dependent either upon the ship alone or the railway alone. These are plain business propositions that are governed and controlled by the logic of business eventualities and they have become so thoroughly the rule in commercial affairs that no one finds fault with the merchants by whom they are enforced.

The Central Pacific and other railroads take these and kindred considerations as the basis of their charges, and yet they are denounced by the very men who are guided by the same motives in dealing with their neighbors. Freight can be transported cheaper relatively for long distances than short ones, and can be delivered more conveniently at the main terminal points than at small intermediate stations.[17]

In view of the above application of the laws of trade and commerce, what becomes of the rabble-rousing cry of the Opposition: "All that the traffic will bear?" What merchant in putting a price upon his goods fails to charge all that the traffic will bear?

The dissatisfaction against the railroads, at that time, was not confined to California, but was general throughout the country. In his article on "Rates of Transportation" published in the *Overland Monthly* for September, 1873, George A. Hart said:

The greatest outcry against railroad charges and discrimination has come from Illinois and the people from that state have led off in the war against railroad companies. A law was recently passed regulating railroad charges in Illinois, and it is already known that the new law will not work. Many of its provisions which were supposed to be equitable act as positive prohibition to many kinds of traffic and will positively injure the people of that state.

The law permits charges, too, which we of California would think unreasonably high, since they exceed, in many cases largely, the rates charged on the Central Pacific, which we have been led to believe were not only high, but extortionate.

Mr. Hart follows this with a comparative table of rates on the Central Pacific and on the railroad of Illinois. In every instance the Illinois rates were higher, except two where they were equal. The last item shows the distance from San Francisco to Colfax, one hundred ninety-four miles; the rates being fifty-three cents, fifty cents, and forty cents respectively, on the three classifications. For an equal number of miles from Chicago, the rates were sixty-three cents, fifty-three cents, and forty-three cents respectively.

It is to be remembered that the railroad in Illinois runs through a rich prairie country, level and well-populated with an enormously greater business than any road in California. Illinois, too, at that time had more railroads than any other state in the Union.

When compared with the Massachusetts system of railroads for that period, it is found that while the cost of the Central Pacific was greatly in excess, yet the earnings were not much more than one-half as much per mile, and its dividends averaged only 2.66 per cent against 5.04 per cent of the Massachusetts roads.

When the enormous difference in density of population, wealth, manufacturing and social development of Massachusetts is considered, the rates of the Central Pacific are surprisingly low.[18]

The Central Pacific Company was charged by the Opposition with "introducing" a system of special contracts, infamous and illegal, which was enforced by boycotting; it prevented competition by water and raised the aggregate cost of transportation. The executives of the company said the railroad simply offered to carry for one year all of a shipper's goods at a contract price somewhat less than the general tariff rates. The system was open to all and a matter of individual interest; it did not increase the aggregate cost of transportation or prevent competition by water. On the contrary, since the advent of the Overland road, freight by the Isthmus had been reduced from $100.00 per ton to $20.00; and the opening of the Southern Pacific had reduced the price by Cape Horn from $17.00 per ton to $10.00.[19]

The company was charged also with giving rebates to favored shippers, a discrimination practiced by every railroad in the country, whether right or wrong; a method of under-bidding competitors to increase business. The rebates on the Central Pacific Railroad for 1884 amounted to $1,062,275.92, it was said. At one time the Santa Fé line extending in California to San Francisco had over $7,000,000 of unpaid rebates.[20] This practice by railroads was strictly forbidden by the Interstate Commerce Committee when assuming control in 1887.

The practice of issuing annual passes over the railroads was another source of antagonism which the railroad companies themselves desired to stop or at least restrict. They were issued to public officials, business men, agents of other roads, the clergy, members of Congress and the State Legislature, newspaper men, and others whose influence would favor the railroad. Mr. Huntington desired to restrict passes, to employees of the road and to persons whose annual salary was $3,000 or less, to enable them to travel and see something of the country.

In a letter to Mr. Stanford, February 4, 1875, Mr. Huntington expressed concern over the passes issued on the Central Pacific:

I have just received memorandum of the number of passengers carried over the C. P. in 1874, and it shows that we have carried 6,186 dead-heads, which is a fearful number to carry free on a road like the Central. I have issued only 14 annual passes and 128 round-trip passes—mostly to Federal officials. I think we make a mistake three times out of four in issuing passes. I have often, and no doubt you have, heard the remark that we give passes to worthless, no-account fellows, and make good men that are our friends pay their fare.

Whenever Mr. Huntington had an opportunity he vigorously defended the fares and freights of his railroads, as the instances given below will show. A letter from Charles Crocker to Mr. Huntington, September 17, 1877, read as follows:

I have just returned from Los Angeles where I have been trying to overcome the discontent of the people there growing out of the agitation of freights and fares. The commencement of the trouble was occasioned by our purchase of the Santa Monica road, and the consequent rising of freights, which was fanned into a blaze by Governor Brown's visit. I was surprised to find at what low rate we were doing business between this city [San Francisco] and Los Angeles. It averaged during the last 11 months only three cents per ton per mile, and two cents per ton per mile from Los Angeles to San Francisco. The fact is, the excitement down there is only a tempest in a teapot.

The cause of the "excitement down there" was told by Mr. Huntington when he appeared before the Senate Railroad Committee in February 1878:

We have built some roads there [Southern California] through lands which went begging at a dollar an acre and which now command $25 to $50 an acre because now they have access to markets. When we commenced building our lines in and out of Los Angeles, it had about 5,500 population, and it has now over 20,000, and ten times the trade; and yet there can be a few people got together to hear stump speeches, declaring that our "monopoly" has "destroyed their commerce"; and to sign petitions asking you to use the national credit to build them a competing line [Texas & Pacific]. The same men would be found petitioning, if their prayers were granted, for a third line to compete with these two.

You will understand that for some years we were maintaining a sharp competition with short rail and steamer lines to Los Angeles by which all parties were losing money. This the citizens mistook for the normal ratio of charges, and so when the competition came to an end—as all such things must end—and remunerative rates were restored, they thought they were oppressed.

It has been said that the rates of fare and freight are enormous. Well, gentlemen, those roads, built and operated under conditions more unfavorable to economy than any roads of the same magnitude in the world, get $100 in currency for carrying a passenger and his baggage between Omaha and San Francisco, a distance of 1,915 miles, or about the same rates per mile as are charged over the easily built and operated roads in the Southern States. I submit, there is nothing very extortionate about that!

From an address of Collis Potter Huntington before the California State Board of Trade, April 2, 1889:

Some of you may wish to know what the railroads will do to help bring the many thousands that we want here and that may wish to come. I will tell you that there is no divided council in any of the companies in which I am a director. We, one and all, have been for low fares, so low that almost any one could come here if he wished; but others have interests, other railroad lines have to be consulted. We of California, I think, have in all cases got the lowest fares that we could get the other lines to agree to. You can see by the reports that the California roads are worked on the smallest possible margins, that they can do no more in the future than they have done in the past unless they reduce the price of labor, which they are not disposed to do.

In an interview with a New York correspondent of the San Francisco *Examiner,* March 4, 1892, Mr. Huntington said:

The way to get lower rates is to increase the tonnage or reduce the wages now paid to those who operate the roads. The latter we would not like to do, but would much like to increase the tonnage. It could be done if the people of San Francisco and California would turn their attention to building the resources of their state. . . . When the people of California make up their minds to bring forth and develop for the use of mankind all that can be produced from the forest, the farm, and the mine, the railroads would soon have a volume of business that will allow of the minimum rates of transportation; and those who by their foresight and industry have made these low rates possible, will have not only the natural reward of their enterprise, but the satisfaction of knowing they have been benefactors of their State; and to learn that it is nobler as well as more profitable to build up than tear down the institutions that were created for their use and benefit.

From an address by Collis Potter Huntington at a reception to his railroad executives, April 23, 1892:

In the early days, merchants sold goods at from fifty to one hundred per cent profit; now the profits are only two and a half to ten percent. Some of them complained and made an effort to blame the builders of the railroads for their loss of profit and they said as much to farmers, but the latter realized that the building of the railroad had increased the value of their holdings as much as twenty times in some cases. One dealer in millinery charged an extra $1.50 for the frame of a bonnet because freights were so high. The purchaser had the frame weighed and it was ascertained that the actual cost of freight paid on the frame was five-eighths of one cent.[21]

Mr. Huntington's discussion of rates and fares when before the Senate Pacific Railroad Committee in February 1896:

As for the rates and fares on the Central Pacific, I am quite sure they are lower than those of any other road in the world operated under the same circumstances. The Central and Southern Pacific west of Ogden have no great tonnage. . . . West of the 100th meridian lies more than one-half the acreage of the United States with not over 4,000,000 people; while east of that line, on less acreage, there are probably 65,000,000 people today. . . . Notwithstanding the light tonnage . . . for the ten months ending October 31, 1895, the average rates were 1.054 cents, which considering the vast mileage and that almost everything that enters into the cost of these roads is much higher than in any other part of the United States, is phenomenally low. The roads could not live unless those controlling them were exceedingly watchful and practiced a rigid and intelligent economy and keeping their rolling stock and permanent way in the very best condition, for these are the tools by which the railroad makes its money.

In an interview with a representative of the San Francisco *Call*, Mr. Huntington was asked to comment on a recent decision of the Supreme Court declaring illegal all railroad associations which had for their object the maintenance of rates and the apportionment of traffic:

I see that the decision has provoked a good deal of talk and much conjecture as to what will be the effect upon the various traffic associations and the business of the roads generally. I don't think there is any cause for excitement or alarm over the matter. . . . It is absurd to say that because of this decision all proper concert of action among the various lines of road must at once be done away with, and a reign of ruinous competition ensue. Some proper and legal way will certainly be found to prevent anything of the kind and enable the roads to do business on business principles.

The Company did not lack for friends to defend them against the attacks of the Opposition. In newspapers, magazines, and in personal articles and letters, the great benefits that resulted from the development of the railroad were extolled. A typical example is an article in *The Railway Age*, May 3, 1884:

> The Central Pacific Railroad Company have done more for the State than any other interest. . . . They disburse millions every year in the employment of thousands of citizens; they have expanded large sums in building and equipping their roads in a first class manner; in constructing great docks and large station houses; in building up suburban stations and inviting immigration and tourist travel from all parts of the world. Yet they have gone on each year voluntarily reducing rates of transportation and increasing the facilities offered. The State and every locality in the State reached by the railways have prospered as a result of receiving railway facilities.
>
> The money which the railways have earned has been immediately poured into a thousand channels of industry giving back to the people of California not only what they have paid the roads for transportation, but the millions obtained from other states and territories. And yet we find demagogues teaching the people that they are "crushed by monopoly" and ruined by the very power that has built them up.

David L. Phillips from Illinois spent several months of the year, 1875, in California with an invalid son. He wrote occasional letters to the *Illinois State Journal* giving his impressions of the state and people. From Letter No. 6, November 1, 1875, we read:

> What are the crimes of this corporation? Two: (1) The men who have poured untold millions of dollars into the various lines of these roads want reasonable passenger and freight rates for persons and property transported of which they claim to be the judges; or, in other words, while they are conferring benefits they want some profits; (2) the associates have grown rich. As to the first, the rates charged are not in disproportion to the general charges of other things in California. As to the second, no decent, reasonable man would say that they have made any more than they should.

They are charged with exacting exorbitant freight and passenger rates from patrons of the road. Now people in California pay Wells Fargo Company, and the Coast Line State Company, never less than from ten to twenty cents a mile and there are no complaints. But when the Central Pacific Railroad Company charges four or five cents a mile on their cars, there is a general outcry among demagogues, politicians and rapacious members of the General Assembly.

In my judgment, the associates have added in fifteen years $300,000,000 to the permanent wealth of California; and have done already, and will do in the future, more for its permanent wealth than all the pseudo reformers who have been, or ever will be, in the state.

Doubtless there were inequalities and occasional unjust discrimination shown by the many persons handling freight on the Central and Southern Pacific Railroads over the long years. The employees were human and liable to err as did those in any other business.

That it was the fixed policy of the Associates to charge extortionate prices and discriminate unjustly among shippers, however, was disproved by the many cases that came before the public in which the Opposition failed to establish their claims.

Chapter XLI

TAXATION AND THE RAILROADS

ONE OF THE MOST controversial subjects connected with the Central Pacific and Southern Pacific Railroads was that of taxation. The counties through which the railroads passed insisted upon the assessment of the roads at their full value, or what the assessors considered their full value, which the railroad companies opposed and resisted. This resulted in innumerable cases of litigation, first one side appealing to the courts and then the other. A case in point is that of Placer County as early as 1864. The District Attorney for that county, not satisfied with the assessment of the Central Pacific Railroad at $6,000 a mile, demanded that the value be raised to $20,000 per mile. This was taken to the courts and the assessment fluctuated from year to year, $12,000, $6,000, $15,000, finally being fixed at $6,000 per mile.[1]

The early annual reports of the Central Pacific Company show that in 1868, before the completion of the road, the company paid a total tax of $122,301.87, which by 1872, three years after connection with the Union Pacific, had increased to $414,507.31, of which $278,252.53 was paid in California.[2]

In 1878, it was stated that in addition to the $140,000,000 distributed in the construction of the road, the Central Pacific Company paid over $330,000 taxes per annum to the State of California alone.[3]

A California State Convention was held in 1879, with the avowed purpose of curbing the "growing strength" of the railroads. A new Constitution was framed in which it was provided that all railroads operating in more than one county should be assessed by a different tribunal and on a different principal from other property.

A Board of Equalization consisting of five members were appointed to assess and tax the railroads, and a Railroad Commission of three members were appointed to regulate the freight rates and fares. Before the adoption of the new constitution, only material and visible railroad property was taxed, excluding franchises, stocks and bonds, etc. The Board of Equalization assessed the roadway, road beds, rails and franchises of the company, and included the mortgages on the roads in direct violation to the law, the whole being assessed at full value, $15,000 per mile. The assessment was then apportioned to the different counties of the State.

The railroad company considered these assessments illegal and unreasonable and refused to pay the tax. In 1883, the taxes for the two previous years having remained unpaid, the State of California and several counties brought suit against the Central Pacific and Southern Pacific companies to compel the payment of those taxes as assessed, with a five per cent penalty attached.

The Circuit Court held that the assessment violated the 14th Amendment in discriminating against the railroad and declared the tax to be null and void.[4]

An interesting feature of this lawsuit was the great stress laid in the arguments of the plaintiff's counsel upon "the overweening power and greed of those corporations." It was vehemently asserted that this lawsuit was a struggle between the people and the corporations for supremacy; that the corporations by corrupt means and through their large and widespread influence were obtaining control over legislatures. Said Judge Sawyer:

If this be so, then it is of the utmost importance to every natural person in the United States that these guaranties of the 14th Amendment to the National Constitution should be maintained in all their length and breadth. They are the only means of protection left to the people. If these unequal taxes can be imposed upon the class of corporations named in the State Constitution, the position of the parties can be reversed, and the unequal tax now thrown upon the corporations may hereafter be imposed on the other parties. . . . There is no safety to the people except in most rigidly maintaining the guaranties of the 14th Amendment.

Notwithstanding the decision of the Court, the railroad company voluntarily paid over $1,100,000 in taxes for the past two years on a sixty per cent valuation placed upon the property by the Board of Equalization. "Such an act has no parallel in the history of the world," said a writer. "I challenge any man to show a single instance save this where any man or set of men, any company or corporation, has ever paid a dime of tax after the Court has decided that the assessment was illegal." The same writer commented as follows upon the new constitution:

When the new State Constitution was framed, it singled out this company—and might as well have named it specifically—by providing that "All railroads operating in more than one county should be assessed by a different tribunal and on a different principle from the assessments of other people's property," making a discrimination against these people and against their property. They were forced to fight or have their property confiscated. They appealed to the court and after the highest court in the land said they didn't owe a dollar, that they had not been legally assessed, they have paid millions of dollars in to the State and county treasuries, when they were not obliged to pay one cent. . . . From the census of 1880, we learn that the aggregate tax per mile of the railroads in fifteen different states was $151.00 per mile per annum. This company has paid down to last year [1887] $250.00 per mile per annum.[5]

After the decision of the Circuit Court and after the company had paid their lawful tax, the Governor of California called a special session of the Legislature for the purpose of enacting special laws that would withdraw the protection of the Federal law from the corporation, but this effort failed.[6] To remove the friction produced by the existing tax system, the Heath Amendment, to substitute a gross income tax of two and a half per cent for all other taxes imposed on railroads, was submitted to the voters, January 5, 1885, and was rejected.

When testifying before the Pacific Railway Commission in 1887, Leland Stanford gave the following statistics on taxes paid by the Central Pacific to December 31, 1886: to California, $3,355,095.75; to Nevada, $2,411,227.60; to Utah, $264,316.38; a total of $6,030,639.73. Mr. Stanford made the statement which he declared was substantiated by records, that since 1880, the Central Pacific had paid more taxes on the same number of miles per road, than any other railroad company in the United States; and he submitted a comparative table of twenty states.[7]

As the railroads of the four associates stretched their lengths from one end of California to the other, and passed on through other states, the increase in the value of property in those states became absolutely incalculable. The estimate of the taxable property from which the states acquired increased revenue varied greatly. In 1872, a writer in a San Francisco journal stated that the values of real estate along or near the Central Pacific Line had been raised more than $30,000,000 on which taxes were being paid.[8]

A visitor from Illinois who spent several months in California wrote to his home newspaper that in fifteen years, the railroad had added $300,000,000 to the permanent wealth of California.[9] With other writers, the estimate went up to "thousands of millions of dollars."

The charge was made by the Opposition that after the completion of the transcontinental line in 1869, a blight had fallen upon the prosperity of the State of California, particularly upon San Francisco, the city of Los Angeles alone being exempt. In answer to this charge, a comparative valuation of property for the years 1867 and 1882 was published showing the following differences: California in 1867, $221,-466,101; in 1882, $666,399,985. San Francisco in 1867, $95,972,470; in 1882, $255,000,000.

One of the subjects assigned to the Pacific Railway Commission for investigation was whether the railroad company had not deliberately neglected to apply for patents on the land grants until they could be sold in order to avoid taxation. The testimony of William H. Mills, Land Agent for the Central Pacific, showed this charge to be untrue. On the contrary surveys had been made and paid for, and applications for patents were then pending on more than 600,000 acres of land on the Central Pacific Line and 400,000 on the California & Oregon Line. The company greatly desired to sell the lands, acquiring thereby an increase in transportation and greater earnings. The directors considered that the company had suffered several thousand dollars loss by not having the patents at the time they were due. Up to the time of this testimony, the records showed that taxes to the amount of $420,743.67 had been paid on the lands.

Over and over again the same question was asked and the same denial given without deviation; but in spite of this testimony made under oath and vouched for by the Federal Land Agent, the Commission reported as follows:

It appears from the evidence that frequently the bond-aided companies did delay in taking out their patents with the object and for the purpose of avoiding the taxation to which they would be subjected after the perfection of their patents.

The minority Commissioner recommended that the Attorney General be instructed to force the company to patent the lands they had received.

In addition to the State, county and municipal taxes paid by the company and the taxes on land grants, the Central Pacific had paid taxes to the United States Government as told by Mr. Huntington in a letter to Philetus Sawyer in May 1874:

The company has paid the United States directly for taxes $598,635.32, independently of a very large amount of taxes paid indirectly in the purchase of locomotives, cars, etc., which had paid manufacturing tax to the Government. This is also independent of the amount paid to the Government for interest on bonds.

The attitude of the Central Pacific Railroad Company toward the payment of taxes was expressed by Charles Crocker, April 12, 1884, in an interview with a representative of a San Francisco newspaper:

The Central Pacific Company does not desire to be taxed less than other railroads in the United States with which it is required to compete, and is willing to pay as much taxes per mile of road as any other railroad in the Union without regard to its locality. The company thinks, however, that it should be taxed no more than other railroads in the country are taxed. If the present Legislature can arrive at some system for the taxation of railroads which will lift that question entirely out of politics and enable the railroad company to walk up to the State Treasury and deposit its money without meeting this man and that man and the other man, each to take a slice out of it, the Central Pacific Railroad Company will favor such a scheme.

Chapter XLII

LAWSUIT OF
SAMUEL BRANNAN

IN JULY, 1870, a lawsuit was brought in the District Court of San Francisco by Samuel Brannan and R. O. Ives against the Central Pacific Railroad Company of California and others, whose charges against the company and exaggerated estimates of subsidies and aids received by them for the construction of the road, had far-reaching and lasting effects. Brannan was the owner of two hundred shares of capital stock in the company, purchased as he claimed, at nominal value on November 1, 1864.[1]

The plaintiffs' estimate of various subsidies and aids granted to the company for the construction of the railroad and telegraph line was as follows:

Value of lands granted by the U. S.	$ 50,208,000.00
Lands granted by corporations in California	5,000,000.00
Lands granted by corporations in Nevada	3,000,000.00
Lands granted by corporations in Utah	2,000,000.00
Donation by the State of California	1,500,000.00
Bonds on which California guaranteed interest	12,000,000.00
Bonds of Placer County	250,000.00
Bonds of the City & County of Sacramento	300,000.00
Bonds of the City & County of San Francisco	400,000.00
Bonds of the U. S. Government	27,389,120.00
First mortgage bonds of the company	27,389,120.00
Second mortgage bonds of the company	15,601,741.83
Second mortgage bonds issued & sold	11,787,378.17
TOTAL	$156,825,360.00

The plaintiffs claimed, according to their information and belief, that all these subsidies and aids had been transferred to the control of the defendants and converted to their own benefit and use. They charged that the defendants and their associates combined to cheat and defraud them and other stockholders, and fradulently to acquire and to appropriate to themselves large profits and gains, large amounts of the assets and property of the railroad. To that end the defendants organized themselves and some of their employees into the C. Crocker & Company for the purpose of taking contracts for the construction of the railroad instead of letting them out to the lowest bidder. . . .

That afterward, about the 18th of November, 1867, the defendants and their associates again combined to cheat and defraud the plaintiffs and other stockholders and fradulently to acquire and appropriate to themselves, with consideration of a just equivalent, large profits and gains, and large amounts of the assets and property of the Central Pacific by organizing themselves and some of their servants and employees, to *plaintiffs unknown,* under the laws of the State of California into a corporation styled Contract & Finance Company for the purpose of taking contracts for construction of the railroad, and its equipment.

That under the fradulent and illegal pretense of paying for said materials and work . . . the directors and their confederates from time to time voted to pay, deliver, and make over in the name of the Central Pacific to the Contract & Finance Co. large sums of money, large amounts of bonds, lands, and other assets of the Central Pacific of great value, to wit: $225,855,618.17. The amount was greatly in excess ($206,632,661.50 1/3) of the actual cost of the work ($19,-

222,956.67 2/3) ; in excess of the sum in which the construction and equipment could have been contracted for by responsible persons and firms who did not intend to cheat and defraud the Central Pacific Company and its stockholders. The greater portion of the work was sublet by the Contract & Finance Co. at more than two hundred per cent below the prices which that company received from the Central Pacific for the same work.

The plaintiffs claimed that, according to their information and belief, the dividends, profits, and gains received in the names of C. Crocker & Co. and the Contract & Finance Co., amounted to the sum of $211,299,308.17. . . .

The charge that the five men, Stanford, Huntington, Hopkins, Charles Crocker, and E. B. Crocker, had divided more than $200,000,000 of the railroad assets among themselves, was soon spread throughout the country. On July 6, 1870 Mr. Huntington sent the following messages to Leland Stanford:

(1) A telegraph from San Francisco is published here in this evening's papers saying that Sam Brannan had commenced suit against the C.P. If possible settle it. . . . It is important that it should be settled immediately.

(2) This Brannan matter, as I understand it, is as follows and I have sent this statement to all papers that publish his complaint so that they will appear in the same issue: President Stanford of the Central Pacific Railroad in his answer to the affidavit of Sam Brannan states that each and all of the allegations contained therein are false, malicious and without foundation of fact. He further states that the suit is not brought in good faith but for the purpose of extorting money from the company and grows out of an old standing enmity against the railroad to which Brannan attributes losses sustained by an inland Express Company of which he was part owner.

Mr. Stanford concludes as follows: The record of the officers and management of the C.P.R. is so clear that all attempts to blackmail have hitherto failed and this one will prove no exception to the rule.

When the junction of the two roads was made on May 10, 1869, the associates had expended all the Government bonds and other aids and were more than $3,000,000 in debt for which they were personally liable. The notes of the four associates were outstanding everywhere that they could get loans, many of them bearing interest as high as from ten to twelve per cent. They held most of the Central Pacific stock, about $54,000,000 par which at that time was not worth more than ten cents on the dollar. Credit alone, largely established by Mr. Huntington, kept them from bankruptcy. They had hoped to keep this knowledge from the general public until the earnings of the road and the increase in the value of the stock enabled them to pay off their debts. Any lawsuit at this time would reveal the critical situation and might result in bankruptcy, hence the decision to settle the Brannan demand out of court.

The Brannan charges, however, made a lasting impression upon the public. Even in later years it was stated that before the road had reached Promontory Point, its builders were millionaires.[2] Proof of the real situation is shown by the withdrawal of the two Crockers from the company in May 1871. They were to receive only twelve and one-half per cent for their share of stock, one-half paid in two years, the other half in three years. When they returned from Europe in 1873, and applied for their money, the company could not pay them and Charles Crocker returned to his old position with the firm "just as if he had never been out, but away on a vacation."

During 1873, the year of the great panic, Mr. Huntington had to make strenuous efforts to meet the demands of the company's creditors. Most of the money had to come from the earnings of the road in California, and again and again Mr. Huntington's appeal went to Mr. Hopkins, the Treasurer: "Help me all you can. . . . Let us prepare for the worst, but don't let the C.P. down."

When the market value of the Central Pacific bonds began to drop due to false statements and figures of the newspapers, Mr. Huntington ordered his agent to purchase enough bonds to keep the price from falling below par. Dividends of three per cent were declared on the stock in an effort to enhance its value, and with the hope of selling it on the market.

In January 1873, resolutions were introduced in Congress to investigate the Central Pacific Railroad Company, and General Franchot, the company's Washington agent, and Mr. Huntington were summoned to appear before the Wilson Committee on February 13 and 14 respectively. On February 27, in a letter to Mr. Hopkins, Mr. Huntington referred to the printed testimony of this interview as being incorrect in many respects, and that the committee was filled with the Sam Brannan and Placer County Complaints. Among the claims of Placer County, was a demand as a stockholder for a share in the profits of the company. After considerable litigation, this was brought to an end by an Act of the State Legislature which required the county supervisors to sell the stock to the Central Pacific Company, and apply the money received to the redemption of the bonds.[3]

A year later on January 12, 1874, Mr. Luttrell, representative from California, introduced in the House another resolution to investigate the Central Pacific. This resolution was accompanied by a copy of the Brannan complaint, upon which the resolution was largely based. In a letter to the Honorable Philetus Sawyer, Chairman of the Committee on the Pacific Railroads, dated May 1874, Mr. Huntington discussed at length the resolution and the Brannan charges:

... On the allegations of that complaint, unsustained by any evidence of their truth, this resolution making grave charges against the Central Pacific Company, its officers, directors, and others, and calling for a committee of investigation, is based. ... Notwithstanding that the suit has been disposed of, you will pardon me for calling your attention to some facts bearing upon the subject of that paper. At the outset, I desire to say that so far as my knowledge and belief Pacific and the Western Pacific that received subsidies of lands and unfounded, and known to be so by their originators. ...

The only companies of those now composing the Central Pacific which received subsidies from the Government are the Central Pacific and the Western Pacific that received subsidies of lands and bonds, and the California & Oregon that received land only. ...

I would respectfully ask your committee to compare the list given below with that given in the resolution and Brannan's verbatim and to bear in mind that these bonds with the stock were all that the company had from which to raise money to apply to the construction and equipment of the road, and they have been honestly and economically used.

Subsidies and Aids	Face Value	Reduced to Gold
C.P.R. Co. 1st mortgage	$25,885,120.00	$18,625,499.75
U. S. Govt. bonds to C.P.	25,885,120.00	19,119,552.95
C.P. 7% bonds of 1883	1,483,000.00	830,025.35
C.P. 7% bonds, State aid	1,500,000.00	978,584.68
W.P.R. Co. 1st mortgage	2,735,000.00	1,975,814.39
U. S. Govt. bonds to W.P.	1,970,560.00	1,616,053.50
C.P. Land bonds ($10,000,000)	9,153,000.00	7,894,345.00
Land sales, net, to Jan. 1874 gold	613,675.69	613,675.69
County bonds, S.F. to C.P.	400,000.00	300,638.80
County bonds, Sacra. to C.P.	300,000.00	192,129.25

Subsidies and Aids	Face Value	Reduced to Gold
County bonds, Placer to C.P.	250,000.00	161,772.89
County bonds, S.F. to W.P.	250,000.00	175,000.00
County bonds, San Joaquin to W.P.	250,000.00	125,000.00
County bonds, Santa Clara to W.P.	150,000.00	101,650.00
Calif. & Ore. bonds	6,000,000.00	4,589,648.16
C.P. on Calif. & Ore. branch ($7,200,000, authorized) sold	1,066,600.00	802,457.20
C.P. on San Joaquin branch	6,080,000.00	4,682,590.83
S.F. Oakland & Alameda	500,000.00	425,000.00
TOTAL TO JAN. 1874	$84,472,075.69	$63,212,438.74

A brief comparison of the two lists will show a vast difference between some of the values on the Brannan list—included also in the Luttrell resolutions—and the amounts actually received. From the $10,000,000 land mortgage and the amount received by sale of the lands, the company received less than one-fifth of the $50,000,000 declared by Brannan. The State did not agree to pay seven per cent interest on $12,000,000, but on $1,500,000, the company to pay the principal. For this interest the company agreed to do certain transportation for the State.

No lands were granted the company by the State of Nevada or the Territory of Utah, and the lands granted by the State of California at Mission Bay added nothing as aid to the construction of the railroad. No second mortgage bonds were ever issued to the sum of $27,387,120, or any other amount. Despite the fact that a number of items amounting to millions of dollars not found in the Brannan list, are given in the factual list the total amount of the face value is less by $72,453,-284.31; and when reduced to gold, less by $93,612,921.26.

Mr. Huntington continued his letter by references to the cost of the road as stated by Brannan and the resolution:

The mover of the resolution [Luttrell] states before your committee that the first 7.18 miles of the road cost less than $11,500 a mile [Brannan's statement]. This would be about $82,570. The American River bridge which is included in this 7.18 miles, itself cost more than that sum; and the road from Front Street at the foot of I Street to the corner of B and 7th Streets in the City of Sacramento—about half a mile—cost more than three times that sum, more than $250,000, I am informed [due to expensive rip-rapping]. The iron alone cost more than $11,500 a mile.

He says also that the next 150 miles cost less than $42,000 a mile, and the remainder of the road less than $21,000 a mile. In regard to these statements, I need hardly say more in reply than that there are some fifteen tunnels on the road; that some of the snow galleries cost the company upwards of $40,000 a mile; and that the railroad is probably the most expensive in the United States.

When it is considered that the larger portion of Government bands and first mortgage bonds were sold for currency; that all the proceeds which were remitted to California to be expended there upon the work had to be converted into gold at enormously high rates of exchange; that the iron railroad supplies, and locomotives for the main line had to be purchased and paid for on delivery on board ship in the Eastern States from six to eight months before they could be placed on the road; that the company was compelled to expend generally from $3,000,000 to $4,000,000 in advance of receiving Government bonds; that the iron and locomotives had to be sent during the war 17,000 miles around Cape Horn at war rates of freight and insurance, or across the Isthmus at most exorbitant rates; the cost of upwards of 1,200 miles of railroad and telegraph line now belonging to the Central Pacific with over 100 miles of side track, and all its depots, shops, machinery, ferry-boats and other appurtenances, will not be deemed extravagant or unreasonable.

It will hardly be pretended that the main line of the Central Pacific with the Western Pacific have not cost a sum far exceeding all the aid granted by the United States which were available for their construction; the vast amount that has been obtained from other sources and expended over that aid has added so much to the value of the property and to the ability of the company to meet the Government bonds at maturity. . . . If the company has faithfully applied the amounts realized from the United States subsidies, has complied with the laws of Congress in building the road, and is now keeping it in running order, should Congress interfere?

If the State of California or any of its counties have any claim for the misappropriation of aid granted, or if any stockholder thinks his money has been improperly used, the Courts of California both Federal and State, are open to any suitor.

This measure did not originate with the mover of the resolution, but with a few men in California who have opposed this road from the beginning and whose hostility and malice seems to have increased by the success of the enterprise; but I am sure that your committee will not recommend an investigation merely to gratify the malice of private individuals. . . .

This letter of Mr. Huntington to the Chairman of the Pacific Railroads must have been effective. On April 30, he replies to a letter from General Franchot:

Yours of yesterday received. Glad the members [of the committee] understand the animus of Luttrell's attack, or rather Sam Brannan's, as it seems to be a rehash of that and of that published in the *Union, Bulletin,* and *Call* once in every six months for the past four years. . . . I was in California at the time the Government supervisors came down to examine the books, which of course they found correct and so reported all the committee except Rogers. He hardly looked at the books but after the rest had signed the report, he kept sauntering about and Crocker told me that Rogers kept saying to him that he was poor, that the company had made a large amount of money, that he would like to make some, that he was poor.[4]

The following letter from Mr. Huntington to Mr. Stanford May 16, 1874, shows the former in a retaliatory frame of mind:

If Luttrell stole hogs in Missouri, give the clue and I will send a man there to work up the case, anything you get against Luttrell, Brannan, or Rogers, sharp and pointed and certified, I will use against them in the Washington papers.

Another result of the Brannan charges was a lawsuit by John R. Robinson, March 15, 1876, who as owner of ten shares of capital stock, sued to recover as his part of the profits made, the sum of $1,200,000 and 15,050 acres of land, which he charged the defendants from attempting to swindle him out of. The list of subsidies and aids was copied verbatim from Brannan's list; and the moneys, bonds, assets and profits that the defendants are charged with having paid to themselves are identical with the sums named by Brannan even to the one-third of a cent! The plaintiff demanded that pending the action of the lawsuit, a receiver be appointed for the company and the defendants be restrained from acting as members of the Board of Directors of the Central Pacific.[5]

On March 30, 1876, Paton, Aspinwall, and Agnew of New York brought suits to recover the difference between the price received for some C.P. stock Mr. Huntington had purchased from them several years previous and $400 each, claiming that they could prove that they were promised as much as any stock sold for. On March 31, Mr. Huntington wrote to Mr. Hopkins:

If they prove that, they will prove what is false. It is possible that Cohen is stirring this up. I have been shown three of J. R. Robinson's complaints to-day, and I am told . . . that many of them have been sent to Europe, and their tendency will be for a short time

to hurt us here and there. I do not think there is any other concern
in the world that has so many personal bitter enemies as the parties
that built the Central Pacific Railroad. When will it be otherwise?

Another suit was brought in 1884 by David Stewart of New
York, likewise claiming the difference between the price received for stock sold and $400 per share, which was won by
the plaintiff. Again and again in Congress the influence of
the Brannan charges was apparent in debates on Pacific Railroad matters, particularly on the Thurman Bill and the bill
in 1887 to appoint a Pacific Railway Commission to investigate the company. This influence was even more evident in
the reports of the Commission, charging the Associates with
"incessant depletion of the treasury and misappropriation of
its property by those whose sacred duty it was to protect and
defend the company"; and "extravagant contracts made for
the company." In reply to this, Mr. Huntington stated:

They may have come to that conclusion honestly from what they
were told in San Francisco, yet a greater lie was never printed for
there never was any depletion of the company's treasury, or misappropriation of its property. No work was ever built where
greater economy was practiced, or more care taken in the expenditure of money than in the building of the Central Pacific Railroad;
and when completed there were not enough assets controlled by the
builders to pay the debt created in building the road; and if
the securities had not largely appreciated, the builders of the
road would have been bankrupted by the debts incurred in its
construction.

Chapter XLIII

HUNTINGTON-COLTON
CORRESPONDENCE

In 1867, Charles Crocker met David D. Colton and their two families became warm friends. Colton received passes on the Central Pacific Railroad and he and Crocker visited the Yosemite Valley together. Colton was made the president and general manager of the Rocky Mountain Coal & Iron Company mine at Ione in Amador County, which belonged to the railroad company. When the Crockers severed their connection with the railroad company in 1871 and went to Europe, the Coltons looked after the Crocker boys who were attending a military academy.[1]

David Douty Colton was a native of Monson, Maine, where he was born July 17, 1832. He came to California in 1849 and served as the Sheriff at Yreka in Siskiyou County. Later he returned to the East, and after a course of study at Albany, New York, he opened a law office in San Francisco in partnership with R. C. Harrison.[2] He was active in California politics, and was the delegate of the Union Democrat Party in 1861. He became Brigadier-General of Militia and Colonel of the U. S. Volunteers. He was of fine physique and quick intelligence.

In 1872, General Colton and his family occupied a handsome house at the N. E. corner of California and Taylor streets on Nob Hill, the third elegant residence to be built there. Its interior arangements were said to be in good taste, the walls embellished by rich and beautiful oil paintings.[3] In 1874, after his return from his second trip to Europe, Charles Crocker built a house on California Street directly across Taylor Street from the Colton residence. The relations between the two families were most friendly.

In 1874, an arrangement was made whereby Colton became a co-worker with the four associates. He went to see Mr. Huntington in New York and an agreement was drawn up for two years which was to be continued if agreeable to all concerned. This agreement was accepted by the other associates and signed on October 5, 1874. An extract from the deposition of Mr. Huntington in the Colton Case gives his reason for Colton's admission to the railroad company:

> I was worked up to my full capacity, whatever that might be. Mr. Crocker was in the habit of going off to Europe and having a good time. The Governor owned ranches and his horses took a great deal of his time; in fact, the Governor never could confine himself to the office; that is, I don't consider that he could do close, hard work, and we needed somebody there to do the work. Mr. Colton convinced me that he of all men was just the man we wanted . . .

Another and an important reason for admitting a fifth man to the company was the declining health of Mr. Hopkins who had previously carried out most of Mr. Huntington's requests in regard to finances. The desire to relieve Mr. Hopkins of a large part of the duties he had assumed was a determining factor in Mr. Huntington's decision.

Colton received 20,000 shares each of Central Pacific and Southern Pacific stock in return for his promissory note for $1,000,000 maturing in five years. He was to share all responsibilities and liabilities in proportion to his stockholding. The shares he received were not salable. His right to participate in the management was revocable by his associates. Early in 1876, he was notified that his connection with the company was to be severed; but upon appeal, it was reconsidered and a second contract made, after which he purchased one-ninth of the capital stock of the Western Development Company, and deposited money there as the four associates did.[4] Mr. Huntington had felt some misgivings as to his value to the company as shown in a letter to Mr. Hopkins, January 4, 1876:

Mr. Colton came in with us to stay two years, then if three of the four (as I understand it) liked the arrangement, he was to remain. The arrangement that I made him (of course, all agreeing) gave him the same share in the Construction Company [Western Development] as his interest in the capital shares have to our interest. When he arrived out in California [after his interview with Mr. Huntington in New York], you made an arrangement that he was to have one-fifth interest in the Construction Company. While I have no particular fault to find with Mr. C. he has not brought us the political or financial strength that I supposed he would, and I do not think I would like to have him come in on the basis talked of. I do not want anyone but yourself to see this, but I wish you would find out how Crocker and Stanford stand, and let me know.

From October, 1874, to October, 1878, Colton was actively in charge of the financial affairs of the Huntington group at the San Francisco end. He attended to short term loans in San Francisco as Mr. Huntington did in New York. He used considerable initiative in his dealings and made decisions which met with the decided disapproval of his associates. His suggestion that the salaries of the directors be increased from $10,000 per year to $25,000 did not carry.

On September 4, 1877, without the knowledge of his associates, he distributed dividends of the Western Development Company consisting of $13,500,000 in Central Pacific stock, $6,300,000 in Southern Pacific bonds, and $1,562,500 in other securities. This was, in fact, a division of capital amounting to from one-third to one-half of the Western Development holdings. Colton's share was one-ninth.

The following year when Huntington was in the West and a meeting of directors was being held in one of the Southern Pacific Offices, Colton came in accompanied by two subordinates with their hands full of bonds.

"Gentlemen," said Colton, "here are your dividends."

The associates were very angry and said the stocks and bonds must be returned at once. However, upon Colton's promise not to part with his share and to "save face" with the employees, it was agreed to let the matter stand.

During his connection with the company, Colton drew and credited to himself considerable amounts of money without the knowledge of his associates, no vouchers being made out. Substantial progress was evidently being made toward meeting the million dollar note. He misappropriated the following funds:

(1) In addition to his salary of $10,000 as associate, he drew from the coal company in 1874, $12,000; in 1875, 1876, and 1877, $6,000 annually. During the years 1874-1877, Colton took $54,966.50 in excess of his agreement with Crocker.

(2) He deposited to his own account and used in his private transactions, balances of the coal company running from $30,000 to $90,000.

(3) An extra payment for coal of $11,622 to increase the price from $2.65 to $2.85 per ton, paid by the Central Pacific Company and not reported.

(4) He clipped coupons from the Southern Pacific bonds given in payment for land purchased by Mr. Tevis in 1876.

These items of excess salary, interest on coupons, and miscellaneous unaccounted for expenses totaled $130,831. These manipulations were revealed only after his death.[5]

Huntington's suspicions had been aroused somewhat as shown by the following extracts from his letter to Colton, March 24, 1877:

> . . . You write: "Our receipts are not enough to meet payrolls and imperative demands here."
> I have no knowledge of what the receipts have been this month, but for January and February of this year, on all our roads they were nearly $3,000,000, which was nearly $400,000 more than in the same month of 1876, and one-half must have been profits. Now just where the $1,500,000 of the months of January and February went to, I do not know, but when John Miller took, say, $1,000,000 without being found out,[6] and Mr. Cohen, it is claimed, took in the course of years some terrible amount from the railroad companies, and he was sued for taking a commission from the Contract & Finance Company when he was not even in the pay of that company, so when I think of these things, I think it is just possible that you are all endeavoring to fill up some other wells with the bottoms out . . .

The following extracts from letters, written to Mr. Huntington by Mr. Colton a few months before the latter's death are of peculiar interest in view of later revelations:

> [April 15, 1878] It seems to me that between the Thurman Bill and the Commissioners Bill now before the House of Congress, that there is not much left for us or the stockholders of the Pacific

Roads. So far as I am concerned, I would have much more respect for a highwayman who stops me on the road *and robs me* than I for these fellows in Washington.

[April 16, 1878] I know you are having a hard time there in Washington. I begin to think it is a dreadful life to live, when you are forced to feel that *everybody wants to rob you*, and steal all we have. We will hope for the best.

In October, 1878, while his wife and daughter were in New York, Colton was taken suddenly and violently ill. A surgical operation was performed which disclosed that he was suffering from a dreadful tumor that had developed beyond the hope of recovery. He died on October 9, 1878.

The first intimation that Mr. Huntington had of any serious irregularities in Mr. Colton's affairs with the company was contained in a letter from Charles Crocker, written December 2, 1878:

I have got the old books of the Rocky Mountain Coal and Iron Co. in the hands of Gunn, and he has just reported to me that the president of that company drew as salary for several years $500 per month, and for eighteen months, $1,000 per month. The investigation has not proceeded far enough to develop whether this salary was authorized by the Board of Directors or not. At any rate it was a surprise to me. I have just talked with Col. Gray (who has been a director ever since we got the mine) and he was as much surprised as I, and said he never heard of any vote or authority from the board for such, or in fact, any salary. I think I will go and have every company and everybody else examined that we are interested in, and take nothing on trust any more.

Again on February 15, 1879, Mr. Crocker writes to Mr. Huntington on the subject:

There is much crookedness being developed in the affairs of the Rocky Mountain Coal & Iron Co., say $100,000; and I have found crookedness in the Ione coal purchase of $30,000, and some other matters of the Central Pacific of several thousands, etc. If things had gone on for three or four years more, Miller would have been small potatoes in comparison. I am waiting for the Governor [who had been ill] to get out to see if we can get at a settlement of these matters; but he scatters so much, and changes his mind so often, that I wish you would come out here and assist in fixing them up; it needs firmness to deal with this matter.

On June 7, 1879, Mr. Crocker wrote an urgent letter to Mr. Huntington:

I hope you can come out here very soon as the Colton estate really ought to be settled up, and I have everything ready now so that it can be quickly done. Governor Stanford has not been in the office since January 5, and there is no immediate prospect of his coming here.

The Huntington group insisted that Mrs. Colton settle Mr. Colton's entire obligations and refused to value his stock at a probable future value, but figured it at its value at that time. By an agreement dated August 27, 1879, Mrs. Colton delivered the following to the company:

(1) 408 shares of capital stock of the Rocky Mountain Coal & Iron Co.

(2) All shares held of the Occidental & Oriental Steamship Co.

(3) All claims to 20,000 shares each of Central Pacific and Southern Pacific stock pledged as collateral for the $1,000,000 promissory note.

(4) All capital stock of the Western Development Co.

(5) Some $587,500 in par value of bonds of the Central Pacific and Southern Pacific system of which $500,000 were first mortgage bonds.[5]

In return, the associates agreed to cancel Colton's note for $1,000,000, and to release Mrs. Colton from any claims on the part of themselves, the Western Development Co., the Central Pacific and its allied companies. This settlement left Mrs. Colton with property valued at $587,000, and with a yearly income of about $28,000.

Mrs. Colton felt that she had been robbed, however, and in May, 1882, commenced a suit to reopen the whole transaction and annul the compromise agreement. The trial opened at Santa Rosa in Sonoma County in November, 1883. Mrs. Colton alleged fraud. She offered to pay the promissory note and other liabilities and asked for a return of the securities she had surrendered. The case dragged on until October 6, 1885, when decision was rendered by Judge Jackson Temple for the defendants.

Mrs. Colton took the case to the State Supreme Court which rendered a decision in January, 1890, and sustained Judge Temple's decision. The case had cost each side an estimated $100,000.[5]

During the trial in December, 1883, the so-called "Colton Letters" were produced by the plantiff's lawyer and admitted as evidence purporting to show how close was Colton's connection with the company. These were business letters written by Huntington to Colton between October 8, 1874, and October 8, 1878, and were stolen from the safe in the office of the Southern Pacific Company. They covered the period of construction of the Southern Pacific Railroad south through California to Yuma and the proposed extension of the line through Arizona and New Mexico. Also, the letters commented freely on Mr. Huntington's controversy with Tom Scott, and his efforts to circumvent Scott in getting the latter's bill through Congress.

The Opposition fell upon those letters like hungry wolves. The anti-railroad newspapers vied with each other in producing extracts of damning import. On December 23, 1883, the San Francisco *Chronicle* published the letters in full, 213 of them, which the editorial claimed:

Exposed the full extent of the arrogance, corruption and duplicity of the Central Pacific monopoly, and the fact that for years past the company had been systematically engaged in debauching Senators and Representatives, buying up Legislatures, presenting fraudulent reports, declaring dividends with borrowed money, buying up newspapers and agents of the *Associated Press*, misrepresenting the status of the Southern Pacific Co., gobbling up steamship and railroad lines and other kinds of wickedness too numerous to mention . . .

These men not content with the enormous profits derived by them from the traffic of the Central Pacific road, conceived the idea of totally monopolizing the railroad business of California, and of shutting out all overland competition from this state.

Had the *Chronicle* not been so intent and bitterly serious in condemning the railroad company, surely the editor would have noticed the humor in a situation in which it is stated first that they "declared dividends with borrowed money," then in the next paragraph comments caustically upon the "enormous profits derived from the traffic of the Central Pacific."

In December, 1883, the New York *World* published the "Colton Letters" in several installments with caustic comments on Huntington, who, upon being shown a column of spicy extracts by a reporter, good-humoredly said:

I have not read them as published but they are probably my letters. I am not afraid of their effect and would not give four cents to prevent their use. When I was in San Francisco in March 1883, four separate persons came to me as my friends and told me the letters would be published. I didn't know who the parties were. One represented himself as a clerk in Wells Fargo & Co., and said he could probably stop publication for $100. They would of course have asked more at first.

When he was asked why *The World* alone of New York newspapers used them, he answered:

I have no idea, but it is welcome to do so. My record as a business man is pretty well known among business men and there is nothing in it I am ashamed of. No, I don't think political hostility or railroad rivalry dictated their publication. I don't see what they are going to prove by those letters.

Here Mr. Huntington glanced over *The World* extracts handed to him reading aloud several passages and asking:

Where's the evidence of corruption in these? I've been in business fifty years, and practiced the usual methods known among business men to accomplish certain objects, but I've never bought votes or bribed men directly or indirectly. . . .

Certainly, I have used money in the passage of bills by Congress, but it was spent in getting information before members concerning our interests, not in buying votes. Witnessess were brought from long distances, and attorneys and agents employed. I have had to do the same thing in State Legislatures. The great difficulty in shaping legislation is to get legislators thoroughly informed concerning measures you wish to carry or to defeat, and this costs time and a legitimate expenditure of money. I have done a good deal of this and references in these letters refer to this work . . .

Yes, I have been offered votes for money by Congressmen. I remember that when the Goat Island bill was before Congress, a member told me that he could control fourteen votes if I would pay $28,000. I said "That cuts you off, and your votes." And it did, for he held the fourteen votes against the bill, and it was defeated by only two votes . . .

When I was a boy trying with other boys to catch on to a bob sled for a ride, if I succeeded, the fellows immediately set up a shout, "Cut behind!" So it is with me and some of the fellows in the race since.

The "Huntington group" were not without friends in this as in other charges and controversies of the Opposition. The following editorial from the December 29, 1883, issue of *The Argonaut* expressed the feeling and opinion of many others:

Thanks to the enterprise that comes from malignity, *The Chronicle* in its Sunday issue sprung the mine and gave us three closely printed pages, the Huntington-Colton correspondence. We have heard of those letters ever since the death of the worthy gentlemen to whom they were addressed, and we are only disappointed that they have not panned out one-hundredth part of the vile calumnies with which they were supposed to be charged . . .

We are not quite certain as we look around us here in San Francisco which one of the men now engaged in throwing stones at the railroad does not live in a glass house. We do not recognize "the man without sin." If there is one man in all our business or professional circles that would have come with cleaner hands from such a contest than Mr. Huntington, we have not made his acquaintance. The accomplishment of so great undertakings as have been successfully carried out by Messrs. Stanford, Hopkins, Huntington, and Crocker could not have been achieved by more intelligent and honorable conduct that has characterized the dealings of these people with courts, the Congress of the United States, Legislatures of states, officials, and private individuals . . .

All through these letters runs the idea of serving the people of California. The Southern Pacific, in opposition to Tom Scott's Texas Pacific, was inspired by the single idea of concentrating the Arizona business in San Francisco and giving California system an independent through line from the Bay of San Francisco to the Gulf of Mexico . . . The means used to accomplish results are not other than those resorted to by all men in like conditions. Mr.

Huntington writes in the darkest hour of his fight: "Tom Scott promises everything; I promise nothing that I do not expect to fulfill. I keep on high ground."

They have lived in and worked for a community that has ever been jealous of them. Political parties have made capital by opposition. A press has lived upon their defamation. They have been the subject of revilings, misrepresentation and blackmailing ... After a patient reading of these letters we find in them nothing on the part of our railroad builders and Mr. Huntington, and the evidence of nothing, that any business man in America would not have done under like conditions.

Among the collection of Colton's letters to Mr. Huntington, nothing has been found to confirm the charge of the Opposition. On the contrary, his letter of May 22, 1876, is considered by many as conclusive proof that the correspondence had no reference to fraudulent or other illegal dealings. The following extracts are from that letter:

. . . I think the mistake you all have made has been in not favoring any legitimate investigation. The facts are that but one side has ever been brought before the public. Your strength in answer to all these lies, Contract & Finance, and all matters connected with building the road is in *having the facts known*. The papers have accused you all of stealing, and the world not knowing the facts and seeing no statements of proof from you to the contrary, take it for granted that what the papers say and what Cohen says is true. People think you four gentlemen have got your safes full of these Government bonds, and that about fifteen or twenty millions have been received from the sale of the land, etc., and now that I know all the facts, I am surprised to find how good a case you have. Its weakness lies in the fact that facts have been kept from the world . . .

I have spent considerable time going through the old books, and have been present when the attorneys had the meeting with our people; and I have no fear as to the ultimate result of these suits and slanders against us. On our side are L. M. Wilson, Hall McAllister, J. B. Felton, and Sanderson.

This great talk about Contract & Finance Company robbing the Central Pacific, and the stock being void is all bosh. As things are I do not think we would pay twenty-five cents to compromise these suits.[7] Whether we will be able to get any of the money back from A. A. Cohen that he has swindled us out of is a question. We will try . . .

A prominent writer on the history of the Southern Pacific Railroad had this to say about the Huntington-Colton correspondence:

A characteristic of the man was that he never gave up. As a whole the letters show that Huntington was a persistent and energetic lobbyist. On the whole, the railroad managers pulled wires with a skill which rapidly increased with experience. These letters tend to show that it was Huntington's belief in the years, 1875-1877, that the influence of the Central Pacific should be used to advance the political interests of persons favorably inclined toward his railroad's system and to discourage those who opposed it.[8]

And why not? "Hostile legislation has been proposed at every session of the legislature since the commencement of the road," said Stanford in 1887. If newspapers and men, affected by jealousy or whatever kind of grievances, united to elect anti-railroad men to the State Legislature, to the Congress of the United States, and to other important offices, even that of the Governor of the State, for the expressed purpose of defeating the policy of the railroad company, devaluating its securities, and breaking up its system, surely the members of the company could not be condemned for whatever legitimate political measures they took in self-defense.

The associates were in complete agreement on the subject which was well expressed by Charles Crocker:

If the legislature and legislative bodies had let us alone, we would have been glad to have kept entirely out of politics . . . We have been two or three times within a few votes of being ruined by legislation that was proposed in the State Legislature . . . We have always tried to prevent the passage of those laws that were going to ruin us, just as any man would throw a bucket of water on a fire that had attacked his house.[9]

That this defense induced the selection of candidates favorable to the cause of the railroad and working for them is understood. As the Opposition grew in strength and malignity, it was necessary for the company to exert greater efforts to counteract their designs.

The following is an account of the efforts of a Congressman against the Central Pacific Railroad Company: On January 12, 1874, John King Luttrell, a representative from California, introduced a resolution in the House concerning the Central Pacific Railroad Company. Attached to this resolution was a copy of a complaint that had been filed in court by Sam Brannan, July 1, 1870. Upon the allegations of fraud and violations of law contained in that complaint, unsustained by any evidence of truth, Luttrell made grave charges against the company and called for a select Committee of Investigation.

While the resolution failed to gain the Committee of Investigation, it resulted in bringing Huntington and Franchot before the Pacific Railroad Committee for questioning, February 13 and 14, 1874.

In May, 1874, Mr. Huntington wrote a long letter to Philetus Sawyer, Chairman of the Committee on Pacific

Railroads, protesting the use of this complaint that had been made by Brannan solely for the purpose of extorting money from the company; it was incorrect in every particular, and contained extravagant and unsupported assertions in regard to the road. These charges Mr. Huntington sought to refute by giving a brief, correct history of the railroad. . . . In view of the above, probably Mr. Huntington might be forgiven for the following letter to Mr. Colton, dated May 1, 1875, and published by the *Chronicle:*

I notice what you say of Luttrell; he is a wild hog; don't let him come back to Washington; but as the House is to be largely Democratic, and if he was to be defeated, likely it would be charged to us, hence I think it would be well to beat him with a Democrat; but I would defeat him anyway, and if he got the nomination, put up another Democrat and run against him and in that way elect a Republican. Beat him . . .

On June 1, Mr. Huntington wrote Mr. Hopkins:

Luttrell was before the Committee bellowing like a mad bull. We could not have a better man to oppose us.

When Mr. Huntington was before the U. S. Pacific Railway Commission in 1887, the following extract from one of the letters was read:

All the members in the House from California are doing first rate except————, and he is a damned hog anyway you can fix him.

Ques. Did you ever write such a sentence as that to anybody?

Ans. Well, I should think that I did. I wrote about one fellow, and I have never passed a hog since that I have not felt as though I wanted to go on the other side of the way, as I had abused him.

Extracts were read from another letter, dated September 27, 1875, which the Opposition had claimed was a proof of the fradulent use of money:

Collis Potter Huntington, ca. 1870

Huntington House at California and Taylor Streets, Nob Hill

Smith C.L. Del.

Can you have Safford [Governor of Arizona] call the legislature together and grant such charters as we want at a cost, say, of $25,000? If we could get such a charter, it would be worth much money to us.

Ques. Would that application of $25,000 be within the domain of what you have described to us as a part of the necessary, legitimate, and proper expenditure of money for the purpose of advancing the interests of the Central Pacific?

Ans. While the expense of passing a bill so much in interests of the people of the Territory should be paid in the Territory, yet rather than not have it, we would be willing to pay the expense of an extra session to pass it. The people of the Territory were poor, and that seemed a large sum to them. There certainly is nothing wrong in that.

Ques. What do you include in their expenses—just the board bill of the members, or their salaries?

Ans. Whatever the Territory was responsible for. Just what that was I could not say.

Ques. Then in order to have such legislation as the Arizona Legislature passed, that in your judgment would be a proper application of money?

Ans. There certainly would be no harm in it, and it would be clearly in the interests of the people.

Another letter, dated January 17, 1876, that had been quoted widely by the Opposition to show the corrupt practices of the writer, was read, of which the following are the portions that caused so much comment:

I have received several letters and telegrams from Washington to-day, all calling me there, as Scott will certainly pass his Texas-Pacific bill if I do not come over; and I shall go over to-night; but I think he could not pass his bill if I should help him; but of course I cannot know this for certain, and just what effort to make against him is what troubles me. It costs money to fix things so that I would know that his bill would not pass. I believe with $200,000 I can pass our bill; but I take it that it is not worth that much to us.

Ques. What do I understand you to say in regard to that last sentence?

Ans. I should say that with $200,000 I could pass a bill that would protect our border for 1,500 miles between Mexico and the United States, where the cowboys have been raiding ever since the treaty of Guadalupe Hidalgo. I should say that with $200,000 I could get such a bill passed when the building of the road would not cost the Government one dollar, and would make land, then entirely worthless, of some value after the road was built. I should say that I could get men from as many districts in the United States as would be necessary to convince members of Congress that this road was in the interest of the people, and was a thing they could not afford to vote against.

Again in 1896, when Mr. Huntington appeared before the Senate Committee for questioning about the Central Pacific Railroad, the subject of the Colton letters was introduced and the questioning by a Senator proceeded as follows:

Ques. What percentage of interest did Mr. Colton have?

Ans. I do not know; somewhere in the neighborhood of one-sixth.

Ques. What did he do with his interest?

Ans. I do not know; he died.

Ques. He did not lose it because he died; what has become of it?

Ans. It was settled by his widow.

Ques. Who got it?

Ans. His widow got it.

Ques. To whom did she sell it?

Ans. I was not her adviser in the matter.

Ques. But still you know?

Ans. I do not.

Ques. You do not know to whom she sold it?

Ans. No.

Ques. Have you no belief or information as to whom she sold it?

Ans. No; she had some bonds, but what she did with them, I do not know.

Ques. She may have all that interest now?

Ans. I hardly think she has got it, she was in litigation a good deal.

Ques. Did you buy her house in San Francisco?

Ans. Yes.

Ques. Did you buy her library?

Ans. No.

Ques. Did you not take the house with the papers in it?

Ans. I took the house with the wall papers.

Ques. No other papers?

Ans. No others that I know of.

Ques. And did you not destroy the papers after you bought the house?

Ans. If you charge me with it, I will answer you.

Ques. It is charged by men who are probably as good as you or I.

Ans. Oh, they are very good men.

Ques. What is your answer?

Ans. I destroyed no papers, and I do not know that such a thing was ever charged, although I suppose that those men in San Francisco, if they had thought of it would have charged it.

Ques. Did you not receive papers which were turned over to you when Mrs. Colton sold you that house, which papers belonged to her husband's estate and were connected with these railroad transactions?

Ans. I did not destroy any papers.

Ques. Did any agent of yours do so?

Ans. No, I am sure that nobody did.

Ques. Did you buy that house for a residence?

Ans. I did.

Ques. Have you lived in it?

Ans. Yes.

Ques. When you took possession of it, did you find any of Colton's papers?

Ans. No.

Ques. That is the first positive answer which you have given.

Ans. I have answered the same question before, but I answer it now in another way. That is all.

Ques. I am so glad you are so emphatic. Did you settle your controversy with Mrs. Colton by buying her house?

Ans. No.

Ques. How did you settle it?

Ans. I paid her the money for the house about two years ago.

Ques. How did you pay for the other part of the business, about which she had that suit against you?

Ans. I think the best way to get at that would be to get the records of the court.

It had been reported that Mr. Huntington purchased the Colton house for the purpose of getting possession of the letters. Since these interviews with the Senate Railroad Committee were for the purpose of inquiring into the condition of the Central Pacific Railroad, its cost, earnings, etc., the questions seem to have gone far afield. The Senator's manner of questioning, too, seems to show at least a taint of the Opposition.

Mr. Huntington purchased the Colton house in 1892, and used it for a residence whenever he and Mrs. Huntington came to San Francisco. Of this house Willis Polk, the architect said that the house had been selected by twenty artists as the most artistic dwelling in the entire city. Of the many and expensive homes that had been built in San Francisco no other approached it in modesty, dignity, and simple grandeur of outline.[10]

Chapter XLIV

HUNTINGTON-HOPKINS
CORRESPONDENCE

IN DECEMBER, 1862, Mr. Huntington, Vice-President of the Central Pacific Railroad Company, took up his residence in New York as financial and purchasing agent for the company. He kept in almost daily—sometimes hourly—communication with his associates in reference to the affairs of the company, most of his letters and telegrams being addressed to Mark Hopkins, the Treasurer, and his former partner in the hardware business.

In the fall of 1873, the main offices were moved from Sacramento to San Francisco, and a year later, D. D. Colton was admitted to the company largely for the purpose of relieving Mr. Hopkins of some of his duties and because of his declining health which was giving his associates, particularly Mr. Huntington, grave concern.

From the fall of 1874 to the fall of 1878, most of Mr. Huntington's letters were addressed to Mr. Colton, but he continued writing to Mr. Hopkins every few days. On March 29, 1878, Mr. Hopkins died at Yuma, where he had sought a warmer climate.

E. W. Hopkins succeeded him as Treasurer of the company. Four years later, Timothy Hopkins, Mark Hopkins' adopted son, was appointed to that position which he held until after Mr. Huntington became President of the company in 1890.

Upon his retirement, Timothy had all his father's letters and other papers that he had found in his father's safe, boxed and shipped to his country home in Menlo Park, where they were during the devastating fire that followed the earthquake in San Francisco, April 18, 1906, and so escaped destruction.

In December, 1923, these letters and documents were presented by Timothy Hopkins to the Stanford University Library. The Librarian of the University, Mr. George T. Clark, realizing their importance, and in order to make these writings more easily available for study and research, had each item mounted upon a sheet of heavier paper, arranged in fourteen volumes, each with an index, an additional volume of a general index, and had the fifteen volumes strongly bound in a good grade of buckram.

There are 1,188 letters in the collection, dating from December 5, 1865 to January 5, 1885; 840 of them addressed to Mark Hopkins of which 653 were written by Mr. Huntington. There are also over 300 letters written by Mr. Huntington to other members of the company and to a few other persons. Two volumes are composed of documents pertaining to the railroad and drafts of charters, etc., in Mr. Hopkins' handwriting.

Another small collection of 54 letters written by Mr. Huntington to Mr. Hopkins are filed in the Henry E. Huntington Library at San Marino, California.

In those days Mr. Huntington used no typewriter or mechanical aid to writing; it was all done by hand. No efforts were made to produce a beautiful chirography nor one easily read. The letters were dashed off by a very busy man, some-times four to the same person, the same day, as matters would occur to him. The number of letters he wrote in addition to his manifold duties is rather astounding. When before the Pacific Railway Commission in 1887, he was asked: "What is the general character of your handwriting? Is it easily read?" Mr. Huntington replied: " I used to flatter myself that I could write a letter in half the time it would take the other party to read it."

Most of the letters and extracts from the letters of Mr. Huntington quoted in previous chapters have been taken from these collections. Mr. Huntington had great respect for Mr. Hopkins, an entire trust, and a warm affection. While his letters were mostly on business matters relating to the railroad they were occasionally confidential, and often had a personal touch.

Whenever the other associates handled a situation in a manner that he did not approve, Mr. Huntington seemed to find relief in writing to Mr. Hopkins about it. During the early years of construction, Charles and Philip Stanford, brothers of Leland Stanford, annoyed Mr. Huntington by demanding of him a return of their moneys that had been invested in the Central Pacific Railroad Company. On May 11, 1866, Mr. Huntington wrote as follows to Mr. Hopkins:

I think you are quite right in keeping all the securities together until the road is completed. It is very uncertain about what a fellow like Phil Stanford would do with his—build a wind mill or do some other foolish thing that would not only put the securities out of the company's reach, but would likely bring the company into bad odor before public with his foolish pranks.

On April 11, 1867, he wrote another letter to Mr. Hopkins marked confidential, a later one of several on the same subject:

I saw Charles Stanford again a few days since, and he said he was interested in the Central Pacific, that it was his money that had carried it through. He said the Boys [his brothers] owed him large amounts and whenever he wrote for money, they answered that they were putting it in the Pacific Railroad, and he was not going to be cheated out of it. If he could not have what belonged to him, he would, like Samson, pull down the building if he destroyed himself in so doing . . . I said to him quietly that if the Boys had used his money, they ought to pay him, that I was inclined to think they would. I thought it just possible that Phil Stanford had gotten some foolish notions and written to Charles.

Some years later, after many appeals, Mr. Huntington made arrangements with Mr. Hopkins to pay Charles Stanford in installments the amount due him. Charles said he had written to his brother Leland six times about the matter but had received no reply. In order to keep Charles quiet, Mr. Huntington attended to it himself.

On December 8, 1867, he wrote to Mr. Hopkins as follows:

I would like very much to see and talk over matters with you, but it has seemed so necessary for the last three years that you should be there and I here, that I could not devise any means by which we could get together without business and railroad interests suffering.

The strenuous years of 1873-1874 had been hard for Mr. Hopkins who had been ever on the alert to respond immediately to the innumerable requests of Mr. Huntington for money to carry them through. Mr. Huntington had become concerned about his health and wrote to him June 23, 1874, urging him to come to New York for a change. "You and

COLLIS P. HUNTINGTON

LELAND S. STANFORD

CHARLES CROCKER

MARK HOPKINS

The Four Associates

Facsimile of an Advertisement

Mrs. Hopkins must get on the office car and come. You owe it to me. I want very much to see you. I have thought much of you lately."

Mr. Huntington's next letter to Mr. Hopkins was dated November 13, 1874, and referred to the latter's absence from the city. He was away about four months. On November 29, Mr. Huntington wrote as follows:

Yours of November—is received, and it is a long time since I have received a letter that gave me the satisfaction that this has for the reason that it tells me that you are in the office and well again . . . I will go over in a few days and will endeavor to convince Delano that honesty is the best policy. It will not do to quarrel with him, but he must be taken into our camp, and then with a good example always before him, he most likely would do what was right.

His reference to Delano and not quareling with him is in harmony with his conciliatory attitude in many of his letters. His attitude toward Governor Booth and his hostility toward the railroad has been commented upon. Two members of the Union Pacific Railroad Company were referred to in his letter of May 27, 1875:

I notice what you write of Gould and Dillon. I shall not disagree with you about those men but if it is possible for us to work in harmony with them I think we should do so, or at least not come to an open quarrel with them, if we can avoid it. Very likely we could harm them as much as they could us, but I cannot see that harming them would help us.

On March 28, 1876, he writes Mr. Hopkins that he thinks A. A .Cohen is "the meanest man on earth," yet three days later he writes about him as follows:

I notice from the California papers that our quarrel with Cohen is growing. It does seem that our close connection with Cohen could have broken off without an open quarrel. Somehow we seem to be very unfortunate in our quarrels in California. No doubt Cohen is a very bad man, so was Morrill and Anthony [of the Sacramento *Union*], so is Booth, but there never was any necessity of our quarrelling with them.

In another letter about Cohen written January 5, 1877, he says:

Saw Cohen last week, had a friendly talk with him. Got him and Stanford together. He said he wanted no quarrel with us, etc. Cohen wants to be friendly, and it would be well to be on good terms with him. Life is too short to have many quarrels on our hands with all our other business. Ask Crocker to make friends with Cohen, but don't say I suggested it. Cohen said he was to have free transportation between his house and San Francisco, that it was so agreed verbally by Stanford. I told him that if Stanford agreed to that it should be done. I am satisfied that we can be on friendly terms. Of course, you understand, it will not be necessary that he and we should sleep together.

And this was the man who in the course of years misappropriated a large amount from the railroad company; who took it upon himself in a letter to a well-known banker in New York, to contradict every statement made by Mr. Huntington in a pamphlet describing the San Joaquin Valley as a desirable place of residence, referring to the pamphlet as "a work of fiction entitled to the first rank"; who later made an address in San Francisco on "The Railroad Evils and Their Remedy"; and who never lost an opportunity to speak disparagingly of every member of the railroad company until 1883, when he was employed by the company on the Colton case; after which he deliberately reversed himself on many particulars connected with the railroad.

Even Luttrell who had tried to injure him and the company with Congress, later when the affair was dropped, won Mr. Huntington's approval as one of the California delegates who was doing "first rate."

It was not generally known that the Central Pacific Company was offered the task of constructing and operating the Canadian Pacific Railway; yet among the collection is a letter to Mark Hopkins from Judge A. F. Scott, Brampton, County of Peel, Ontario, dated October 4, 1876, and enclosing a letter of introduction from the Attorney-General of Ontario. In this letter Judge Scott refers to the friendship between his late cousin, Jeremiah O'Leary of Sacramento and Mr. Hopkins, and offers him and his company the "construction and control" of the Canadian Pacific Railway which it was the intention of the Canadian Government to have built.

In his reply, October 12, 1876, Mr. Hopkins said that he and his associates had noted with interest the preliminary progress of that undertaking, but never with a thought of engaging in its construction and management, etc., etc.

During the years 1875 to 1878, Mr. Huntington was endeavoring to get two bills through Congress, his sinking fund bill and the bill for a franchise to build the Southern Pacific Railroad across Arizona and New Mexico under the land grants that had been assigned to the Texas & Pacific Company, neither of which was passed. At the same time he was fighting to prevent the passage of two bills, Scott's bill for a large subsidy toward extending the Texas & Pacific Railroad to Yuma, and the infamous Thurman bill, of which only the former failed to pass. The great strain of this work at Washington in addition to his other manifold duties, is revealed in these letters:

I am having a very rough time in Washington this winter. You can hardly know how ugly matters are. Just how we shall come out, I cannot tell. I have strong hopes that we shall get through all right, but it will cost fearfully . . .

It looks as though all our enemies from California and Tom Scott and all his friends here and elsewhere had united to pass this bill, but I think not. The fight is a rough one as it now stands . . . Three calls to Washington to-night . . . We have against us the worst fight our enemies can make . . . Just returned from Washington very nearly used up. Things look bad there. It looks as though the Devil, the Commissioners and the Pennsylvania Railroad [Scott's] had united against us . . .

When the new residences for Charles Crocker, Leland Stanford and Mark Hopkins were in the process of construction on California Street, Mr. Huntington wrote to Mr. Hopkins, March 23, 1877, enclosing a clipping with the following headlines: "Millionaires' Palaces. Residences That Cost Altogether Over $7,000,000."

This article is going the rounds of the papers on this side. This clip is from *The Commercial* of yesterday and is really hurting us, and is calculated to hurt us in Congress as well as financially. If you could have a truthful article published in the *Bulletin*, or some other San Francisco paper, then let it travel through the papers on this side, it would do us good. Of course I can say nothing and know nothing to say. It is hurting us more than you think, but this is an aggressive age.

A few days later on March 26, he sent Mr. Hopkins a clipping from *"The Banker and Capitalist"* which read as follows:

A paragraph is going the rounds of the so-called "news" papers to the effect that four of the Central Pacific Railroad managers in

San Francisco have built for themselves Palaces on top of California Street Hill costing two or three millions apiece. Of course this is a mistake. Palaces more splendid in papers than in fact; all wooden buildings and with furniture and all may have cost $200,000 or $300,000 each. Represents a net profit of a little real estate speculation, a comparatively worthless knob transformed into the best building site in the city.

A note from Mr. Huntington was added:

Friend Hopkins—As I suppose you do not want to sell your house, I thought it would be well to reduce the price a little.—H.

At the time of his death, he and Mrs. Hopkins were living in a small cottage on Sutter Street, while awaiting completion of the new home. Several years after Mr. Hopkins' death the house on Nob Hill was given to the California School of Fine Arts.

Mr. Hopkins was regarded by his associates as the "balance wheel" of the organization. His advice was always sought whenever difficult problems arose and his decision was seldom at fault. Mr. Huntington said of him:

He was one of the truest and best men who ever lived, a very correct man in everything, a very able man . . . He always seemed to know just what was the best thing to do in all cases. I never considered anything finished until Hopkins had looked at it.

It was to this associate and trusted friend that Mr. Huntington addressed those letters. Unfortunately the replies of Mr. Hopkins have never been located; they were probably destroyed many years ago. The Huntington-Hopkins correspondence covered three years of the Huntington-Colton correspondence. Frequently the letters in both groups dealt with the same subject and refer to the high cost of getting bills through Congress; the cost, as Mr. Huntington repeatedly said, of hiring persons to explain matters to uninformed senators and members of Congress; yet nothing in these letters to Mr. Hopkins have any reference whatever to "debauching senators and representatives, buying up legislatures," etc. such as the Opposition claimed to have found in the letters to Colton.

From an article about the Colton letters, we give the following excerpts:

> . . . If the public could only be privileged to read what he wrote to Leland Stanford and to Charles Crocker and to Mark Hopkins— as well as to David Colton—there would be much to reflect upon. But the public never will see such letters, the nature of them required their immediate destruction . . . That was the safest way. It is not wise to allow great numbers of thinking people to read that they are victims of chicanery, corruption in high places, bribery, and oppression through conspiracy. There might be something more than a spice of danger in such carelessness.[1]

NOTES AND REFERENCES

CHAPTER II

1. Huntington, Elijah. *A Genealogical Memoir of the Huntington Family in this Country.* Stamford, Conn., 1863.
2. *Ibid.*
3. *Ibid.*
4. Huntington Family Association. *The Huntington Family in America, a Genealogical Memoir of the Known Descendants of Simon Huntington from 1633 to 1915.* Hartford, Conn., 1915.
5. Huntington, *op. cit.*
6. Huntington Family Association, *op. cit.*

CHAPTER III

1. Nunan, T. E. *Birthplace and Early Life of C. P. Huntington.* (San Francisco *Call*, Feb. 2, 1896.)
2. Huntington, Archer M. Stories of his father, C. P. Huntington.
3. Bancroft, Hubert Howe. *Chronicles of the Builders of the Commonwealth.* San Francisco, 1891. v. 5, p. 22.

CHAPTER IV

1. Bancroft, H. H. *Chronicles of the Builders.* San Francisco, 1891. v. 5, p. 25.
2. *Ibid.*
3. Sacramento *Union,* Aug. 13, 1872. Reprinted from The Tulare *Times,* Aug. 10, 1872.
4. Ferguson, Homer L., formerly President of the Newport News Shipbuilding & Dry Dock Company.

CHAPTER V

1. Campbell, Dudley M. *A History of Oneonta.* New York, 1901, p. 178.
2. Huntington, Willard Vincent. *Oneonta Memoirs and Sundry Personal Recollections.* San Francisco, 1891.
3. *Ibid.*
4. Campbell, *op. cit.,* p. 180.
5. *Ibid.*
6. Huntington, Archer M. Stories of his father.

CHAPTER VI

1. Howe, Octavius Thorndyke. *Argonauts of '49.* Cambridge: Harvard University Press, 1923. Pp. 4, 6.
2. *Ibid.,* p. 16.
3. *Geographical Journal.* London, v. 22, Dec. 1903, p. 680.
4. Anderson, C. L. G. *Old Panama and Castilla del Oro.* Washington, 1911, p. 8.
5. Robinson, Fayette. *California and Its Gold Fields.* New York, 1849. Appendix, Anonymous letter, Dec. 17, 1849, p. 130.
6. Abbot, Willis J. *The Panama Canal.* New York, 1914, p. 190.
7. Robinson, *op. cit.,* p. 130.
8. Bancroft, H. H. *Chronicles of the Builders.* 6 vols. San Francisco, 1891. v. 5, p. 32.
9. Robinson, *op. cit.,* p. 130.
10. Bancroft, *op. cit.,* p. 33.
11. Howe, *op. cit.,* p. 26.
12. Several writers have stated that Mr. Huntington walked the twenty or twenty-odd miles *across* the Isthmus which is only the distance from Panama to Gorgona. The rest of the way across was impassable except by boat, forty miles from Gorgona.
13. Bancroft, *op. cit.,* p. 34.
14. Comstock, Sarah. *Story of the Ship* HUMBOLDT *Which Arrived at San Francisco, Aug. 30, 1849.* (In San Francisco *Call,* Sept. 2, 1900, p. 11.)

CHAPTER VII

1. Taylor, Bayard. *Eldorado; or, Adventures in the Path of Empire,* 8th ed. New York, 1856, v. 2, p. 55.
2. Upham, Samuel C. *Notes of a Voyage to California . . . 1849-1850.* Philadelphia, 1878, p. 225.
3. Taylor, *op. cit.,* p. 58.
4. Upham, *op. cit.,* p. 310.
5. Dana, Julian. *The Sacramento, River of Gold.* New York, 1939, p. 159.
6. Upham, *op. cit.,* p. 310.
7. Taylor, *op. cit.,* p. 219.
8. Upham, *op. cit.,* p. 313.
9. Miles, George E. *Collis Potter Huntington.* [New York, 1896?], p. 13.
10. *Ibid.,* p. 17.
11. Phelps, Alonzo. *Contemporary Biographies of California's Representative Men,* 1881, pp. 390-395.
12. Bancroft, H. H. *Chronicles of the Builders.* 6 vols. San Francisco, 1891, v. 5, p. 37.
13. *Ibid.*
14. *Ibid.,* p. 38.
15. Sacramento Directory, 1853-1856.

CHAPTER VIII

1. Sacramento Directory, 1850-1852.
2. Democratic State Journal letter sheet for the steamer, December 1, 1852.
3. Directory, *op. cit.*, 1853-1855.
4. Bancroft, H. H. *Chronicles*, v. 5, p. 39.
5. Transcript on Huntington, Hopkins & Co. in the Bancroft Library, University of California, Berkeley, Calif.
6. *Ibid.*
7. *Ibid.*
8. Huntington, Collis P. *Letters to Mark Hopkins*, 1865-1878 in the Archives at Stanford University, Stanford, Calif.

CHAPTER IX

1. Sacramento *Union*, December 5, 1885.
2. Parkinson, R. R. *Pen Portraits*. San Francisco, 1878.
3. Sacramento *Union, op. cit.*
4. Manuscript Transcript of Huntington, Hopkins & Co. in the Bancroft Library, University of California, Berkeley, Calif.
5. *Ibid.*

CHAPTER X

1. Dunbar, Seymour. *History of Travel in America.* 4 vols. Indianapolis, 1915. These items on Pacific Railroad projects are from the above work, v. 4, p. 1330-
2. *Ibid.*, v. 4, 1334.
3. *Daily National Intelligencer,* Washington, D. C. Nov. 10, 1849.

CHAPTER XI

1. U. S. War Department. *Reports of Explorations and Surveys.* 12 vols. Washington, D. C., 1855-1860. Vol. 1: Report of Jefferson Davis, Secretary of War.
2. *Ibid.*, Preface.

CHAPTER XII

1. *Alta Californian,* Sept. 8, 1851.
2. *Ibid.*, Dec. 6, 1851.
3. San Francisco *Bulletin*, Nov. 3, 1859.
4. Sacramento *Union,* April 29, 1861.

5. Robinson, L. L., Director Sacramento Valley Railroad Company. Evidence given at the Nevada Assembly, Carson City, in July, 1864.

6. *History of Sacramento County,* Oakland, 1880, p. 199.

7. Sacramento *Union,* March 28, 1861.

8. *Ibid.,* May 11, 1861.

9. *History of Sacramento County, op. cit.,* p. 196.

10. Sacramento *Union,* March 13, 1858.

11. *Ibid.,* March 3, 1858.

12. *Ibid.,* March 20, 1858.

CHAPTER XIII

1. San Francisco *Bulletin,* Sept. 17, 26, 1859.

2. Hittell, Theodore H. *History of California.* 4 vols. San Francisco, 1885-1887. v. 4, p. 454.

3. San Francisco *Bulletin,* Oct. 20, 1859.

4. *Ibid.,* March 8, 1860.

CHAPTER XIV

1. Daggett, Stuart. *Chapters on the History of the Southern Pacific.* New York, 1922, p. 8.

2. *Ibid.,* p. 9.

3. Sacramento *Union,* June 12, 1857.

4. Willis, William L. *History of Sacramento County.* Los Angeles, 1913, p. 193.

5. Bancroft, H. H. *Chronicles of the Builders.* v. 5, p. 48.

6. Crocker, Charles. Manuscript in the Bancroft Library. University of California, Berkeley, Calif.

7. Nordhoff, Charles. *The Central Pacific.* (In Harper's Magazine, v. 45, 1872, p. 68.)

8. Sacramento *Union,* Sept. 20, 1862.

9. *Ibid.,* June 29, 1861.

10. Bancroft, *op. cit.,* p. 40.

11. Document No. 29 in the Hopkins Collection, Stanford University Labrary, Stanford, Calif.

CHAPTER XV

1. Bancroft, Hubert Howe. *History of California.* 7 vols. San Francisco, 1886-1890. v. 7, p. 566, note.

2. *Congressional Globe,* 37th Congress, 2nd Session, 1861-1862, p. 1912.

CHAPTER XVI

1. Several writers on the subject of the Central Pacific Railroad have ignored the presence of Collis Potter Huntington in Washington at this time and the important part he had in the passage of this bill, even to the extent of attributing to another the humorous telegram he sent to his associates when the bill was passed:

   (1) Wheat, Carl I. *A Sketch of the Life of Theodore Judah.* (In the California Historical Society Quarterly, v. 4, Sept., 1925, p. 243.)

   (2) Lewis, Oscar. *The Big Four.* New York, 1936, p. 35.

   (3) Holbrook, Stewart H. *The Story of American Railroads.* New York, 1947, p. 164.

2. Huntington manuscript in the Bancroft Library, p. 102.

3. *Congressional Globe,* 37th Congress, 2nd Session, 1861-1862, p. 1947.

4. *Ibid.,* p. 1710.

5. Sabin, Edward L. *Building the Pacific Railway.* Philadelphia, 1919, p. 38.

6. *Congressional Globe, op. cit.,* p. 2786.

7. *Ibid.,* p. 1947.

8. *Ibid.,* p. 2788.

9. *Ibid.,* p. 1580

10. *Ibid.,* pp. 1590-1592.

11. *Ibid.,* p. 1593.

12. *Ibid.,* p. 1595.

13. *Ibid.,* p. 1710.

14. *Ibid.,* p. 1593.

15. *Ibid.,* p. 1593.

16. *Ibid.,* p. 1891.

17. *Ibid.,* p. 3754.

18. *Ibid.,* p. 2757.

19. *Ibid.,* p. 2757.

CHAPTER XVII

1. *U. S. Statutes at Large,* No. 12, p. 489.

CHAPTER XIX

1. U. S. Pacific Railway Commission. Report, 1887, p. 68.

2. Bancroft, H. H. *History of California.* 7 vols. San Francisco, 1886-1890. v. 7, p. 557.

CHAPTER XX

1. Documents in Stanford University Library compiled by Mark Hopkins, v. 1, p. 8.

2. *Ibid.,* p. 10.

3. Mr. Pratt's daughter, Sarah Pratt Carr, author of *The Iron Way,* a fictional account of the Central Pacific Railroad, accompanied her father as he directed construction of the wagon road, living with her mother in a house that was moved along the road as it progressed.

4. Stanford, Leland. Testimony before the U. S. Pacific Railway Commission, v. 5, p. 2927.

5. Heath, Erle. *From Trail to Rail.* (In *Southern Pacific Bulletin,* April, 1927.)

6. Stanford, *op. cit.,* p. 2927.

CHAPTER XXI

1. Quiett, Glenn C. *They Built the West.* New York, 1934, p. 76.

2. Stanford's testimony before the Pacific Railway Commission. v. 5, p. 2927.

3. *Ibid.,* p. 2670.

CHAPTER XXII

1. Holmes, Henry Thomas. Transcript in the Banford Library, p. 13. Both Oliver and Oakes Ames were connected later with the Union Pacific Railroad, the former being the President of the company from 1868 to 1871.

2. Bancroft, H. H. *History of California.* v. 7, p. 565n.

3. Bancroft, H. H. *Chronicles of the Builders.* v. 5, p. 57.

4. Clark, George T. *Leland Stanford.* Stanford, 1931, p. 206.

5. Bancroft, *Chronicles,* v. 5, p. 61.

6. Bancroft. *History,* v. 7, p. 567n. A quite different version of this episode is given in Bancroft's *Chronicles of the Builders,* v. 5, p. 63, substituting the name of Judah for Peel, and changing the time from the beginning of construction to the fall of 1863.

7. *History of Sacramento County,* 1880, p. 198.

CHAPTER XXIII

1. Sacramento *Union,* Jan. 9, 1863.

2. Willis, William Ladd. *History of Sacramento,* 1913, p. 198.

3. Haymond, Creed. *Argument before the Senate Committee,* March, 1888, p. 102.

4. *Ibid.,* p. 108.

5. Judah, T. D. *Report of the Chief Engineer,* July 1, 1863.

6. Wheat, Carl I. *Life of Theodore Judah.* (In California Historical Society Quarterly, v. 4, Sept., 1925, p. 261.)

7. Fisk & Hatch. *Railroad Communication Across the Continent, 1868.*

8. Lewis, Oscar. *The Big Four.* New York, 1938, p. 44.

9. Conkling, Roscoe and Shipman, Wm. D. *Review of the Testimony Presented Before the U. S. Pacific Railway Commission.* New York, 1887, p. 68.

10. Huntington manuscript in the Bancroft Library, University of California, p. 13.

11. Heath, Erle. *From Trail to Rail.* (In *Southern Pacific Bulletin*, April, 1927.)

12. Phelps, Alonzo. *Contemporary Biography of California's Representative Men.* San Francisco, 1881, p. 59.

CHAPTER XXIV

1. The actual time required to construct through six tunnels and across the summit from the time of this prediction was eleven months—fourteen years and one month less than the time the distinguished engineer said would be required.

2. Sacramento *Union*, Jan. 28, 1864.

3. Heath, Erle. *From Trail to Rail.* (In *Southern Pacific Bulletin*, Dec., 1926.)

4. Railroad Pamphlets, v. 1, No. 5, in California State Library, Sacramento.

5. Sacramento *Union*, Jan. 28, 30; Feb. 6, 1864.

6. Heath, *op. cit.*, March, 1927.

7. Hittell, Theodore H. *History of California,* 4 vols. San Francisco, 1885-1897, v. 4, p. 480.

CHAPTER XXV

1. Wheat, Carl I. *Biography of Judah.* (In the California Historical Society Quarterly, v. 4, Sept., 1925, p. 261.)

2. *Ibid.*

3. Lewis, Oscar. *The Big Four.* New York, 1938, p. 45.

4. Daggett, Stuart. *Chapters on the History of the Southern Pacific.* New York, 1922, p. 59.

5. Heath, Erle. *From Trail to Rail.* (In the *Southern Pacific Bulletin*, May, 1927.)

6. Holbrook, Stewart H. *Story of American Railroads.* New York, 1947, p. 164.

7. Heath, *op. cit.*, Dec., 1926. Quoted.

8. *Around the World by Steam via Pacific Railway.* By a Traveller. London, 1871.

9. Phillips, David L. *Letters from California.* Springfield, Ill., 1877.

10. Bancroft, H. H. *History of California.* 7 vols. San Francisco, 1886-1890, v. 7, p. 190.

11. Heath, *op. cit.*, April, 1927.

12. Clark, George T. *Leland Stanford.* Stanford, 1931, p. 190.

13. Judah manuscript in the Bancroft Library.

14. Clark, *op. cit.*, p. 191.

15. Judah Manuscript in the Bancroft Library.

16. Hopkins, Mark. Documents relative to the Central Pacific Railroad Company. v. 1, p. 29.

17. *History of Sacramento County,* 1880, p. 198.

CHAPTER XXVI

1. Sacramento *Union,* March 21, 1864.

2. *Ibid.,* March 26, 1864.

3. *Ibid.,* April 26, 1864.

4. Heath, Erle. *From Trail to Rail.* (In the *Southern Pacific Bulletin,* May, 1927.)

5. Crocker manuscript in the Bancroft Library.

6. The *Evening Bulletin,* March 22, 1864.

7. McCormic, George. *Motive Power in Western Development.* (In the Society of Engineers' Yearbook, 1928, p. 44.)

8. Sacramento *Union,* Jan. 28, 30; Feb. 6, 1864.

9. *Ibid.,* July 2, Dec. 5, 1864.

10. *Ibid.,* Nov. 3, 1862.

11. *Congressional Globe,* 37th Congress, 1862, p. 1580.

12. Railroad Pamphlets in the California State Library, Sacramento, v. 1, no. 5, p. 62; no. 7, pp. 4-12.

CHAPTER XXVII

1. *Congressional Globe,* 38th Congress, 1864, p. 3022.

2. Cole, Cornelius. *Memoirs.* New York, 1908, p. 179.

3. *Congressional Globe, op. cit.,* p. 1142.

4. *Ibid.,* p. 3022.

5. *Ibid.*

6. U. S. Statutes at Large, XIII, p. 356.

7. Crocker manuscript in the Bancroft Library, p. 20.

8. Clark, George T. *Leland Stanford.* Stanford, 1931, p. 213.

9. *Ibid.,* p. 207.

10. *Ibid.,* p. 208.

11. Haymond, Creed. *Argument Before the Senate Committee,* March 17, 26, and April 7, 1888.

CHAPTER XXVIII

1. Sacramento *Union,* Aug. 3, 1865.

2. Heath, Erle. *From Trail to Rail.* (In the *Southern Pacific Bulletin,* May, 1927.)

3. Haymond, Creed. *Argument Before the Senate Committee.* March 17, 26, and April 7, 1888.

4. Heath, *op. cit.,* June, 1927.

5. Huntington, C. P. *The Central Pacific Railroad of California, 1866.* A knowledge of this extra work through hard rock for future tracks should have given pause to those writers who claim that the builders did the work hurriedly and flimsily in order to get the Government subsidy as soon as possible.

6. Heath, *op. cit.,* July, 1927.

7. Arthur Brown's testimony before the U. S. Pacific Railway Commission. v. 5, p. 2581.

8. Huntington, *op. cit.*

9. *History of Sacramento County,* 1880, p. 199.

10. Haymond, *op. cit.,* p. 63.

CHAPTER XXIX

1. Lansing, Gerrit L. *Relations Between the Central Pacific Railroad Company and the U. S. Government.* San Francisco, 1889, p. 76.

2. His testimony before the U. S. Pacific Railway Commission. 1887, p. 10.

3. Lansing, *op. cit.,* p. 82.

4. Carmen, Harry J. and Muller, Charles H. *The Contract & Finance Co. and the Central Pacific Railroad.* (In the Mississippi Valley Historical Review, v. 14, Dec., 1927.)

5. Heath, *op. cit.,* July ,1927.

CHAPTER XXX

1. Sacramento *Union,* March 22, 1867.

2. San Francisco *Bulletin,* Feb. 28, 1867.

3. Statutes of California, 1867-1868, p. 473.

4. Hopkins documents, v. 2, p. 5.

5. Cornelius Cole, Senator from California.

6. Hittell, J. S. *History of the City of San Francisco,* 1878, p. 390.

7. Clark, George T. *Leland Stanford.* Stanford, 1931, p. 321.

8. Cole, Cornelius. *Memoirs.* 1908, p. 266.

9. California *Spirit of the Times,* May 4, 1872.

10. Huntington-Hopkins Correspondence, v. 11, p. 117.

CHAPTER XXXI

1. Hopkins documents, v. 1, p. 5.

2. Hopkins, *op. cit.,* p. 4.

3. Sacramento *Union,* March 7, 1868.

4. *Ibid.,* March 9, 1868.

5. San Francisco *Bulletin,* March 9, 1868.

6. Sacramento *Union,* March 28, 1868.

7. Statutes of California, 1867-1868, p. 716.

8. Sacramento *Union,* May 13, 1869.

9. Clark, George T. *Leland Stanford.* Stanford, 1931, p. 315.

10. *California Mail Bag,* v. 1, 1872, p. 33.

11. Clark, *op. cit.,* p. 320.

12. Cornelius Cole, Senator from California.

13. San Francisco *Call,* Nov. 1, 1892.

14. San Francisco *Daily Record,* Nov. 7, 1892.

CHAPTER XXXII

1. Letter from Mark Hopkins to C. P. Huntington, Feb. 15, 1873.

2. Huntington manuscript in the Bancroft Library.

3. Crocker manuscript in the Bancroft Library, p. 35.

4. *Ibid.,* p. 35.

5. *Ibid.,* p. 36.

6. California *Spirit of the Times,* Aug. 5, 1871.

7. Clark, George T. *Leland Stanford.* Stanford, 1931, p. 285.

8. *Ibid.,* p. 303.

9. Huntington-Hopkins Correspondence, v. 10, p. 117.

CHAPTER XXXIII

1. Letter from Mark Hopkins to C. P. Huntington, Feb. 15, 1873.

2. Heath, Erle. *From Trail to Rail.* (In *Southern Pacific Bulletin,* Aug., 1927.)

3. An Act of Congress permitted construction crews to grade 300 miles from the end of the completed line.

4. Stobridge, J. H., engineer. Testimony before the U. S. Pacific Railway Commission, 1887.

5. Phillips, David L. *Letters from California.* Springfield, Ill., 1887. Letter no. 2.

6. Hammond, Creed. *Argument before the Senate Committee,* March 17, 1888, p. 24.

7. Heath, *op. cit.,* Aug., 1927.

8. Williams, H. J. *The Pacific Tourist, 1879,* p. 164.

9. Heath, *op. cit.*

10. Sherman, Gen. T. Testimony before the U. S. Pacific Railway Committee, 1887.

11. Curtis, Wellman. *Biography of Leland Stanford.*
12. Del Mar, Alexander. *Our Road Builders and the State.* (In *The Californian,* 1880, v. 2, p. 360.)
13. *Around the World.* By a Traveller.
14. *Spirit of the Times.*
15. Sacramento *Union,* June 19, 1868.
16. *Ibid.,* March 19, 1868.
17. Myers, Augustus. *History of Great American Fortunes.* 1936, p. 519.
18. Russell, Charles E. *Stories of the Great Railroads.* 1912, p. 127.
19. Cohen, Alfred A. No. 1 in each pair is an extract from his *"Address on the Railroad Evil and Its Remedy,"* delivered at Platt's Hall, San Francisco, Aug. 2, 1879, p. 9; while no. 2 in each pair is an extract from his testimony before the U. S. Pacific Railway Commission, p. 2398.
20. California *Spirit of the Times,* Sept. 25, 1869.
21. *Ibid.*
22. United States vs. Central Pacific Railroad Company, Circuit Court, District of California. Oct., 1877.
23. Hopkins documents, v. 2, p. 34.
24. United States vs. Central Pacific, *op. cit.*
25. *Ibid.*

CHAPTER XXXIV

1. Huntington manuscript in the Bancroft Library.
2. Letter from Huntington to E. B. Crocker.
3. Town Topics. *A Great American.* Sept., 1900.
4. Boruck, Marcus D., in the California *Spirit of the Times.* Oct. 15, 1870.

CHAPTER XXXV

1. Curtis, Edward. *What the Locomotive has Done for California.* (In *California Mail Bag,* v. 4, March, 1874, p. 97.)
2. *Ibid.*
3. *Ibid.*
4. *Ibid.*
5. Report No. 440. 44th Congress, 1st Session, 1876.
6. Vernon, Edward, comp. *American Railroad Manual for the United States and the Dominion.* 1874.

CHAPTER XXXVI

1. *History of Sacramento County.* 1880, p. 200.
2. Clark, George T. *Leland Stanford.* Stanford, 1931.

3. History, *op. cit.*

4. Trinity *Journal,* Jan. 12, 1867.

5. Shasta *Courier,* May 29, 1869.

6. Sacramento *Record-Union,* Jan. 24, 1881.

7. Root, Henry. *Personal History and Reminiscences,* San Francisco, 1921.

8. Hopkins documents, v. 2, p. 17.

9. Van Nostrand Engineering Magazine, March, 1871, p. 331.

10. Felton, John P. *The Railroad System of California.* San Francisco, 1871.

11. Hopkins documents, v. 2, p. 6.

12. Huntington testimony before the Pacific Railway Commission, 1887.

13. Heath, Erle. *From Trail to Rail.* (In the *Southern Pacific Bulletin,* June, 1928.)

14. Hittell, John S. *History of the City of San Francisco.* 1878, p. 385.

15. Daggett, Stuart. *Chapters on the History of the Southern Pacific.* New York, 1922, p. 108.

16. Root, *op. cit.,* p. 35.

17. Trinity *Journal,* Dec. 8, 1866.

18. Yreka *Journal,* Feb. 21, 1865.

19. Redding *Republican,* Oct. 31, 1865.

20. Yreka *Journal,* Dec. 21, 1887.

21. Daggett, *op. cit.,* p. 127.

22. Hopkins documents, v. 2, pp. 18, 19.

23. Daggett, *op. cit.,* p. 127.

24. Heath, *op. cit.,* Aug., 1928.

25. *Ibid.,* Sept., 1928.

26. Hopkins documents, v. 2, p. 20.

27. Hittell, *op. cit.,* p. 417.

28. Heath, *op. cit.,* July, 1928.

29. *Ibid.,* June, 1928.

30. *Ibid.,* Aug., 1928.

31. Letters from Chas. Crocker to C. P. Huntington, 1882-1883.

32. Heath, *op. cit.,* Oct., 1928.

33. Powell, Fred Wilber. *Railroads of Mexico.* Boston, 1921, p. 137.

CHAPTER XXXVII

1. Hopkins, Mark. Collection of documents relative to the Central Pacific Railroad Company, v. 2, p. 28.

2. McCreary, George W., Secretary of War. *Letter to the Speaker of the House of Representatives,* Jan. 13, 1878.

3. Hopkins, Timothy. Explanatory note in the Huntington-Hopkins correspondence, v. 9, p. 181.

4. Haymond, Creed. *The Central Pacific Railroad, Its Relations to the Government.* San Francisco, 1886. p. 75.

5. Heath, Erle. *From Trail to Rail.* (In *Southern Pacific Bulletin*, Dec., 1928.)

6. Dictionary of American Biography, v. 3, p. 165.

7. White & Kemble. *Report on the Physical and Financial Condition of the Southern Pacific Company.* Aug. 1, 1902.

8. *The Argonaut*, April 26, 1884.

9. House ex. doc. no. 60, p. 6, 49th Congress, 1st Session, 1885-1886.

10. Clark, George T. *Leland Stanford.* Stanford, 1931. p. 437.

11. Thelin, Max. *The Proposed Central Pacific and Southern Pacific Unmerger.* (In railroad pamphlet, Bancroft Library.)

CHAPTER XXXVIII

1. *Bay Memories.* Reprinted from the *Southern Pacific Bulletin*, edited by Erle Heath.

2. San Francisco *Call*, May 8, 1913.

3. Willis, Wm. L. *History of Sacramento County, 1913*, p. 204.

4. His testimony before the Pacific Railway Commission, 1887.

5. The history of the Pacific Mail Steamship Company has been ably written by John Haskell Kemble in his *The Panama Route, 1848-1849*, and *The Transpacific Railroads, 1869-1915.* The brief account given here is to review Mr. Huntington's connection with the company.

6. Curtis, William Elroy. *Trade and Transportation Between the U. S. and Spanish America, 1889.* pp. 184, 188.

7. Kemble, John Haskell. *The Transpacific Railroads.* pp. 334-337.

8. Clyde, William B. (President of the Pacific Mail SS Co.) *Report, April 3, 1887.*

9. *Ibid.*

10. House ex. doc. no. 60, p. 12. 49th Congress, 1st Session, 1886.

11. His testimony before the Pacific Railway Commission, 1887, p. 3787.

12. *Report of the Pacific Mail for 1899.*

13. The history of the Occidental and Oriental Steamship Company has been told by John Haskell Kemble in his *The Big Four at Sea.* The brief account given here is derived from this work together with some original letters.

14. *Dictionary of American Biography*, v. 13, p. 165.

CHAPTER XXXIX

1. Dunbar, Seymour. *History of Travel in America.* 4 vols. Indianapolis, 1915. v. 4, p. 1405.

2. Letters of C. P. Huntington to Mark Hopkins, March 31, 1876, and to Jas. W. Throckmorton, chairman of the Committee on Pacific Railroads, Jan. 25, 1886.

3. Madden, Jerome. *Lands of the Southern Pacific Railroad Company of California.* San Francisco, 1876.

4. Haymond, Creed. *Argument before the Senate Committee,* March 17, 1888, p. 58.

5. Bond, Frank S. (Vice-President, Texas & Pacific Railroad Co.) *Address before the House Committee on Pacific Railroads,* Jan. 29, 1878.

6. Hopkins documents, v. 2, p. 26.

7. Del Mar, Alexander. *Our Roadbuilders of the State.* (In the *Californian,* v. 2, Oct., 1880, pp. 359-363.)

8. San Francisco *Bulletin,* April 11, 1884.

9. Sacramento *Record-Union,* April 25, 1881.

10. *Memorial and Biographical History of the Counties of Fresno, Tulare, and Kern, California.* Chicago, 1892, p. 166.

11. *Ibid.*

12. Smith, Wallace. *Garden of the Sun.* Los Angeles, 1939.

13. Bancroft, H. H. *History of California.* 7 vols. San Francisco, 1886-1890, v. 7, p. 617.

14. Smith, W. *op. cit.*

15. Bancroft, *op. cit.,* p. 618.

16. Sacramento *Record-Union,* April 25, 1881.

17. Bancroft, *op. cit.*

18. San Francisco *Examiner,* Aug. 28, 1893.

19. *Ibid.*

CHAPTER XL

1. Sacramento *Union,* Feb. 7, 1868.

2. Young, John Park. *San Francisco.* Chicago, 1912, p. 355.

3. Poor's *Manual of Railroads,* 1881-1885.

4. Sacramento *Union,* Dec. 14, 1867, and Jan. 11, 1868.

5. California *Spirit of the Times,* Feb. 15, 1878.

6. Hittell, John S. *Commerce and Industry of the Pacific Coast,* 1882.

7. California *Spirit of the Times,* Feb. 16, 1878.

8. Sacramento *Union,* Jan. 6, 1868.

9. Hopkins, Mark. Collection of documents relative to the Central Pacific Railroad Company, v. 1, p. 20.

10. Bancroft, H. H. *History of California,* v. 7, p. 625.

11. California *Mail Bag,* April, 1874, v. 5, p. 44.

12. Bancroft, *op. cit.,* v. 7, p. 626.

13. California *Spirit of the Times,* July 14, 1883.

14. Walker, David H. *Pioneers of Prosperity, 1895,* p. 89.

15. Hart, George A. *Rates of Railroad Transportation.* (In *The Overland Monthly,* v. 11, Sept. 1873, p. 254.)

16. Fink, Albert. *Legislative Regulation of Railroads.* (In *Engineering Magazine,* July, 1895, p. 623.)

17. John Shertzer Hittell was a journalist from 1853 to 1880 on the staff of *The Alta Californian,* a San Francisco newspaper bitterly opposed to the railroad.

18. *The Railway Age,* May 3, 1884.

19. *The Argonaut,* Aug. 22, 1882.

20. Huntington testimony before the Pacific Railway Commission.

21. Sacramento *Record-Union,* April 25, 1892.

CHAPTER XLI

1. Hittell, T. H. *History of California.* 4 vols. San Francisco, 1885-1887. v. 4, p. 483.

2. Hopkins documents, v. 1, p. 40.

3. *Pacific Coast Mining Review,* 1878-1879, p. 6.

4. State of California vs. Central Pacific & Southern Pacific, Sept. 17, 1883.

5. Vrooman, Henry. *The Hon. Leland Stanford.* (Typescript in the Bancroft Library.)

6. California *Spirit of the Times,* June 14, 1884.

7. Stanford, Leland. *Testimony before the Pacific Railway Commission,* p. 2511.

8. California *Mail Bag,* Jan.-June, 1872.

9. Phillips, David L. *Letters from California.* Springfield, Ill. Letter no. 6, p. 62.

CHAPTER XLII

1. Samuel Brannan was born in Maine in 1819, and had become a Morman when he arrived in California in 1846. He was a printer by trade and published the weekly California *Star,* the first journal to appear in San Francisco. He was also the projector of *The Alta Californian.* He dealt in real estate and accumulated a fortune. He was active in organizing the Vigilance Committee and became one of its officers. His later years were marred by strong drink and his mind became clouded by dissipation; his wealth melted away, and he died in obscurity in San Diego County in 1889. As early as August, 1871, the California *Mail Bag* referred to him as "poor, demoralized Sam Brannan."

2. Hittell, John S. *Commerce and Industry of the Pacific Coast.* San Francisco, 1882, p. 170.

3. Hittell, Theodore H. *History of California.* 4 vols. San Francisco, 1885-1887, v. 4, p. 483.

4. The officials of the company ignored Supervisor Rogers' hints, and as a consequence, he made a separate and adverse report concerning the financial condition of the company to the Secretary of the Treasury.

5. Robinson was represented in this suit, which was settled out of court, by the lawyers A. A. Cohen and Delos Lake. In 1894, Robinson published a book entitled: *The Octopus; a history of the construction, conspiracies, extortions,*

robberies, and villainous acts of the Central Pacific, Southern Pacific of Kentucky, Union Pacific, and other subsidised roads, in which he charged Cohen with compromising with the plaintiffs, compelling the Central Pacific to employ him and Lake at large salaries, and returning to the plaintiff only a fraction of the amount paid for his ten shares.

CHAPTER XLIII

1. Daggett, Stuart. *Chapters on the History of the Southern Pacific.* New York: 1922. pp. 154-168. Chief source of the data on D. D. Colton contained in this chapter.

2. Bancroft, H. H. *History of California.* 7 vols. San Francisco, 1886-1890. v. 7, p. 611.

3. California *Spirit of the Times,* July 4, 1876.

4. Hopkins, Timothy. *Huntington-Hopkins Correspondence in the Stanford University Library.*

5. Daggett, *op. cit.*

6. John Miller, secretary and bookkeeper for the Contract & Finance Co., embezzled over $700,000 from the company, of which the company got back about one-half.

7. Four stockholders—Samuel Brannan, John R. Robinson, Charles A. and Orville D. Lambard—filed suits against the Central Pacific for an accounting of profits which they claimed had been diverted.

8. Daggett, *op. cit.,* p. 208.

9. Crocker manuscript in the Bancroft Library.

10. *The Wave,* Oct. 1, 1892.

CHAPTER XLIV

1. Moore, Joseph H. *How Members of Congress Are Bribed.* San Francisco, 1895.